P9-CIT-863

Washington Through a Purple Veil

Washington Through a Purple Veil

MEMOIRS OF A SOUTHERN WOMAN

࿐

Lindy Boggs

WITH KATHERINE HATCH

HARCOURT BRACE & COMPANY

New York   San Diego   London

To the valiant women who keep our Republic

Library of Congress Cataloging-in-Publication Data
Boggs, Lindy, 1916–
Washington through a purple veil : memoirs of a Southern
woman/Lindy Boggs, with Katherine Hatch. — 1st ed.
p.   cm.
Includes index.
ISBN 0-15-193106-2
1. Boggs, Lindy, 1916–   .   2. Legislators—United States—
Biography.   3. Women legislators—United States—Biography.
4. United States. Congress. House—Biography.   I. Hatch,
Katherine.   II. Title.
E840.8.B6A3   1994
328.73′092—dc20   94-27838

The text was set in Janson
Designed by Camilla Filancia
Printed in the United States of America
First edition   A B C D E

ACKNOWLEDGMENTS

A BOOK like this, covering my life and career of more than three-quarters of a century, obviously draws on the help and devotion of scores of people—my family, my staff, and the countless friends who have contributed so much over the years. To transform the story into a book has taken the dedication of professional archivists and researchers who are also my dear personal friends: Dr. James Billington, the Librarian of Congress; Dr. Raymond Spock, the Historian of the U.S. House of Representatives; Dr. Richard Baker, the Historian of the Senate; Dr. Wilbur Meneray, Tulane University Librarian for Special Collections; Honorable Clarence H. Brown, President of the U.S. Capitol Historical Society; Daniel P. Mulhollan, Director, Congressional Research Service; Honorable J. Walter Stewart, former Secretary of the Senate; Honorable Donnald K. Anderson, Clerk of the House. And then there are those who have become dear friends in the process of writing this book: Kate Hatch, my collaborator; Claire Wachtel, my senior editor; Celia Wren, my book editor; and Dori Weintraub, who made sure that the public knows this story is here to read. Thank you all.

᭡᭡᭡

*M*Y DAUGHTER Barbara studied the family tree and told me that every generation of my family, since the first William Claiborne came ashore at Jamestown, has included at least one public officeholder.

I grew up hearing the stories about Thomas Claiborne, a Virginia congressman when George Washington was president, and about his son, Thomas, also a Virginia congressman, who was on Andrew Jackson's staff during the Creek War. I heard about William Charles Cole Claiborne, the member of Congress from Tennessee, the territorial governor of Mississippi, the first territorial governor of Louisiana Territory, and the first elected governor of the state of Louisiana; and John Francis Hamtramck Claiborne, a Mississippi congressman who loved the U.S. Constitution too much to vote for secession. And I rejoiced in the service rendered during my generation by Herbert Claiborne Pell, a New York congressman, and by his son, Senator Claiborne Pell of Rhode Island.

I learned the stories by heart, but I never expected that I would share directly in that heritage. I never dreamed I would lead the life that I have led.

CHAPTER ONE

I FIRST WENT to Washington to live in 1941 when my husband, Hale Boggs, was elected to Congress. We had been active in New Orleans in a reform movement to break the grip of the scandal-ridden incumbent political machine, and Hale was swept into office on a wave of public support. At twenty-six he was the youngest member of Congress. I was a twenty-four-year-old wife and mother in love with my tall, handsome husband and in awe of his innate political skills, which had brought us to official Washington so early in our careers. He was my brilliant mentor in the world of public service. If I had not been married to him, I would have nonetheless been his enthusiastic supporter anyway.

The Speaker of the House of Representatives was Sam Rayburn, a shrewd Texan and strong leader known for recognizing leadership qualities in young, untested congressmen. Assessing Hale's political and intellectual abilities, he assigned him to the prestigious Banking and Currency Committee just as the committee began its debate and public hearings on Lend-Lease.

Newly empowered by his third-term election victory, President Franklin D. Roosevelt was pushing Congress to authorize sending millions of dollars' worth of war supplies and food to Great Britain and China through direct sales, as a loan, or by lease arrangements. German air raids had the British fighting for their lives, while the Chinese battled a Japanese invasion. Although the president likened the aid to lending a neighbor your garden hose to put out a fire, the opponents of the Lend-Lease Bill saw it as an irrevocable step into another world war.

The prevailing mood of the country was one of isolationism, with which Hale and I and most of our friends, the children of the World War I generation, agreed. We were reluctant to be associated with other countries' wars, as we had noisily demonstrated while we were in college.

The Lend-Lease hearings were the most popular events in the capital. Everyone seemed to have a strong opinion one way or the other on sending supplies to our allies. As soon as the doors of the hearing room were opened each day, people streamed in to take every seat and listen to the arguments. There was always a long line of those hoping to get in, standing for hours in the hall.

Hale called me at our apartment one morning and asked me to come and listen. He felt I wouldn't understand the serious nature of the arguments in favor of the necessity for the Lend-Lease Act unless I heard the testimony. The international situation was more complex and threatening to democracy than we had recognized, he said.

I threw a jacket over my sweater and skirt, and made up my face, brushed my hair and put on high heels, I left little Barbara, who was nineteen months old, and baby Tommy with Lucy Boutwell, the nurse who helped me, and rushed down to the Capitol.

We had no specific Congressional identification cards in those days, no picture on a driver's license, no credit cards. I walked past the line of people waiting and went directly to a young clerk who stood at the closed door of the hearing room.

"My husband is a member of the committee," I said, "and he

has asked me to come down to the hearing. May I go in, please?"

"Oh, sure, honey," he said, looking away. He totally disbelieved me.

It was imperative that I get into the hearing room. Hale was expecting me. I suddenly thought of Mrs. Dugas, a beautiful New Orleans socialite who had told me, when I was leaving for Washington, that the most sophisticated and becoming thing a woman could wear was a purple veil.

I dashed back to the apartment and changed into my best outfit—a black Davidow suit, a pretty silk blouse with my pearl circle pin, a little black velour hat, and kid gloves. At the Palais Royal, a store near the Capitol where on our very first day in Washington I had opened a charge account in order to purchase a baby bed for Tommy, I hurried to the veil and scarf counter and had the saleslady drape a purple veil on my hat.

When I returned to the hearing room, the same clerk was guarding the door. I took off one glove and then the other with as much authority as I could muster. In my sweetest Southern accent, I said, "I'm Mrs. Boggs. I'd like to be seated, please."

"Oh, yes ma'am. Come right in." He opened the door and led the way. That day I became a true believer in Mrs. Dugas's purple veil theory.

During the next fifty years I often thought of the lesson I received from the purple veil story. I recognized that you played the Washington game with confidence and authority and graciousness, and so I was prepared to accept the challenges, the triumphs, and the heartaches of life in the shadow of the Capitol dome.

Chapter Two

I WAS BORN on March 13, 1916, in the four-poster bed in which my mother and her father before her had been born, on Brunswick Plantation, Louisiana. When my great-grandfather was a young man, he had planted an avenue of live oak trees, and the big white house sat at the end of this avenue, raised off the ground to avoid flooding by rains or a rampaging river.

My great-grandfather had rebuilt Brunswick around an older dwelling—one of the oldest in Louisiana—of fortresslike heavy beams and timbers, which local historians believe was built by French Army engineers in the 1700s as the residence of Nicolas de la Cour.

When I was a few days old, I was baptized at Saint Mary's Catholic Church in New Roads. My parents named me Marie Corinne Morrison Claiborne. My daddy was Roland Philemon Claiborne, a handsome, twenty-seven-year-old lawyer with fine features, dark brown hair, and blue eyes that sometimes seemed to change to hazel, just as mine do. He had graduated from the Louisiana State University law school and was popular with everyone who knew him, men and women. They affectionately called him Rollie.

Mamma was Corinne Morrison Claiborne, a beautiful petite young woman of nineteen, the only blond in her family and blessed with brilliant blue eyes and the fairest skin I've ever seen. They were both from large families. My daddy was the next to youngest of eleven surviving children, out of fourteen born to his parents, and Mamma was the third oldest in her family, with seven siblings.

Brunswick was a Mississippi River sugar plantation in Pointe Coupee Parish (a parish is the Louisiana political designation for a county), where the rivers rule life, and it was home to Mamma's parents, Edward Seghers Morrison and Florette Harriss Morrison, "Wampa" and "Rets" to me. My mother's natural mother, Eustatia Harriss, had died a few weeks after Mamma's little sister Maybart Frost was born, and Wampa had married her sister Florette, my "Rets," the only Grandmother Morrison I ever knew. (I called him Wampa because I couldn't say "Grandpa.")

On the first floor were the double parlor where Wampa played his piano; the dining room that was filled every afternoon with Rets's good food, friends and relatives, and lively conversations; the kitchen with a glowing stove and oven spreading tantalizing aromas in the adjoining rooms. A summer kitchen separated by a covered walkway was out back, separate from the house so the heat wasn't felt in the house on summer days.

Rets planted her own garden close to the house and grew prized lemon and kumquat trees. Camellias lined the center walkway and sweet olives, magnolias, and gardenias provided fragrance and year-round greenery.

My parents and I lived in New Roads, the parish seat, where my daddy practiced law with his father, Louis Bingaman Claiborne, "Biz," the judge of the 18th Judicial District and the founder and owner of the local newspaper, the *Pointe Coupee Banner*. Biz was devotedly married to Rose Porciau Claiborne, "Gom," and they lived in a fine house with a big garden a short walk from

Biz's downtown office. We occupied their *garçonnière*, the separate quarters families built for the teenage boys to get them out of the house when they reached the rambunctious stage of life.

Because of the parish's numerous navigable waterways, it was always a prosperous trade center, and New Roads was a fairly important town with railroads serving the sugar and cotton plantations and State Highway 1, a two-lane gravel strip, running down to the capital, Baton Rouge, and up to Alexandria. The Mississippi River had flowed through town until 1722, when its course changed, leaving behind an expansive horseshoe lake called False River, which abounds in a large variety of fish and wildlife. White egrets fluttered up to fill the sky, wild swans did their graceful swirls, and always there were *poules d'eau*—literally, water chickens—dipping for fish and ending up tasting fishy themselves. We usually ate them in gumbo.

Most of my relatives lived beside False River, either on its grassy bank or across the road in their "Louisiana cottages," houses built up off the ground and sheltered by magnolias and great old live oak trees with huge branches. Porches, galleries, and dormers invited the breeze and sunshine indoors and everyone had a long pier for fishing and swimming and boating.

Four of us who were neighbor children were born the same year and remained closest lifelong friends: Katherine ("Doozie") Kearney, who was born in February; Angelique ("Dicky") Provosty, who was born in March, as was I; and Elizabeth ("Chuckie") Bouanchaud, who was born in April. Doozie and her sister, Genevieve, had two older brothers, Ross and Robert, who were especially kind to us, and my mother's younger brother, Stanley Morrison, who was about six years older than I was one of my pals. Happily Stanley later married Hale's sister, Claire.

When I was born, the nurse present at all family births, Mrs. Fazende, decided I looked more like my daddy than my mamma and she called me Rolindy. Eventually, it was shortened to Lindy, and that's remained my name ever since, despite efforts on my part from time to time to change it.

The experience of having been named by a baby nurse served me in good stead much later in my life. After Lyndon Johnson became president, he and his wife, Lady Bird, received volumes of mail from all over the world, and several of Lady Bird's friends volunteered to help her answer it. We all went over to the Elms, their personal residence in which they were still living because Lady Bird didn't want to rush Jackie Kennedy in her move from the White House. In a big unused room on the third floor, we set up a long table and chairs and began digging into the mountain of mail from people offering their prayers and hopes for the country and the new president.

Among the heartfelt notes were several directed to Lady Bird, saying, "Why on earth do you have such a name as 'Lady Bird'? Why aren't you called by your given name, 'Claudia'?"

I said, "Give me those letters. I can answer them. She received her name the same way I received mine, from her baby nurse, who declared, 'She's as pretty as a little lady bird.' "

When my daddy was twenty-nine, he died in the 1918 influenza epidemic. He had taken Governor Pleasant and several other politician friends to Brunswick on a deer hunt when he fell desperately ill. Mamma and I had accompanied him so that she could help entertain his guests, and she became sick, too, but she was able to tend to Daddy, who rapidly became too ill to be moved. Dr. J. C. Roberts, our close family friend, had a hard time getting out to Brunswick because so many people had the flu. By the time he arrived my precious daddy had died.

Asleep in her house in New Roads, his mother knew it before anyone told her. Gom awakened Biz and said, "Roland is dead." About that time my daddy's favorite bird dog, Napoleon, had begun to howl. "Nap knows Roland is dead," Gom said. Then the phone rang with my mother's call, confirming Daddy's death. Gom thought it was religiously unacceptable to have that kind of psychic talent, so she never openly used it, but she knew before she was told of the death of each of her children who preceded her. The next time the bird dogs were fed, Gom, who had a reputation for fairness, said, "Feed them all equally, but just a little bit more for Nap."

After my daddy died Mamma and I moved back to Brunswick and lived with her parents, Wampa and Rets. Everyone was especially sweet to me because I was two and a half and had lost my daddy, whom they all loved. Bessie Rogers, my baby nurse, who was very young herself, brought me two little white mice as pets. I learned that two white mice become a hundred white mice very quickly. They ate their way out of any cage or box I put them in, and they ran all over the house. The cute little pair became a swarm of rodents taking over the place.

In the mornings as soon as I awakened, I went into the dining room to sit on Wampa's lap while he was having his first cup of coffee. He saved a little bit at the bottom of the cup and added a couple of spoonsful of sugar so that I could have my "morning coffee" with him. One morning I discovered that all my white mice were dead. Wampa said, "Huh? Huh? What happened to your mice? Oh, girl, look at that. Oh, my goodness, what happened to your mice? Oh, terrible, terrible." Years later I discovered that he had mercifully had them all chloroformed. He spoiled me so, but a house swarming with mice was too much for my indulgent Wampa.

Many things in life influence a person, not only physical surroundings and the natural environment but the social environment affect the way you feel. As an only child growing up in the country, I had a special rapport with God's creatures. My pets were my constant companions. There was Speedy (because she was so slow), my Shetland pony I brought with me from Brunswick to our next home, Moreau, and progressively my other horses: the slightly larger Creole Tacky and my gloriously beautiful saddle horse Ramona. There is no sensation more satisfying than feeling one with your horse galloping through a pasture or trotting along the road back home savoring the fun of an outing. Among my dogs, I loved three most especially. They were Fanny, a silky-haired collie benign in her treatment of little children, Cleve, my huge yet gentle Great Dane, who became my fierce protector by night, stretching his large frame diagonally across the thresholds of my bedroom doors, and my tiny Toby, a Boston bullterrier, who lived long enough to see me off to college. Among my mother's beautiful Siamese and Maltese cats there were always several who favored me (gingerly to be sure) with special affection. And then there was Polly, my parrot of irrepressible spirit, raucous in his remarkably large vocabulary, who twitted parents, household workers, gardeners, hunting dogs, and gamecocks, alike. His nemesis was the Victrola. He was jealous of this inanimate object that could talk.

In addition to my pets we had farm animals and wild animals and birds in great abundance. The cycle of life was my natural environment; births and deaths, sickness, and accidents all were part of the everyday fabric of my existence. My grandmothers, Rets and Gom, instilled in me that we humans are the stewards of God's creation.

I spent so much time with my grandparents that I had a special opportunity to know them well and to be the beneficiary of their love and training, their codes of morals and behavior, their stores of knowledge. Grandmothers Gom and Rets were the underpinnings of my whole being, and they continued to exert influence on me and shower love on me all their lives. They were strict in their way, wanting me to respect others and not think only of myself. The most valuable lesson I learned from Rets was that you can succeed at anything if you give somebody else the credit for doing it.

When Rets would get provoked with me and look for me, Wampa would come and swing me up in front him on his horse. I'd hold onto the pommel of his saddle, and off we'd go on his rounds of the plantation. We'd stay far from the house while he'd make up stories to tell me until he was certain that Rets had forgotten the cause of her provocation. He didn't want to confront her directly or defy her, but he helped me escape.

He was a wonderful man who could play the keys off a piano. Many times I would run into the parlor when he was playing and flop down and listen. He loved people and music, and he could play by ear anything you could name or hum.

Wampa was born during the Civil War, when the plantation lost its workforce, livestock, and crops to the Yankees. Despite the hardships of Reconstruction, he was sent to a Jesuit school in Cape Girardeau, Missouri, but he returned home when he was eleven because his father died. His mother took over the plantation and opened a finishing school for young ladies to supplement her income. She died of tuberculosis when Wampa was twenty-one. By then he was running the plantation himself.

Wampa also suffered from tuberculosis. It was devastating to me when this beloved father figure and friend would leave for weeks at a time to be treated in the drier air of North Carolina or Arizona. He died in 1922 while he was in Phoenix on one of those health-restoring visits, and his body was brought back to Brunswick on the train.

The day it was to arrive, I was sent out of the house with friends to divert me. The casket was brought in and placed in the parlor. When the mortician was finished "laying Wampa out," he went to fetch family members for their approval.

At that minute I came back, unaware of what was going on. I went skipping into the parlor, expecting to see Wampa at the piano, and there he was in a coffin. I was so horrified that years passed before I could force myself to look at family members and friends in their coffins. I preferred to remember them as they had been in life. In time I overcame these inhibitions and learned to confer some finality on my good-byes.

Without Wampa to run Brunswick, Rets had to relinquish it. As with most plantations, a big mortgage had been imposed on it, and Rets had sons to see through high school and college. Drawing on the skills and talents she had developed through her expert organization of the large plantation household, she decided to open a guest house in New Orleans. It was a brave move on her part, to a very different kind of life, but she saw no alternative. She found a house large enough for her family, paying guests, and the two Brunswick household employees who wouldn't let her go to the city alone.

There is a bond among Southern women, a powerful shared tradition of carrying on our lives with grace and dignity regardless of personal loss or hardship. This bond was forged in a very dramatic fashion following the Civil War, when everybody was impoverished together and the women, black and white of all generations, borned one another's babies, nursed one another's sick, and buried one another's dead.

In many cases that bond predated the war. My great-grandmother Virginia Seghers, aware that African families were often deliberately separated in the slave trade, insisted that her husband try to find the relatives of people who worked for them. They were able to find several, and those who went with Rets to the city were their descendants.

Rets was forged of strong character, a direct descendant of Elder William Brewster and his wife, those privileged children of affluent parents who had protected the religious separatists, the Pilgrims, and allowed them to hold meetings in their home. When they sought religious freedom in the New World, William Brewster's young wife became the great strength, the nurse, the consoler, the servant of fellow passengers who were sick and dying, as their tiny ship, the *Mayflower*, made its desperate and hazardous voyage through wintry seas.

Once they arrived in Plymouth at Christmastime 1620, my Brewster ancestor performed every strenuous domestic chore that was required to establish and maintain their settlement. By leaving the plantation and moving to New Orleans, completely changing her life, Rets was responding in the same sort of brave and adventurous manner.

My grandfather and grandmother Claiborne were sweethearts all the days of their lives and celebrated their sixty-seventh wedding anniversary before Biz died. He was a student at Georgetown University when the Civil War began, and his parents, worried about his safety in the war zone, wrote him to return home immediately by riverboat and ferry.

When he arrived he told his parents that he wanted to join the Confederate Army. He was seventeen years old and they couldn't hold him back, so he went off with the Pointe Coupee artillery and participated in the battles of Shiloh Meeting House and Corinth, Mississippi; in the defense of Vicksburg, which Union General Ulysses S. Grant broke with a torturous siege of the city; and in the defense of Atlanta under General John Bell Hood. He followed General Hood to Tennessee, where they were defeated at Nashville. When the war ended, Biz returned home safe and sound and studied for the law.

He devoted his life to public service. Whenever an issue excited him, he felt an obligation to get involved. He'd be elected to the state legislature, preside over the school board, be superintendent of schools, or serve on the levee board. He was parish attorney and then he was district judge, training generations of young lawyers in his office.

I don't know where he found the time, but in 1880 he established the *Pointe Coupee Banner*, which is still the local newspaper. He was seventy-two when I was born, and he lived to be ninety-two, so I knew him quite well and I always looked up to him. He had high expectations of what his children and grandchildren should do: He expected you to live up to your own potential. Before the turn of the century all his children, including the girls, attended college.

Renowned for his photographic memory, Biz could tell the young lawyers to look up something in a certain volume, and he would name the page, column, paragraph, and line, and there it would be. But as he grew older he developed cataracts in both eyes. He was persuaded to go to New Orleans and be examined by my Aunt Rowena Morrison's husband, Dr. Wiley Buffington, a renowned ophthalmologist.

In those days cataract removal was considered a very strenuous operation, requiring a long hospital stay with your head held perfectly still. On elderly people Dr. Buffington performed an initial operation, a preliminary iridectomy, to determine how successful it would be, before he removed the cataract. Biz went into Baptist Hospital for his preliminary surgery, and he was miserable as a man can be, all those miles away from Gom, deprived of his daily toddy and his Picayune cigarettes. When they released him he determined he was never going back.

When he went home he pretended that he could see. My aunt Ethel Claiborne Dameron, Biz's youngest child, who had lived away, returned to New Roads to look after him and Gom. Biz never caught on that everyone knew he couldn't see. He would have Ethel's young daughter, "Wink," read the newspaper to him every morning and then he'd discuss the news with her. He thought it was a good lesson for the child to know what was going on.

Everybody in town watched out for him. His law clerks would ask his advice on cases and as usual, he would tell them exactly where to find what they needed. Instead of handing Biz his mail, they would tell him what correspondence had been received, and he would tell them which case it related to and what they should do about it. "You should learn about that," he would say, and they would.

Gom was petite and French, a descendant of the earliest French settlers in neighboring Avoyelles Parish. I was twenty-one when she died, and the whole time I knew her, she was not in good health; it was always *"comme ci, comme ça,"* the main difficulty being a kidney ailment. She had a prescription to drink two glasses a day of Vichy water, which she guarded in her armoire.

Because drop-in visits were inconvenient for her health and her medical routine, she had calling hours every afternoon from three until five. People would drive for miles to call on "Lady" Claiborne, as she was known. This diminutive Frenchwoman who lived with the high-powered Claibornes was the person who was sought out by her sons' friends for her blessings and advice.

Every morning my grandfather brought Gom her coffee in bed. She would put on her bed jacket, secured with the gold bar pin Biz had given her when their first child was born, and he would bring her a red flower to put in the pin. After he developed cataracts, we couldn't figure out how he could find a red flower every day in every season in their huge garden. Once when I was spending the night, I heard a sound around five o'clock in the morning and peered out in time to see my grandfather taking a freshly picked red flower from the hand of a little black boy. Biz smelled the flower and handed the boy a dime. It was their grand secret.

Gom was known for being just and fair, and as she had to exercise this balance among their fourteen children, most of whom lived to adulthood, she had a good system: As each little one was born, one of the older ones became that child's special protector and nurturer. My daddy, who was the youngest son, was assigned to Ferdinand, the oldest. I was told that after my daddy died, I climbed onto Uncle Ferd's lap and said he would have to be my "Uncle Daddy."

Uncle Daddy was a grand figure, with handsome features and beautiful white hair, favoring white linen suits and fine Arabian horses. He wasn't always a regular churchgoer, but somehow a young priest in New Roads lured him back to the sacraments. The priest told me, "Mister Ferd comes to mass in his white suit, and he looks like he's dressed for his first communion."

I said, "Considering the number of years he was away from the church, that's the appropriate garb."

The two families, Morrisons and Claibornes, were on different political sides locally, but everyone was a Democrat, the only political affiliation compatible to the needs of the post–Civil War, post-Reconstruction era. In national politics sugar planters sided with the Republican candidates, wanting high tariff barriers, while cotton planters tended to vote Democratic, all for free trade. I was curious about the danger that must have lurked on the other side of the high tariff wall. Could Uncle Joe build a stile high enough so that I could climb over the wall to investigate, I wondered. In this comparatively small town and parish all these volatile, rigorous, energetic people were fighting each other politically, and they were all my family members.

The first political conversation I remember took place between my great-uncle on my mother's side, Jake Morrison, and my Claiborne Uncle Daddy, on the day of Wampa's wake. They were sitting on a banister at the far end of the front porch at Brunswick when I wandered out. I remember their conversation because I was surprised that Wampa's brother and my daddy's brother were talking about politics without fussing. One of them told a story, and they both laughed so hard I wondered how they could be so jolly at my adorable Wampa's wake.

Uncle Daddy had been in the state legislature when he decided to campaign for the lieutenant governorship, but he needed a timely issue. A state highway system was being put through, and there was a public uproar about cattle and other farm animals that might wander onto the highways and cause accidents. People were demanding that fences be constructed by the property owners, who had already been paid for the right-of-way for the new roads. This angered the property owners, and they were up in arms. It promised to be a long, noisy battle.

When a no-fence law was proposed, Uncle Daddy became one of its most energetic defenders, making impassioned pleas for the poor "widow women" who lived along the highway route and would have to spend their meager finances to construct fences that were not necessary. His speech struck a chord with his eldest sister, my Aunt Celeste, an energetic suffragette. Celeste and some suffragette cohorts undertook a census of every property owner along the route of the proposed highways, and when they finished they had found not a single "widow woman." Uncle Daddy's no-fence bill was defeated and, worse for him, he didn't win the lieutenant governorship either.

I had an unusual childhood. After I lost my daddy, my mother was wonderful in her willingness to share me with many people and make certain that I knew my father's family members well. She was close to me, yet she understood my need to develop on my own. "You need to know about initiative," she'd say. At the same time she seemed to enjoy doing things for me and making *my* plans. She came from a large, gregarious family, and it was sometimes difficult for her to understand my personal exclusivity when I'd be at my desk, absorbed in something. She was generous about having many young people visit, however, never wanting me to feel that, as an only child, I didn't have an opportunity for companionship and friendship.

My cousins from both sides of my family were an important part of childhood. Haywood and Claiborne Dameron who were near my age, and I spent many summers with our grandparents Gom & Biz. Their little sisters, Ethel Mary ("Shingo") and Dorothy ("Wink") would come for shorter stays. And on my mother's side, Ben and deLesseps ("Chep") Morrison were close, and their mother, Aunt Anita Morrison, and my mother were dear friends. My aunt Martha Morrison Brady's little sons Hiram, "Bookie," and Judge, "B. B.," were especially dear to me.

Mamma had become a widow when she was twenty-two and a half. Her sister, Maybart ("Frosty") Morrison, who lived in New Orleans, was sixteen months younger, and naturally they liked to enjoy the city. Often, I went along on their jaunts, which was unusual for a child. We'd go shopping or to visit friends or relatives in New Orleans, Alexandria, or Baton Rouge, and these excursions never ceased to be an adventure for me.

In New Orleans we always dined in one of the fine old restaurants. Once we arrived and were seated, I would open the menu and pretend that I could read. When the waiter came, depending on the time of day, I ordered scrambled eggs and bacon or a club sandwich. I knew they had to be listed somewhere. I have earlier memories of places than most people, because they didn't frequent Arnaud's, Antoine's, or Commander's Palace when they were small children.

Mamma's many beaux courted me as much as they doted on her. The one I liked the best was Hamilton Lewis of the Corps of Engineers from New Orleans. One day "Ham" accompanied

Mamma and me on a shopping spree in New Orleans. As we were leaving Gus Mayer's store on Canal Street, I saw a red-haired baby mannequin in the window, and I thought it was the most beautiful doll I had ever seen. I wanted it more than anything in the world, so I began asking for it. Ham tried to explain the impossibility of the request.

He said, "You see the lady mannequin standing in the window? She's not a lady, she's a mannequin. This is a little girl mannequin. It's not a doll."

"But I want her," I said. "I don't care what you say. She's a beautiful doll."

"It isn't a doll, and it isn't for sale. It's part of the window decorations," he said.

I said, "I'm just going to sit here until you get me that doll." I sat down on a bench in front of the store.

After a few minutes he went in to see Mr. Mayer. "The child isn't going to leave until I buy her that baby mannequin in the window," he said. I was exultant when "Doll" became mine. What a pain I must have been, but at least I had the first successful sit-in on Canal Street.

My future stepfather, George Keller, "Daddy George," was considered an old bachelor at twenty-nine when he and Mamma were married. Because he was a Protestant, they couldn't have the wedding in a Catholic church, so they were to be married by Father Beaver, a beloved Jesuit priest, at Aunt Frosty's house in New Orleans. Wampa had died by then, so Uncle Daddy came from New Roads to "give Mamma away." Although the Morrisons and Claibornes were political rivals, they loved my mother and they loved me. It didn't seem strange to anyone that my father's brother should be the one to officially present my mother to her new husband. I was Mamma's only attendant.

I was crazy about George, but the day before the wedding I

was out of sorts and unhappy that he and Mamma would be leaving soon on their honeymoon to New York. To get me out of the way of the wedding preparations, Uncle Daddy invited me to go to Commander's Palace restaurant for a treat. In my evil little mind I decided that if I could get sick, Mamma would have to stay up all night with me and she would look so ugly the next day George wouldn't want to marry her.

When the waiter came to take my order, I asked for a quart of chocolate ice cream. Uncle Daddy insisted he serve it, and I ate as much as I could. Right on cue I was sick that evening, and Mamma was worried and concerned about going away the next day. Everything was working out just as I'd planned until a friend of Mamma's showed up. "Miss Nan," Anna Bolton Ellis, the society editor of the *New Orleans Times-Picayune*, saw what was going on and she said to Mamma, "Oh, Corinne, you go and get your beauty sleep. I will take care of Lindy." I was the only one who looked awful the next day, and I had to wear the yellow dress that had been selected for me, which I hated.

We went to live at Moreau, a cotton plantation farther up in the country than Brunswick. Daddy George's family owned three plantations in a row, and you couldn't tell where one ended and the next began. As at Brunswick a long avenue of live oak trees led to the raised, two-story house, whose main rooms were on the first floor. A gallery ran around the entire first floor with floor-to-ceiling windows opening onto the rooms.

The house commanded a large natural knoll that stretched out in front about three quarters of a city block until it sloped into Bayou Lettsworth, which ran through the front yard to meet Bayou Moreau at its western corner. The lovely, large pool formed by the convergence of the bayous provided a welcoming baptismal opportunity for many of the neighboring church congregations. Down one side and up the other of the bayous' banks a profusion of wildflowers bloomed progressively throughout the year: primroses, Langlois irises, and bird's-foot violets, goldenrods, orange flowered azaleas, coral honeysuckle, morning glories, moss verbena, chain leaf asters, mock thistles, wild ageratum, sunflowers, lady slippers, white flowered milkweed and the especially lovely Louisiana irises, copper colored and blue to deep indigo. I can still conjure them up in the memory of my senses. Between Bayou Lettsworth and the main road that ran along Old River was the traditional plantation home avenue of live oak trees spreading the beauty of their ample ancient limbs with year-round shade against the unyielding Louisiana sky. Out back were a rose garden, a kitchen garden, and a long covered walkway, laden with fragrant clusters of wisteria, that led to Daddy George's office, the commissary, and Uncle Posey's room. Uncle Posey was an elderly African-American who had been orphaned early in life and had always been taken care of on the place. Farther on were the dairy; the Delco electric generating plant, which provided all of our power; the stables, barns, hunting dog kennels, hutches for my mother's rabbits, and cages as big as piano crates for the gamecocks. It was quite an establishment!

Mr. Lafayette Keller, Daddy George's father, had a sizable fortune and properties that included three buildings on Canal Street in New Orleans. When George and his three sisters Chlotilde, Barbara, and Ada were in their teens, their father decided to buy a house in New Orleans; his daughters were going there for parties all the time, and the eldest would soon be entering Newcomb College, and he thought it would be better if they owned a house appropriate to their needs. After he found a place he liked, he took Joe Trueblood, who supervised all the buildings on Moreau, down to check it over.

The house was in the University District on Saint Charles Avenue, next door to beautiful Audubon Park. Joe, who had never been to New Orleans, was enchanted with being in the city, and he took a long time going over the foundations, the plumbing, the wiring, the roof, the floors, and the drainage. When he had finished Mr. Keller asked for his appraisal. "It's a fine sturdy house," Joe said. "Course, it's not as fittin' as Moreau, but look at that nice side yard."

Many more boys than girls lived around Moreau, which meant we rode horseback and fished and played boys' games, but I would never go hunting. Daddy George used to tease me and say I ate everything he killed but I wouldn't kill anything myself. My closest girl neighbor and friend was Vera Lee Hopgood, who had four brothers, the eldest of whom, Jack, was my very first beau.

My empathy with people whose rights are denied probably began at Moreau, when the others ganged up on me—the favorite and an only child—and I always had to be the enemy. I was the British when we played Revolutionary War, the Yankee in the War between the States, and an Indian in cowboys and Indians. I have often wondered if these experiences made me sympathetic with people who are the underdog.

I grew up without sibling rivalry and with a great amount of love from my cousins, but I always wished for a little brother. (I wasn't too interested in having a little sister. Perhaps I thought she'd be competition.) My children tell me that because I had no siblings, I don't understand that people have differences and compete within a family or among close friends. They say, "You don't understand that there are rivalries. You don't understand that people sometimes feel that way about you, Mother."

I'm blissfully unaware of other people's competitive feelings about me, and it's too late to change now. My children are right: I could never understand it when they fussed with each other. I thought the Lord made us a family and we should be supportive and loving and never get in fights. It's all right to disagree and to respond to provocation, but never to have a real fight. Hale, who was one of six children, used to roar with laughter at my pacifist views of family relationships.

In the plantation house much of the wife's activity was geared to the big midday dinner. She had to procure the goods, store them, and assemble an enormous and delicious meal without ever knowing exactly how many people were going to be there to enjoy it. She ran a complicated, autonomous organization, and she started from scratch every day. There were no freezers or microwaves, no supermarkets or neighborhood convenience stores—in fact, there were few stores of any kind out in the country. Whatever you needed that you didn't grow, shoot, or catch came by boat up the Mississippi River from the stores in New Orleans. Solari's could supply great quantities of fancy groceries; J. L. Lyons was the sundries and drug company everyone used.

Rets used to buy fancy artichokes from Solari's, but at certain times during the year they were not in season. She decided that artichokes were nothing more than thistles and that she could grow them on the plantation. With determination, good soil, and a green thumb, she was soon growing so many beautiful artichokes that she was supplying Solari's.

Many years later, when Hale and I were driving through the fertile fields of coastal California, we came upon a vast expanse of unusual-looking plants in varying stages of development. Hale mused aloud, "I wonder what those plants are," having no notion that I could possibly know. From somewhere way back in my Brunswick memory, I responded, "They're artichokes." Both of us were stunned a few miles later when we saw a large sign stretched across the highway proclaiming, WELCOME TO CASTROVILLE—THE ARTICHOKE CAPITAL OF THE WORLD.

My expectations as a child reflected the life I saw around me: to be a good wife and a mother, keep a pretty house, and foster and participate in some cultural outlets. I didn't expect to live on a plantation; I knew that way of life was on its way out. I recognize now that the women not only ran the households, they took care of their husbands and children and made their own entertainment, often working as hard on cultural activities as they did on keeping everything on their extensive premises running smoothly.

The midday table was the social center. Besides the immediate and extended family of cousins, aunts and uncles, and in-laws, other friends and neighbors would drop in. Rocking chairs in the dining room accommodated those who had already eaten but came for coffee and the conversation. The talk always covered local politics and the weather, and it might take off from there to what Washington was doing about the price of cotton or sugar, the merits or follies of the world war and of the incumbent peace proposals, or the latest activities of Huey Long, a brilliant, brash young state official who was raising Cain with the big oil companies.

Everybody talked, and if you were a kid and you were there and behaved, nobody sent you away. You were treated like an adult and were expected to act like one. The only time I was ever banished from the table was once when Haywood, Claiborne, and I were visiting Gom and Biz, and Claiborne and I had a fight over the last helping of tiny green beans. We were a happy threesome, never a cross word, never a fight, but we misbehaved so badly that day we were sent from the table without dessert. The next time those tiny beans came to the table, one dish was in front of me and one dish was in front of Claiborne. For a split second we were too embarrassed to eat them. (What an impression that punishment must have made, for me to remember every detail after all those years!)

At Moreau we were on a party line of seven telephones that were connected to the Feduccia family's general store in the little town of Torras, and to the operator in New Roads. Everyone had an individual ring—ours was two longs and a short—but when Vera Lee and I would call each other, we could usually hear other phones being taken off the hook. Listening in on the party line was one of the favorite activities of rural life, especially when the weather was bad and you were housebound. The party line provided plenty of information and gossip on what was going on, and oftentimes the eavesdroppers became so interested that they broke into the conversations.

Every once in a while Vera Lee and I would pretend we had a secret we didn't want anyone to hear. We'd say, "Miss Amy, would you please hang up?" "Miss Ruby, would you please hang up?" and we'd hear the clicks as the ladies on our line hung up their receivers. Sometimes when we knew they were listening to us and it was close to mealtime, we would come right out and ask them what they were having for dinner. If we liked what they were having better than what we were having at home, we'd invite ourselves to dinner and get on our horses and go.

Miss Hazel Bondy was the telephone operator at New Roads. She could always find your Mamma for you, but she might tell you something like, "Oh, honey, I wouldn't call her right now. She's at Miss Gert's and she's bid three no-trump doubled and redoubled. Let's wait a little while, and I'll give her a ring and have her call you."

I took dancing lessons from the time I was six, and I still love to dance. The study of dance was considered a proper kind of exercise for a young girl, to make her graceful. Mamma or Louis Sturgis, our butler/chauffeur, would drive me to classes in New Roads and Baton Rouge during the school year. In the summertime, I'd visit Grandmother Rets and my aunts in New Orleans and take my lessons there.

The summer I was ten, the Chicago Opera was developing its own ballet corps, holding auditions and making inquiries among ballet schools around the country. I was offered a scholarship to study with them, and I was thrilled beyond belief. In my mind I was already boarding the train to Chicago, but ballerinas frequently look so much alike that it's difficult to tell much difference in their ages or what age one of them might be. When the Chicago Opera recruiters learned how young I was, the invitation was withdrawn. My parents had of course never intended allowing me to go. I was crushed.

We grew one crop of cotton a year at Moreau and a successful yield depended on the weather. First, cotton plants need rain to grow, but then they require hot dry weather right through picking season; everyone prayed it wouldn't rain when cotton was being picked. People who worked in our house got time off to pick cotton because it was a cash crop and they could make extra money.

"Aunt" Hannah Hall, my nurse of the ample lap and cushiony bosom, would take me out with her. Picking cotton was hard, especially if you had a tiny hand. You had to put your hand in and pull out all of the little flowerets, the cotton balls, at one time. When your sack was full, you put it up on a sled and a team of mules pulled it over to the weighing station.

My sack never weighed anything, so one of the men would stand on the scales. "Oh, Baby," he'd say, "you picked one hundred and eighty pounds!" The workers were all so nice to me, and I relished being out with them despite the fact Aunt Hannah made me wear long sleeves and a hat to protect my fair complexion.

The household workers and some of the fieldworkers at Brunswick and Moreau were our close companions, privy to our private lives as we were to theirs. We were all family in our hearts, with love and respect for one another, and through good times and bad we were dependent on them as they were dependent on us. There was never a need for a discussion of race relations; the ties that bound us were so strong there was nothing more to say.

Segregation of the races was the law of the land, and few people, black or white, publicly questioned it. It was a fait accompli. I came to realize that there is no true democracy unless all its citizens have equal opportunity, and that all people should be able to participate in their government. I'm sure that the love I felt from the African-American women who raised me contributed greatly to those realizations and to my activism to make them come true.

Calling close family friends "Aunt" or "Uncle" was a way of showing "endearing respect," and we used it for white friends as well as for older black people who served us, such as Hannah Hall, who had been Daddy George's nurse. She came willingly out of retirement to take care of me, and she ruled the roost at Moreau. At supper Daddy George had acquired the habit during his bachelor days of serving the plates of the people who had served us.

Aunt Hannah would plant her hands on her hips and say, "Serve mine while you're still hungry, Mr. George," and she would laugh as he piled on the food. When the price of cotton began falling, Daddy George invested in equipment the field hands could use to cut the weeds on nearby levees so they could supplement their income. I still hear from children and grandchildren of the people who worked for us, and when Hale and I were active in politics they were among our most loyal supporters.

I went to grade school briefly. The school had only one or two rooms, but we were all different ages and levels of learning and I'm afraid we overwhelmed the teacher. Otherwise, I was tutored at home by a talented local woman. I ended up learning a great deal about literature, geography, and history but not much about long division or things you learned by rote like the multiplication tables.

Aunt Rowena paid me twenty-five cents for every book I read, and I found a collection of Shakespeare's plays in my stepfather's library, each play in a separate little red leather book I could hold in one hand. I made money on Mr. Shakespeare and became a great lover of his work, but my education was weak in other areas until Mamma and Daddy George made a decision that dramatically expanded my world.

CHAPTER THREE

ᕔᕀᕲ

WHEN I WAS NINE years old, I went off to Saint Joseph's Academy, the convent school in New Roads, to board during the week. I had been well prepared by Mamma and Daddy George to like boarding school, and I was excited about going. I had grandparents, aunts and uncles, and friends living right there in New Roads. It wasn't as though I would be all alone, Mamma said. But Aunt Hannah was so apprehensive that I began to have squeamish feelings about being so far away, forty miles from Moreau.

The day Biz took me to enroll, he took along two bottles of Rock & Rye whiskey and gave them to Mother Gertrude, the mother superior. They were for medicinal purposes, he said, one for the nuns and one for me if I had a cold. Mother Gertrude winked and thanked him.

I responded fairly well my first day at the convent, but that night I decided that I really wanted to go home as soon as possible. When bath time came, I told Sister Mechtilde, who was in charge of our dorm, that I didn't know how to bathe myself because my Aunt Hannah had always bathed me. It was a big fib, but I thought it might hasten my departure.

Sister Mechtilde said, "That's interesting, dear. I will bathe you." The nuns always wore a big linen body covering when they bathed, and she got out one of these coverings and put it over me. Then she took a long-handled scrub brush and began scrubbing away. I decided that I knew how to bathe. She had administered an effective punishment that was typical of her guidance of the boarders.

I soon found myself having worlds of fun, and I couldn't imagine that I had wanted to leave. Every weekend, Aunt Hannah would send me back with two dozen Milky Way candy bars, and I'd use them as barter, especially with two town students whose parents owned fruit stores. I never needed the medicinal Rock & Rye, but I grew to love Mother Gertrude. After my grandparents and my mother, the nuns became major figures in my life.

I was put in a grade appropriate with what I had learned at home, and they kept advancing me. I loved learning. Besides classes we twenty boarders had a two-hour study period with recess and a *goûté*, a little bite to eat, usually root beer and cookies. I was so young, the youngest of the boarders, that I was given a light load of homework, which I usually finished before recess.

The rest of the time, I was asked to do things like set the refectory tables for supper or put out fresh chalk in the classrooms. Sometimes I sat in the kitchen with Sister Stephanie, a beautifully educated retired nun from Cincinnati, who seemed to love talking to me. I learned a great deal from her, the most enduring lesson being the simple one that when you're a great intellectual and what you've always wanted to do is bake bread, when you retire you can bake bread and still be a splendid intellectual.

I was greatly influenced by the nuns. Living with these women, who were dedicated to what they were doing and had a high sense of responsibility and a caring and loving regard for God's human beings and all creatures, molded the way I approached life. Because nuns were presidents of colleges, directors of hospitals, principals of high schools, it didn't occur to me that there were things women couldn't do. Nuns did everything and still baked bread if they wished to do so. The nuns also instilled in me a lifelong devotion to Mary, the Mother of Jesus, that strong and virtuous woman, and unfailing guide to the paths of justice and peace.

My mother used to pick me up on Friday afternoons and drive me home, but as I grew older I sometimes went to high school parties in Baton Rouge with my cousins or the children of family friends who lived there. Once, when I was twelve, I was going to spend a Friday night with Jeanne Perkins and her family because the party was expected to last later than usual. Mamma impressed on me the fact that it was a big deal to be allowed to spend the night, and I was very excited about it.

I must have been terribly sassy in the car, because when we arrived at the landing at Port Allen, instead of driving onto the ferry and going across the Mississippi to deliver me to the Perkinses' house as she ordinarily would, Mamma stopped the car and snapped, "All right, young lady, if you think you're so smart you can get out of this car and get yourself to the Perkins house the best way you can." She, who had always arranged things for me, was suddenly sending me off on my own.

I don't know whether she expected me to take her up on it, but I shouted back, "All right!" I got out of the car and boarded the ferry with my overnight case. I knew what to do on the ferry—sit down, don't talk to strangers, hold on to my case—but I didn't know what to do when I got off. I thought about the times Mamma had shopped at Rosenfield's store in Baton Rouge and I'd hear the clerks say as we were leaving, "If there's ever anything we can do, don't hesitate to call us."

When we docked I used the telephone at the ferry landing to call the manager of Rosenfield's. I explained who I was and where I was going and he sent a chauffeured car to take me to Jeanne's house. I realized then that if you want something done, go to the top. I didn't know until later that my mother had phoned Mrs. Perkins, worried to death, wanting to know as soon as I arrived.

From the age of seven, when I received my first Holy Communion, I was required to attend Sunday Mass regularly. Daddy George was a fairly active member of Saint Stephen's Episcopal Church, a little Gothic gem on the river near Moreau and the only non-Catholic church for white people in the area. He used to send me with Louis Sturgis, for early mass at Saint Mary's, and then Daddy George and I would go to the eleven o'clock service at Saint Stephen's.

Before so many people began leaving their hometowns to seek their future or fortune, relatives lived within a fairly small radius of where everyone had been born and family connections often took interesting turns. The Saint Stephen's church organist, Mrs. Platt, was a close friend of Rets and her family going back several generations, and she was related to Mary Byrne, who became the mother of Barbara Denechaud, who, years later, became my son Tommy's wife.

The pastor of Saint Mary's was Father Hoes, a Dutchman we knew especially well because Gom became his surrogate mother. (His own mother lived in Holland.) In those days good Catholics were not supposed to attend any but a Catholic service with a clear conscience. I felt perfectly natural going to church with my stepfather, but the prohibition itself bothered me and at recess one day, I asked Mother Gertrude's permission to talk to Father Hoes.

When I arrived in his study, I said, "You have to do something about the nuns."

He said, "What do I have to do about the nuns?"

I said, "That catechism they're teaching us says it's a sin for me to go to church with my Daddy George on Sunday."

Father Hoes thought a minute and replied, "I think it would be wrong if you *didn't* go to church with your Daddy George on Sunday." That settled it.

A depression in agriculture, which began several years before the stock market crash of 1929, brought hard times to Pointe

Coupee Parish, and it became increasingly difficult for the Saint Stephen's congregation to support a full-time minister. The church finally attracted a retired British minister, the Reverend Crompton Sowerbutts, and his lovely Irish-Canadian wife, Emma. They were nature lovers and fond of historic buildings, and he, unlike most of his parishioners, was a High Church Episcopalian.

When Uncle Crompton heard that I attended the convent school, he asked me, "Do the good nuns teach you to genuflect?"

I said, "Yes they do, Uncle Crompton."

"Would you please teach my heathens how to genuflect?" he said.

"Not unless you require me to, Uncle Crompton," I said. Thank goodness, he never did.

One of my teachers was Sister Dorothy, a lovely girl from New Orleans who had made her debut and was extremely popular with everyone, courted by many beaux. At the end of her debut season, she had stunned her family when she told them she wanted to become a nun. She was so absolutely beautiful that we used to conjecture that young men had swooned when she went by and had died of broken hearts when she joined the nunnery. The nuns of the St. Joseph Order changed their names, but schoolgirl sleuthing discovered hers: Andrée Lanusse.

Many years later I was working on the renovation of La Maison Hospitalière, a residential home in New Orleans that was begun after the Civil War as a residence for impoverished ladies of the Confederacy. It had to be upgraded to meet twentieth-century standards without altering its historic appearance, and I was assisting with the project. Among the rooms to be preserved and refurbished was a glorious little chapel.

I was in the chapel one day when I encountered a stranger. Since I knew most the people around La Maison, I smiled and introduced myself.

The man said, "Mrs. Boggs, I understand you are from New Roads, so you will understand if I tell you something about this chapel."

I couldn't imagine what he was going to tell me.

"I was in love with a beautiful girl who joined the convent," he said. "Every morning the postulants used to come to this chapel to early Mass, and I would come every day to look at her and to hope that she was not going to go through with all of that, but she did. She became a nun."

I said, "Andrée Lanusse, by any chance?"

"Yes!" he declared.

Our convent days conjecturing had been correct all along.

For years La Maison has been one of *the* places to live, even when a woman still had to be impoverished to be accepted. Hale's great-aunt Cornelia Robelot and her husband, Mortimer, lived in the French Quarter until Mortimer died when Cornelia was in her nineties. All her friends were in the French Quarter, most of them at La Maison Hospitalière, so she sold her house and gave all her money to La Maison and thus impoverished, happily moved in.

My cousin Chep Morrison's mother, Aunt Anita Morrison, wanted to move in after Chep died in an airplane accident; her only other child, Dr. Ben Morrison, was living and practicing medicine in Alexandria. She had two grandchildren in New Orleans, and she called her granddaughter, Corinne, and said, "I have decided I'm moving into La Maison Hospitalière. I've been wanting to get in there for two years; there's a room for me, and I'm going."

Much earlier, after she had lost her husband, Aunt Anita had realized that what she did best was to run a big house: oversee the kitchen, direct the servants, and feed a great many people. She managed the French House at LSU while she put her boys through college, and then she was made manager of the Baton Rouge Country Club. When she got to La Maison, she was over ninety and hadn't worked in years, but a new nutritionist sought her out for advice on preparing meals for the home's residents.

"People react most specifically to the aroma of food," she told the young woman. "If something smells the way they remember a good dish is supposed to smell, they assume it's going to taste good. The aroma helps whet an appetite. If people can't have salt or hot pepper, use herbs—bay leaf, thyme, rosemary, all the things we think of as meaning good food." Then she devised some recipes the nutritionist gratefully used, with great results.

A devastating flood swept through Louisiana when I was eleven years old. It began at Cairo, Illinois, where the Ohio River meets the Mississippi, after days of rain drove the big rivers out of their banks and into swollen tributaries that couldn't hold the water. It kept raining, and by the time the churning waters reached us, the Mississippi was eighty miles wide in places, and a million and a half people had to run to higher ground with whatever they could carry out of their barns and houses.

The flood of 1927 had already reached national disaster proportions when it hit us. Because Moreau was on a knoll, it was spared. But the major rivers and bayous around us overflowed their banks—especially the Mississippi, Old, Atchafalaya, and Red Rivers—and our house became the center for relief activities and for dignitaries visiting the flood area. Mamma was in charge of Red Cross operations, overseeing the distribution of food, clothing, and medicine to the homeless and finding space for them in emergency tent shelters.

Secretary of Commerce Herbert Hoover was sent by President Calvin Coolidge to supervise and coordinate flood recovery and to make recommendations for flood control. Because of Mamma's and Daddy George's prominence in the area and Mamma's Red Cross activities put her in the front line of flood relief, they were asked by the organizers of the trip to entertain Mr. Hoover when his special train arrived in Pointe Coupee Parish.

As you can imagine, much folderol surrounded Mr. Hoover's visit. His inspection tour was scheduled for the middle of the day, which meant we had to move our main meal to the evening. My mother called in the help to inform them of this major shift in household routine, making certain they understood what time they would have to come back to prepare and serve dinner.

She asked Louis to chill a good wine, and she persuaded my stepfather to break out one of his precious pints of prescription whiskey to be served to Secretary Hoover's group when they returned from their tour. She knew they would be tired and wet, and she asked Louis to pour the whiskey into a fancy decanter for serving. This was during Prohibition, when everyone made wine at home and pints of whiskey were available only with a doctor's prescription.

Everybody except Aunt Hannah was going to have an opportunity to meet Mr. Hoover and his group, but Mamma wanted to make sure that no one was left out. After giving it some thought, Mamma decided Aunt Hannah could meet him by announcing the dinner. Since this was not her regular duty, Mamma rehearsed her on what to say: "Come into the parlor and you say, 'Dinner is served,' in a low voice." Aunt Hannah practiced until Mamma said, "Oh, that's just perfect."

We were ready, but the group touring the flood was later and later. Dinner was put off time and again, and Aunt Hannah became more and more provoked with the whole arrangement. At last Mr. Hoover and the other dignitaries arrived. Louis brought in a beautiful silver tray with the decanter, glasses, and ice, but none of the visitors would touch the whiskey. In those days all sorts of bootleg whiskey was available, some not so good, some downright dangerous. Mamma hadn't thought of that, but Daddy George did.

He excused himself and returned with a full bottle of whiskey with the labels still on it, making sure it was sealed before he handed it to Louis. Louis passed the bottle around, inviting the first man to open it and then whoever wanted some to have a welcome swig. All of that delayed dinner even longer, and Aunt Hannah was now extremely tired.

Her moment finally arrived. She walked into the parlor and announced: "Dinner is served, in a low voice. Now y'all come and get your supper."

The next day Uncle Daddy took me in a motorboat to see the flood around Moreau. We made our way across the Atchafalaya River onto the opposite bank and into Bayou des Glaises, where tall native grasses were completely submerged. The water swirled around us and splashed over the sides of the boat, bloated bodies of animals and household furniture swished by, and although I was scared, I was more excited to be out in the flood everyone was talking about. I remember the boat ride specifically because Mamma was beside herself when we returned home and she found out where Uncle Daddy had taken me.

Her role in the flood exemplified Southern women's performance in the face of adversity, corralling their own strengths and the diverse goods and services others rendered to organize everything while maintaining great composure. Seeing my mother's willingness and ability to gather all the forces of the household and environs to entertain and calmly feed large numbers of people and adjust schedules under the most disorganized conditions prepared me as well as anything could (not to mention the many campaigns—local state and national—that I would eventually run) for being married to Hale Boggs.

Even in normal times the rivers were eating away the earth beneath our feet. It was a simple law of nature: The twisting Mississippi was seeking a more direct route to the Gulf of Mexico. At its intersection with the Old River, a mile and a half from Moreau, part of its water was going into the Old to join the Atchafalaya's comparatively straight course southward a few miles farther on—a course to the gulf half the length of the Mississippi's.

By 1977, fifty years later, all of Moreau's large front yard and the land that had been occupied by the house were gone. Where the kitchen garden had been was a levee on the Old River. My firsthand experiences prepared me well for future service with congressional committees dealing with river and flood control because I could make other members visualize the flood as I had lived it, and comprehend the pain and losses it had inflicted.

During congressional hearings on funding a system to control the Old River, I came across a yellowed newspaper article tucked into an old Bible. It was from the *New Orleans Daily Picayune* of October 13, 1887, quoting a prominent general who said it was "imperative" to keep the Mississippi River from changing course at the Old River. I took the article to the hearing room the next day.

The flood of 1927 finally brought about extensive federal involvement in Louisiana flood control. It was obvious that the state couldn't do what was needed on its own, even though everyone detested giving up any rights. Mr. Hoover's plan, which included floodways and levees in Louisiana, was passed by Congress in 1929, and right away young Corps of Engineers officers began working up and down our rivers.

On most weekends a public dance would be held in a high school auditorium and the engineers and local people would attend. Mamma and Mrs. Hopgood allowed Vera Lee and me go with the older boys in her family. We were twelve or thirteen, and we would put on our mothers' high-heeled shoes and Tangee lipstick and dab a little Vaseline on our eyelashes and off we'd go. We didn't dance a whole dance with anybody; the boys "tapped"—cut in—and our older escorts were always there so if any unsavory person cut in they could come right back to us. Sometimes the engineers asked us to dance.

During peach season Vera Lee and I picked peaches in the Moreau orchard, and when we would fill a basket, we'd sit on the fence by the road and sell them. We were sitting there one day, scruffy little girls in our jeans, when a group of engineers came by and stopped to talk. We'd been to a dance the night before, and one of the boys had asked me for a dance. When his buddies got a look at me in the daylight without Mamma's makeup or high-heeled shoes, they saw how young I was and they began kidding him unmercifully.

Twenty years later Hale and I were coming back from Germany by ship when we encountered a terrible storm that had everyone sick and clinging to the bunks. It was so severe we averaged only 1.5 knots in twenty-four hours. I was lying in my bunk feeling awful when an officer in the Army Engineers stepped into our stateroom. Hale was one of the few people still up and about, and I guess he had met him and brought him around.

The officer looked at me and said, "Lindy Claiborne, I hope you die." He was the one who'd asked me to dance and been ridiculed by his friends that day Vera Lee and I were selling our peaches. If I had had the strength, I would have thrown something at him.

I was asleep in my bed in the school dormitory one night when a familiar voice roused me, saying, "Don't be alarmed, dear, but please get up because the convent is on fire." I opened my eyes to see one of the nuns. Around me other boarders were being awakened. We had heard nothing, and we never did anything without a bell—we lived by the bells. Despite the nuns' urgings, none of us budged until one of them had the presence of mind to ring a bell. We all immediately recognized it as the get-up bell and we thought, My Lord, it really is a fire!

The convent burned down, but no one was hurt. The next day, help came from everyone in town; they all loved the nuns. A widower moved out of his house and gave it to them for their convent, the owner of a dry goods and furniture store provided all of the furnishings they needed, and the Masons donated their Masonic Hall to be the school. We instantly began calling it "Saint Mason's Academy." By the time I graduated, the townspeople had built a new school in which we were living comfortably.

A much more personally devastating fire struck Moreau two years later, on a night when my parents had gone to a party in New Roads. I was fourteen and an older cousin, Miss Florence Kingsbury, had come to be with me, staying in a guest room on the opposite side of the house from my room and my parents' room.

I was feeling lonely that evening because Mother Gertrude had recently died. Her death and the wake and burial had been a traumatic experience, and I was physically fatigued, feeling kind of forlorn. I asked my cousin if I could sleep in the other bed in her room and we were fast asleep when we were awakened by Joe Trueblood and Nelse, the hostler, banging on the doors and windows and yelling at us to get out of the house—that it was on fire.

The fire had begun above my parents' room, ignited by a fireplace spark that had landed on the wood-shingle roof. A hard wind was blowing, and the fire spread faster than the eye could follow it. Joe and Nelse had thought that I was in my room, and they ran around the gallery to wake me, worried to death that the roof had already fallen in. When I didn't answer their calls, they entered the room through the tall gallery windows and saw I wasn't there. They knew Cousin Florence was visiting and they rushed to the guest room to lead us to safety.

It was bedlam. The fire whipped through the house, and sparks showered onto the outbuildings, until almost everything was ablaze. The air was filled with shouts from the workers and a terrible roar and crashing of burning timbers. All the people who worked on the plantation came running from their houses to help. Because it was a Saturday night, many of them had been partying, and they were climbing on top of buildings to throw off flaming boards, being braver than they ordinarily might have been when they were cold sober. I begged them to come down, but they were determined to help.

I had always been the favored child, with people doing things for me, but in this awful emergency without parents, grandparents, aunts, or uncles, "Miss Baby" had to take charge, telling people what to do and keeping them from killing themselves as the fire roared out of control. I thought of Grandmother Rets and Mamma, and I knew that I could do what they would do.

"Get down off that roof!" I can hear myself shouting it all these years later. I felt the responsibility as a terrible and heavy burden, but there was nothing else I could do.

The wind kept changing. People dashed through the flames to bring things out of the house and put them where they seemed safe, and then the wind changed and everything they had rescued was burned to ashes. Among the few things saved was a portrait of Daddy George's great-uncle. I was scared to death of that old man when I was a little girl, because the eyes in the portrait seemed to peer right into my bedroom door and follow me around.

We had water wells, but with the plantation's power plant in flames, there was no electricity to pump the water; it was the same as having none. The house and several buildings burned to the ground, but no one was badly hurt. We got all the animals out, and the barns and kennels and cock cages were spared, but we were too late to save Mamma's rabbits.

My parents had left their party and started home before we tried to get in touch with them. I knew they would see the fire long before they reached us—it was so huge everybody for miles could see it—so a neighbor drove up the road to meet them and tell them I was safe.

That awful night was a revealing experience. It showed me the devotion of the people who worked on the plantation—not only their physical protection of me but the care they had for the place and the tenderness with which they treated the animals. I was also made aware of the strong ties of friendship that brought distant neighbors hurrying to help, even at the risk of their own welfare.

There wasn't sufficient insurance to rebuild the house, and we were, as they say, land poor, so we moved into an unoccupied house that had once been the residence of the plantation superintendent and that fortunately had its own electrical generating plant. Animals had roamed through it while it was vacant, and we cleaned it up and then Mamma went to work on it.

She had a special talent for pulling together diverse furnishings and decorative pieces to create attractive places, which was put to the test as she combined and coordinated family pieces with comfortable upholstered furniture and practical chests and cupboards that she bought. She worked miracles and created an extremely bright, comfortable, and pleasant home. When Aunt Paule Parlange, an old family friend, came to call, she looked around and exclaimed, "Corinne, dear, you have done such a marvelous job with this house! You've given it a wonderful atmosphere."

Mamma laughed and said, "The goats got here before me."

Our household staff moved with us, although there didn't seem to be as much to do in the smaller house, and Mamma and Daddy George added a glassed-in room and bath so Mamma's brother, Harriss ("Chic") Morrison, could leave the Tuberculosis Hospital in New Orleans and live with us. Louis assumed the role of caretaker and companion, often rising in the night because, he would explain, he "just knew Mr. Chic was awake and lonesome."

The Moreau fire marked the beginning of the end of my childhood. I grew up that night, proving to myself that despite my fears and anguish and my years as "Miss Baby," the pet, I knew what to do in a real-life, adult emergency, and I had acted with authority. I still own a little piece of Moreau. I lease it out to a tenant who grows soybeans and corn. He'd so love to buy it, but I can't make myself give it up.

I don't know how I ended up graduating from high school two months after my fifteenth birthday, but I did, and for Daddy George's sake, I was glad to be the valedictorian. But Saint Joseph's taught me in areas beyond the academic. A reporter asked me once what preparation I had received for political life, and I said I had received perfect training for serving on the House Appropriations Committee because I had been taught by the nuns that I was doing people a favor when I gave them the opportunity to contribute to a good cause.

But that was far down the road as I left Saint Joseph's Academy on a day sweet with the scent of magnolias and sad with the tears of good-bye. As I turned my thoughts toward college, I didn't dream reporters would one day be asking me questions; I dreamed *I* would be the reporter.

CHAPTER FOUR

***

I FIRST MET Hale Boggs at a fraternity dance my freshman year in college. I was a student at Newcomb College for women in New Orleans, the coordinate college to Tulane University, where he was a freshman.

The very first week of the sorority and fraternity "rush season" while I was dancing with someone at the Beta Theta Pi fraternity house, Hale had a friend of his come to tap and introduce me to him, and then Hale and I began dancing. He was good-looking, over six feet tall, with wavy brown hair above a high forehead and expressive dark blue eyes.

He swirled me around for a moment, fairly awkwardly, and then he said in a pleasant, mellow voice, "I'm going to marry you someday."

I was shocked. I don't remember saying anything; I just looked desperately around for somebody else to come tap. As soon as someone did and Hale walked away, I said, "Who was that crazy boy?"

Hale had arrived at Tulane with an honors scholarship and thirty-five dollars—the first bestowed because of his special gifts as an orator and leader at Long Beach (Mississippi) High School; the second saved from summer jobs. He received the four-year scholarship because Tulane President A. E. Dinwiddie had heard from the Long Beach school superintendent about the boy's exceptional abilities and the family's scant means imposed by the economic depression.

In high school Hale repeatedly won a newspaper contest that challenged students in Louisiana and Mississippi to choose the most important news item of the week and explain why it was important. First prize was ten dollars, with lesser amounts down to fourth place. He won a total of four hundred dollars and helped his school win the grand prize. Unusually poised for a teenage boy, he honed and practiced his speaking skills, consistently winning or placing in regional oratorical contests. In his junior year, fellow students voted him "Best All-Around Student" and "Best-Looking Boy." The next year he was president of his senior class.

His parents, William Robertson ("Will") Boggs and Claire Josephine Hale Boggs, were from the Mississippi Gulf Coast. Hale was born in Long Beach on February 15, 1914, and named Thomas Hale Boggs. He was the third of six children, four boys and two girls.

Their father was a dear man, strong-minded and often argumentative about politics. He worked in a bank in Gulfport and later in banks around New Orleans until the depression deepened and the family moved back to Long Beach to try to hold on to its property. Will built tourist cabins on it in an attempt to make ends meet, but there were few tourists. Like many families at that time, the Boggses' financial situation was precarious.

Hale's mother was energetic and pretty and quite religious. When the boys were young, she sent them off to be altar boys, and she got everybody to church and into Catholic grade schools. Even when the children were grown and raising their own families, she reminded them to go to Mass.

When Hale's younger brother, Robert ("Robbie") was offered a baseball scholarship to Loyola University, Josephine moved the family to New Orleans so that the boys could live at home and afford to go to college. Besides Robbie, who became the dean of students at Loyola and a Jesuit priest, Hale's siblings were William ("Billy"), the eldest; Mary ("Sissy"), who worked as a secretary to help put her brothers through college; Claire ("Tootsie"), who married my mother's youngest brother after Hale and I were married; and Archie, who became a lawyer and judge.

Newcomb and Tulane offered some complementary courses, enabling students to take classes at both institutions. Most of my friends had gone to LSU—among them Jack Hopgood, Vera Lee's big brother, who was a childhood beau—but I was steered toward Newcomb by my aunts, especially Aunt Frosty, who was a graduate. I lived with Grandmother Rets at her apartment near her guest house on Neron Place, not far from the campus, but before I made many new friends I went up to LSU so many weekends my buddies up there began calling me "the Tiger Lady," for the school's tiger mascot.

My role-model was Margaret Bourke-White. A prominent photojournalist and a dashing character accepted in the mostly male professional world, she was a great heroine to my generation. I wanted to be like her and go all over the world covering stories, learning about different cultures and civilizations, photographing people's lives and their habitats. I wanted to participate in great events and be where the action was.

I took a general freshman course and studied journalism in the afternoons at Tulane. I tried to learn photography—Newcomb had an excellent department—but I didn't have the knack. I loved journalism, history, and English, and I made good grades in them; but I had trouble with French when I was put in an advanced class I couldn't handle and it pulled down my average. That didn't worry me as much for myself as for Daddy George, because he was trying to give me every advantage and I hated to disappoint him.

Newcomb's art department was renowned, and we had a young, extremely attractive art history professor who had an absolute hatred of anything rococo. Imagine someone living in New Orleans with a fixation against all those ornate, treasured buildings and furnishings that had been there since the first French inhabitants!

A few of us who weren't art majors and didn't need an A in the class became weary of his tirades, and we wrote a composite letter, pretending it was from one girl. "I have been in love with you since the moment I laid eyes on you," it said, "and lately, I have the feeling that there is a spark of interest on your part, too. I hope and pray this is true. I will know it is true and that you will meet me here tonight at six-thirty if you mention the word 'rococo' in your class today."

The next day the poor young man was talking away and every once in a while, he'd start to rail against rococo and he'd suddenly have to catch himself. It was all we could do to keep from laughing out loud, but we didn't dare give it away. He must have suspected the letter was a joke or a trick, but we had upset him sufficiently that he quit reviling rococo.

Everybody in college went out with worlds of people. We were gregarious and cordial, the whole crowd getting along and doing things together. Two special friends of mine were Bob Haynie and John Kostmayer. Initially I'd date one of them, and the other would bring along his girl, but after a while the three of us began running around and we became great buddies and sustaining friends. John's daddy was dean of the Tulane Medical School and our beloved family surgeon, and many years later I served in Congress with John's son, Peter, a representative from Pennsylvania who enjoyed the tales I told him of his father's college days.

Donald McKay, whom I still hold as a good friend, was my most consistent date my freshman year. I didn't date Hale, and although he later was one of the regulars, we didn't become sweethearts until I was out of school. By then he claimed he had forgotten all about saying he was going to marry me, but it made an indelible impression on me.

On dates we would go to the movies, a dance, or a fraternity party. Nobody had much cash, but at any neighborhood drugstore with a soda fountain a couple could split a big Louisiana poor-boy sandwich and a quart-size milk shake for twenty-five cents. The new Pontchartrain Beach opened with rides and little restaurants and inexpensive places to dance, and occasionally we splurged and went to La Lune in the French Quarter after a fraternity dance. Most places in the Quarter were closed during Prohibition, and besides I was too young to go to speakeasies.

Fraternity dances ended at eleven-thirty, but the Saturday night dance at the New Orleans Country Club, with Papa Celestin and his jazz band, lasted until twelve-thirty so everybody rushed out there for an extra hour of fun. Every once in a while I'd sneak out and have a late date. That was adventurous and had me wondering if I were going to get home in time, if my early date was going to stick around, and if the second one would run into him.

A Jefferson Parish nightclub was another of our favorite places. It had a separate gambling casino, and the gaming profits enabled the owners to book the best dance bands in the country. When Guy Lombardo and his orchestra were appearing, I wanted to go. A Southern orchestra leader, Gus Arnheim, had written a song I loved, called "Sweet and Lovely," and I told one of the boys I dated that Lombardo's recording sounded better than Arnheim's.

The seventh consecutive night that a date took me there and we came swinging past the band, Mr. Lombardo leaned over and said, "I know. Miss Claiborne would like to hear 'Sweet and Lovely.'"

The poor guys. I didn't tell any of them that everyone else was taking me there.

In my sophomore year I began living with Mamma's eldest sister, my devoted godmother Aunt Rowena Buffington and her husband, the ophthalmologist who had intended to perform Biz's cataract surgery. I lived with them in the Garden District until I finished college, working sometimes in Uncle Wiley's office and sharing an apartment in their house with his young niece, Jane Buffington, who had come from South Carolina to attend Newcomb. Rowena and Wiley did not have children, though they nurtured, educated, and housed many nieces and nephews and eventually great-nieces and nephews and children of good friends. They always had so many houseguests that once, when Uncle Wiley suggested to the mother of a young out-of-town patient that she and her son stay with them, the woman replied, "But, Doctor, we've been staying with you for ten days!"

Hale majored in journalism and was campus correspondent for the *New Orleans States,* working on their copy desk at night and in the summers. He was also campus representative for Beech-Nut chewing gum, servicing stores around the university and giving away lots of gum to pretty girls. He distinguished himself early by being only the second freshman ever to win the Carnot medal, Tulane's highest debate award.

As a sophomore Hale was cited for outstanding general achievement in journalism and he was appointed by the faculty advisor to be news editor of the Tulane student newspaper, the *Hullabaloo.* His coworkers elected him president of Theta Nu journalism fraternity, and he was a natural leader among his Beta Theta Pi social fraternity brothers, who nicknamed him Senator, in recognition of his political prowess in campus activities, including the Theta Nu election.

As an upperclassman I joined the staff of *Hullabaloo* and reached the highest position open to a woman, Newcomb editor—the women's news editor. It was a fascinating job and great fun, mostly because of the others on the staff. Hale was editor in chief, trying to decide if he wanted to be a journalist or a lawyer. He loved newspaper work and thought it was the ideal field for his talents and energies.

Coworkers included Howard K. Smith, who went on to a brilliant career in radio and television news; Herman Neugass, a 1936 Olympic athlete who refused to compete after Hitler insulted Jesse Owens; Moise Dennery, who became a law-school classmate of Hale's, a devoted friend and a prominent New Orleans civic leader; Larry Eustis, future invaluable aide in Hale's and then my campaigns for Congress and a successful New Orleans businessman and state senator; and Thilo von Kurnatowski, whose Russian family had fled the Bolsheviks and who was killed in World War II.

Our biggest foray into political journalism came when United States senator and former Louisiana governor Huey Long tried to censor the LSU student newspaper, the *Reveille*, by ordering it to not print articles critical of him, even though he was openly meddling in university affairs. Its editors refused to acknowledge Long's authority, and to protest against his censorship, the entire staff followed Editor in Chief Dave McGuire and resigned. We had already put the weekly *Hullabaloo* to bed when we heard this news, and we all dashed down to the printshop, tore up the front page, and remade it with an impassioned editorial supporting McGuire and the *Reveille* staff.

Huey Long championed many populist causes and put into practice programs for social welfare. He certainly wanted to upgrade educational opportunities with free textbooks and improved university and medical teaching facilities, and he improved the basic infrastructure with farm-to-market roads and bridges. We agreed with all of that, but his methods were extremely antidemocratic and his muzzling the student newspaper served simply as the latest outrage. We were incensed by his dictatorial meddling.

Those were the exciting days of the New Deal. While it was met with resistance in the more conservative Southern areas, Hale had a vision that was remarkable for a college student. I admired his interest in national and international affairs, his quick understanding of issues, and his aspirations for the United States and the world. He was excited about the efforts of President Roosevelt to lift the nation out of the economic depression by sweeping economic and financial rearrangements and by the President's inclusion of social services as part of an economic recovery package and of government-sponsored work programs, not only to hire the unemployed but also to extend the physical infrastructure of the nation. Hale wrote thoughtful editorials about the long-term beneficial effects of the Social Security system when many leaders were damning it as socialism. I began to share his vision as he led me and others in an exciting intellectual experience that gave us, as well, the satisfaction of being campus leaders.

Many of us were strongly against U.S. participation in the war in Europe, and we showed our disapproval with noisy rallies and marches that always drew big campus crowds. Hale dressed in a mock-military uniform to represent "the General" at one rally, cosponsored by the Young Men's Christian Association, and his picture ran on the front page of the *New Orleans States*.

He and some buddies formed an organization called Veterans of Future Wars, which brought an amused reaction from Tulane's acting president, Douglas Anderson. But President Anderson was immediately criticized by the local American Legion, an indication of the pro-military attitude of World War I veterans. Hale was a strong advocate of an international organization to achieve and maintain world peace, or at the least a United States of Europe.

Owing to his leadership and skill as a speaker, he was appointed student chairman of a university campaign to construct a student union building. In that capacity he addressed campus organizations to promote the building drive, and as a favor to a friend, he spoke to a handful of would-be organizers of the American Student Union, which hoped eventually to have official representation on the campus. Little did we know how these college activities, so harmless at the time, would come back to haunt us in later years.

When I began dating Marvin Harvard, a medical student, Hale used to place an apple on my desk every day "to keep the doctor away." I was very fond of Marvin, and he was a wonderful dancer, but there was no exclusivity about our relationship. He eventually became head of the Medical Department at Yale University.

Newcomb had a rule that any student who married had to resign. It seems ridiculous now, but because of the rule, it wasn't until the senior year that most students began to settle down and get serious about anyone. Everyone in my family who met Hale was crazy about him, but that was not the determining factor in the way I felt. Even though I found him very good-looking and greatly admired his intellectual abilities, we weren't ready to say we were serious.

As graduation approached Hale made up his mind: Instead of attending law school he would go into newspaper work. He went down to see Major Crown, the quintessential newspaperman and his editor at the *States,* to tell him of his decision. He expected to be congratulated and offered a permanent job, and he was eager to accept it.

Crown, who had a special fondness for Hale and who admired his abilities and expected him to become a successful attorney, listened quietly and then snapped, "Too bad. You're fired." Hale was stunned and he tried, unsuccessfully, to change the editor's mind. Major Crown had a great influence on Hale's future by seeing a potential other than journalism and forcing him to reconsider career choices. Hale thought about his future and changed his mind. Once he was enrolled in the Tulane Law School, Crown rehired him for his part-time jobs.

Honors came pouring in as Hale headed for law school. He was chosen for membership in Phi Beta Kappa, the national honor society, and he received a scholarship to law school. Then he was chosen for the board of editors of the *Law Review* and then he ran for president of the College of Law student body.

It was his first real political race, and I helped as much I could, talking up his candidacy without imposing myself too much, but he was defeated in the runoff by Charlie Marshall, who wanted the position more. It was a lesson Hale never forgot.

When I graduated from Newcomb, jobs were scarce and everyone was scrambling for them. Saint James Parish had an opening for a history and English teacher with a library certificate. I took a short course in library science at Loyola, qualified for the job, and was hired. At the age of nineteen, off I went to Romeville, a little river town in an area of old plantations sixty-five miles from New Orleans. Students came from all over the area, and as was usual in those days of legally enforced segregation, all of them were white. Black students went to separate schools.

The home economics teacher, Agnes Duncan, and I shared a rented cottage with the agriculture teacher and his wife, the Duhons. Our school principal, Mr. J. B. Dicharry, was a darling man, but he had fourteen children of his own and there was very little formal discipline in the school.

I taught English and literature to freshmen and sophomores, world history to juniors, and American history to seniors (some of whom were my age or older). To celebrate the Sesquicentennial of the U.S. Constitution, I held a constitutional convention, and all my students became the delegates. I wanted them to realize the difficulties involved and the compromises necessary to create a document that had endured 150 years, and to be aware of their responsibility to protect and advance it.

I still meet elderly gentlemen who say, "You remember me, Miss Claiborne. I was James Madison" (or one of the other delegates).

All my life I had heard the adults in my family talk about being loyal to the federal Constitution, yet being loyal to the South's place under it. When I was about five, everyone was interested in the state constitutional convention. Later, Hewitt Bouanchaud, who was from Pointe Coupee Parish and had been chairman of the convention as well as lieutenant governor and speaker of the state legislature, was married to my Aunt Eustatia Morrison, which brought home to me those discussions.

Hale dated many girls in college and for a while, he had a special girlfriend, Mary Louise ("Weezie") Tobin, but a mutual friend of ours, Louise Tarlton, didn't think Weezie and Hale belonged together. She thought Hale and I did, so she began pushing us toward each other, and it worked. We were friends before we began dating seriously, having fun together and developing mutual respect while we were working on the *Hullabaloo*. Our getting together was "just one of those things," as a popular song of the day declares, that are meant to happen, with a little push from our friend.

Hale still lived in New Orleans, and he would get out of law school on Friday, pick me up in Romeville and take me home to New Roads or to stay with one of my relatives in New Orleans, then drive me back on Sunday. The first time I took him to New Roads was the day after Uncle Daddy had been elected district attorney.

We stopped at his house to congratulate him and Aunt Adrienne, and to celebrate with them and their friends. Hale was fascinated with their romantic story. Aunt Adrienne had been the Mardi Gras Queen of Rex in 1906 and was engaged to be married when she and Ferd met. After a whirlwind courtship, they eloped to be married. They didn't have children, and they both loved being with young people. Aunt Adrienne's niece Joel Lawrence lived with them during her school years, and we remain good and close friends.

We were all having a grand time until Mamma sent over Louis who interrupted the festivities to tell me, "We've been holding up dinner for two days for you so it's time for you to leave, but you better go by Miss Eustatia's house because your mamma's over there."

We went to see Aunt Eustatia, who was married to Hewitt Bouanchaud. He was the incumbent district attorney who had lost the election to Uncle Daddy. Everyone at their house was long-faced and quiet, still shocked that Hewitt had lost. I was ashamed that I had celebrated so with Uncle Daddy when it was Uncle Hewitt he had defeated.

Hale teased me unmercifully about what a hypocrite I was to be celebrating with the winner and weeping with the loser. I felt so bad about it that I sought out a priest for advice. I said, "I guess I'm a terrible hypocrite. I celebrated with the winner and I wept with the loser."

The priest laughed and said, "It's a shame you're a girl, my dear. You should have been a Jesuit."

One of the most jarring turning points in my life occurred around this time. Hale was studying for exams, and the beau of a chum, Marie Louise Tessier, was on his initial voyage following graduation from Annapolis, so Marie Louise and I went to her family's place in Pass Christian, Mississippi, for a few days at the beach.

Our first night there we went to the movies and won a pass that meant we could get in for nothing, and we ended up going to the movies every night. When we returned home, we'd stay up late yakking about the movie we'd seen or our families or talk about books we were reading or current events or boyfriends. The next morning we would be really tired.

We had been determined to teach ourselves how to cook and had told the family's cook, who lived there, we wouldn't be needing her, but we never did get around to learning to cook. A group of friends came on Saturday, and Mrs. Tessier arrived from New Orleans to chaperone the house party. The cook was reinstalled and "the big groceries were made," as we say in Louisiana (we "make groceries," "catch a Mass," "and pass a good time").

At Pass Christian the sand slopes so gradually beneath the water that everyone builds a long pier in order to reach water that's deep enough for swimming. We all went out on the end of the Tessier pier to play cards and swim. I went out even though I was tired, and I noticed it was a choppy, blustery day on the water. Ignoring that, however, I decided to go for a swim.

I swam out a short distance when I realized that the waves were extremely high and battering, so high it was ridiculous of me to be in the water in the first place. All of a sudden I felt so exhausted and devoid of energy that if one more wave hit me in the face, there was no way I could make it back to the pier. I began yelling for help, but the waves were so high and loud no one noticed until Steve Weissinger caught on to my predicament and dived in to save me.

I'd been taught to put my hand on the shoulder of the rescuer, but when I tried to do that Steve thought I was fighting him, and he gave me a little knockout blow and dragged me in. Later I remembered being on the pier and somebody pushing water out of my lungs, crawling the last two steps of the stairs into the house, and lying on a bed with the canopy above me spinning around. I went to bed with a small concussion and didn't wake up for hours.

Until that day I had been daring. Early experiences had induced in me a fear of fire, but otherwise I remained adventurous. When I had started driving, the New Roads town marshal declared, "I've been with you through roller skates, bicycles, horses, and water skis, but I am not ready for Lindy Claiborne driving a car."

The experience of nearly drowning fundamentally changed my behavior and attitude toward my expectations in life. I became much more cautious, realizing that I was vulnerable and that perhaps I wasn't going to escape from all those wild horse rides or automobile turnovers forever. I was very much in love with Hale and that made me want to protect our future together. Whatever and wherever that future might be, I knew that life with Hale Boggs would never be boring.

CHAPTER FIVE

*H*ALE AND I decided to be married in the fall of 1937. I
finished teaching school that summer and went home to be with
my family, but I had an emergency appendectomy, and my recu-
peration caused us to postpone the wedding until January.

Because I expected to stay for several months in Pointe Coupee,
when a teacher friend asked me to substitute for her until Christmas, I gladly accepted. She was expecting a baby, and teachers
were not allowed to be in the classroom during pregnancy. I filled
in at the Livonia School near New Roads and was able to be with
my parents, cousins, and friends and to plan my wedding.

Mamma found me fretting one day because there were so many
people I wanted to ask to be in my wedding party that I was afraid
it was becoming too big. Mamma said, "What difference does it
make if it's ten people or fifteen? Why should you agonize over it,
and why should you hurt anybody's feelings? It's your wedding."
I invited them all.

I designed my wedding dress and had it created by the local
woman who was the most popular dressmaker in New Roads. It
was white satin, a very simple cut with a long train, which the
dressmaker said was like hemming Pointe Coupee Parish. I carried

a bouquet of white roses and camellias. Although the fashion in clothes was Chanel, tailored and sophisticated, for my bridesmaids I chose the new-again feminine Southern look in pink and blue. I almost felt I was imposing on them to make them buy sissy-looking dresses, but they were especially pretty and it turned out to be a gloriously beautiful day, warm enough to wear the dresses without a wrap.

Because I was required to fast from midnight until the Nuptial Mass, I spent the night before my wedding at Uncle Daddy and Aunt Adrienne's home, which was near the Church, hoping to sleep until an hour before the ceremony so I wouldn't be too hungry and feel faint. About six o'clock in the morning, Uncle Daddy came bouncing into my room, laughing and calling to me. I yelled at him as I buried my head under the pillow.

"Ohhh, beautiful is the bride the rain rains on," he exclaimed, "and happy is the bride the sun shines on, but glorious is the bride the cock crows on!" I threw my pillow at him.

He stayed a few minutes, and we talked about Hale, how everyone recognized him as a natural leader and a natural politician destined for great things. Uncle Daddy warned me that even though people sometimes wouldn't agree with Hale's views and they said so, I shouldn't be concerned about their criticism.

Hale was a forceful person, intellectually oriented and an omnivorous reader, able to absorb a tremendous amount of information, glean from it the important elements and marshal everything to create understanding. At Tulane he had been a hail-fellow-well-met when necessary, and he did it very well, but I had also seen a side of him that was self-examining and driven.

I told Uncle Daddy that as Hale's wife, I knew I could handle everything except the criticism. I wasn't sure how I might react to that.

"Everybody in politics is adversely criticized," Uncle Daddy said. "When people criticize Hale, don't let it bother you. Remember, nobody kicks a dead dog."

We were married on January 22, 1938, in the presence of my beloved Father Hoes in Saint Mary's Church in New Roads, where my mother and daddy had been married and I had been baptized, received my first Holy Communion, and been confirmed. I was twenty-one and Hale was twenty-three.

Fifteen bridesmaids and fifteen groomsmen made up the wedding party, and my maid of honor was Halcyon Colomb—who was being married three weeks later—a Catholic girl in love with Billy Holmes, the son of a Methodist bishop. When Halcyon decided to be married by Billy's father in his church, her Catholic friends were not allowed to participate in the wedding and we weren't supposed to attend, so strict were the rules of the Catholic church at the time. I respected what she was doing, and she understood why we couldn't participate, but thank goodness all that has changed. I chose Halcyon to show her how much I loved her and how sorry I was we couldn't be with her.

The church was overflowing with guests. My countless relatives, scores of our friends, and members of Hale's family were joined by the forty-four out-of-town wedding party guests who were staying with our friends in New Roads. The main altar and two side altars were beautifully banked with huge sprays of Pink Perfection camellias, gifts from the trees of generous family friends, amid gleaming Ligustrum leaves.

One of the groomsmen, Arthur de la Houssaye, was a camellia fancier and just beginning his own garden. While he was standing at the altar, I heard him mutter, "My God, seven years' growth in one vase. How could they do it?" He was horrified that people had cut their precious old camellia limbs. Because fasting before mass sometimes caused me to faint, Arthur was carrying a little bottle of ammonia for me, but when I heard his comment, I urged *him* to use it.

After the wedding we and our witnesses went to a side altar to sign the marriage certificate. My two uncles, who had run against each other for district attorney, were witnesses, and they had a good time joshing each other:

"Will you respect my signature?" Uncle Daddy asked.

"I don't know. Will you respect mine?" asked Uncle Hewitt.

"I'll have to think about that," Uncle Daddy said.

I had such a good time at the reception at Uncle Daddy's house that I didn't want to leave. The only disturbing note came from Archie, Hale's youngest brother, still a teenager, who looked as though he had been crying. I was apprehensive, thinking something terrible had happened, and when he reached us in the receiving line, I said, "Archie, what's the matter? Anything wrong?"

" 'Anything wrong?' " he repeated. "Hale's going to go away and live with you and not live with us any more!"

"If you feel that way about it, you can come and live with us," I said.

"It wouldn't be the same."

Dear Archie. Many years later during Hale's most difficult campaign, Hale and I stayed with him and his wonderful wife, Sally, who sustained us through that trying experience.

After the reception we drove past the church so we could always remember how beautiful it was, then we set off for a Mexican honeymoon in a Model A Ford Hale had acquired in school. A new highway was open to Mexico City and Acapulco, and we were eager to use it. Everybody had either wanted to lend us a better automobile or insisted that we buy a new one, but the Model A was serviceable and, most important, we could afford to fix it in the event of trouble.

We went by to see Hale's brother Robbie, at the Jesuit Seminary in Grand Coteau, Louisiana, and after we left, I began feeling ill with the flu. We stopped in Houston with Hale's Uncle Robbie and Aunt Delia until I was better, and then, because we had lost some time, we decided to go only as far as Monterrey, Mexico.

We stayed downtown at the Gran Hotel Ancira. The weather was delightfully warm, and we strolled among the flowers and palm trees in the main plaza, listening to a band concert and exploring the cool, austere recesses of the massive old cathedral. It was a very relaxing time. As soon as we crossed the bridge back into the United States, the Model A went into a coma and quit. We stayed in Laredo until it was fixed.

Ten days after we had left, we returned to New Roads for a visit and discovered some of the out-of-town wedding guests, still having too good a time to go home. However, we didn't tarry long; we were anxious to set up housekeeping in New Orleans.

Hale and I took over the lease on some friends' apartment on Valence Street until October, when we could move into our own place. All New Orleans leases ran from October 1 to September 30, which meant everybody moved in October. We had fallen in love with a raised cottage on Louisiana Avenue, near the Touro Infirmary, and we were lucky to make a deposit on an apartment there. The location proved convenient: Our first three children, Barbara, Tommy, and Cokie, were born at Touro.

Hale joined a general law practice with a longtime mentor and friend, Walter Barnett, and was hired as the general manager of the Tulane Alumni Association at a most welcome eighteen hundred dollars a year. I worked part time in Uncle Wiley's office, which was always packed with patients who would wait for hours to see him. He'd operate very early in the morning, then work in the office, go to lunch at one of his clubs, take a little nap, and come back ready to keep going. If he saw someone he knew with an eye problem while he was at lunch, he would bring that person back and take him or her in a side door ahead of people who had been waiting. I served as a peacemaker, mostly, and I kept track of some of his instruments, which he had a habit of misplacing.

A political revolution swept Louisiana in the late 1930s as a reaction against the excesses of the late Huey Long's political machine. As a Louisiana governor and senator, he had become so powerful that he was often called the "Kingfish," personally controlling appointments to local and state offices, state banking, the production of oil and natural gas, and highway construction. He controlled the government and the elections, and the administration at LSU, in the city of New Orleans and in other jurisdictions of his choosing. It was a situation ripe for crisis.

After he was assassinated in 1935 by Dr. Carl Austin Weiss, his far-flung organization became difficult to control, and evidence surfaced of widespread corruption and graft among his followers in public office. In the private sector the element of greed entered into the picture, and it was almost impossible for anybody to do business unless they did business with the Long people still in power.

A group of young New Orleans business and professional people formed a crusading organization called the People's League. We realized that we were never going to have a part in the future of our state unless we were able to break the grip of the machine and "throw the rascals out." That was our rallying cry as the league became a tremendous movement for reform.

Hale of course was our chairman. The organizers included most of his Tulane Law School class of 1937, spearheaded by Jimmy Coleman and including Marian Mayer, one of two women in the class, and other civic-minded young men and women such as Dave McGuire, who had left LSU when Huey tried to censor the student newspaper. After graduating from the University of Missouri on a journalism scholarship, Dave had come home to help get rid of the Long machine. He eventually became Hale's first campaign manager and first congressional administrative assistant.

Moral and financial support came secretly from a group of prominent, reform-minded businessmen who were apprehensive about being publicly involved. As lawyers, brokers, and major construction contractors, they felt compelled to go along with the machine or risk losing their livelihoods. Herman Kohlmeyer, who became a special friend of mine and Hale's, was their treasurer. The sole purpose of the group, which became known as "the Cold Water Committee" for throwing cold water on the hopes of some prospective candidates who sought its aid, was to pick candidates and spend what was necessary to elect them and get rid of the existing machine.

Women as well as men worked for reform, some as officeholders who saw corrupt situations from the inside and others who were our contemporaries or older, wiser heads, anxious to clean up the state. Activists included Blondie Labouisse, the daughter of U.S. Senator Edward James Gay; Marian Abramson, Phyllis Dennery, and Polkey McIlhenny, future pioneers in public television in the South; Edith Stern, an ardent fighter for human rights and justice; Martha Robinson; Sarah Sharp; Norma Lee; July Waters; Gladys Reily; and Bland Bruns, who later was elected to the state legislature.

From their early efforts were formed two enduring civic organizations: the New Orleans chapter of the League of Women Voters and the Independent Women's Organization, a ward/precinct association to back candidates and issues. Louisiana was basically a one-party state: The Democratic Party had statewide and local organizations, but separate, opposing Democratic factions and splinter groups were numerous. A state Republican Party existed, and when Republican presidents were in office, those Louisianans received federal appointments, but there was little Republican support on the state or local level of government.

The People's League's first public act was a dramatic confrontation with the New Orleans district attorney, Charles A. Byrne, a Long man accused of impeding a grand jury investigation of political corruption. As our chairman Hale led the group up the courthouse steps, demanding that Byrne resign. The resulting public furor had its desired effect and pressured him into doing so. The League next focused on corruption in the State Conservation Department, insisting on public disclosure of all of the oil and mineral rights leases it had authorized. Big headlines and lively news reports of these activities quickly caught the public's attention.

I had grown up with politics as the family vocation, and had helped Newcomb and Tulane students to conduct their campaigns for campus positions. I liked running campaigns for a good cause or a good candidate, and I loved being involved in the People's League, but I never wanted to be a candidate myself. In fact, it never occurred to me. When you're an only child, you want to be accepted by the group, and you're not anxious to get out in front or distance yourself from the others, as a candidate must do.

While Hale and I continued our involvement in reform activities our personal lives took a new turn. I became pregnant and in May 1939 I gave birth to our first child, a beautiful blond-haired girl we named Barbara Rowena Boggs. She was enchanting, unusually smart, and always determined in whatever she did. She looked very much like Hale, with the same expressions he had shown as a baby. When she was a few months old, it was hard to tell from photos of Hale at the same age which was which, except that Hale had worn an old-fashioned baby gown.

Our first foray into statewide politics came that fall, when Sam Jones, a blunt-talking anti-Long attorney from Lake Charles, decided to run for governor against Huey Long's brother, Earl. Hale and some of our other high-powered League leaders met with him and he accepted the League's endorsement, beginning a long association between Hale and Sam, who became close political friends. Statewide offices and seats in the state legislature were being decided, too, and Chep Morrison and Larry Eustis were among our friends who were running for them.

We all worked hard, knocking on doors and talking to people about honest, efficient government; a realignment of state funds to benefit more people, and the need for voting reforms to pave the way to the future. Our idealism and determination carried us many miles. I was asked by the party leaders if I would serve as precinct captain for the 5th precinct of the 12th Ward. Puzzled, I asked, "Don't the police do all of that?" The only time I had been to a precinct station was with a friend who was guilty of a traffic violation. Before long, precincts would become part of my daily vocabulary as I commenced my first formal political participation. I pushed little Barbara in her stroller as I went up and down the blocks ringing doorbells and asking people to vote for Sam Jones and the other league candidates. Barbara declared years afterward that she learned to read upside down from the precinct lists I carried.

One woman I called on was the precinct chairman for an opposing gubernatorial candidate, Jimmy Noe, a former governor.

"I admire Mister Noe, but if I hadn't been committed to him, I probably would be campaigning for Mister Jones," she said. We agreed that if one of our candidates lost in the first primary, we would support the other in the second, the runoff between the top two candidates for the Democratic nomination, which was tantamount to election.

I couldn't wait to tell the other precinct captains that I had found a well-organized woman, highly motivated toward good politics, who would work for us. I announced it at our next meeting, expecting some sign of approval or enthusiasm similar to mine. Instead there was dead silence in the room. I said, "Don't you think that's a good idea?"

A woman looked at me and said, "Honey, haven't you ever heard of patronage?"

Our greatest challenge was voter registration. During the Long years, it had fallen dreadfully low because it seemed not to matter if you voted. Hurdles were placed in the way of white independent voters, and black voters had an especially difficult time because they were subjected to questions that were almost impossible to answer. We thought that everybody should be able to register and to vote—that all people ought to be able to participate in their government.

Only two years earlier, when I reached voting age, I had been required to pass a literacy test and to take three documents with me to the polls: a registration certificate, which I had to remember to get ahead of time, because the registration office closed a month before elections, and poll tax receipts for two years. Huey Long had eliminated the poll tax so that the poor whites would be able to vote, but the receipts were still required to prove one had been a Louisiana resident for two years.

While the Long machine kept many people off the voting rolls, in some precincts names were routinely copied from tombstones and secretly registered, their "votes" to be delivered on election day to the machine's candidates. Years later Rick Tonry, a young Louisiana congressman, had difficulty with similar infractions of the voting laws by some of his people and was confronted on the floor of Congress by a New York Tammany congressman who declared, "What's the matter with you people down in Louisiana, disenfranchising the dead?!"

Black ministers and the Christian black women's organizations rose up and led the way in registering black voters, organizing classes on how to register and car pools to take people to be registered. They were the forerunners by twenty years of the Southern Christian Leadership Conference (SCLC) with young leaders such as Jackson Acox, an organizer of the Orleans Parish People's Voting League, an African-American Democratic organization; the Reverend A. L. Davis, pastor of the New Zion Church and New Orleans's first black city councilman; and the Reverend Avery Alexander, for many years a member of the state legislature.

To protect the integrity of the vote on election day, the League recruited and trained its own poll watchers and commissioners. It wasn't easy to place them because the old system was hard to crack. For us a lot of blind luck was involved. Several watchers or commissioners were allowed at each polling place, and supposedly there was a drawing to see who would go, but we learned as long as we had even one woman at each poll, our group was in good shape.

People did go to prison because of voting irregularities, we constantly reminded one another, and we had help in that respect from O. John Rogge, sent by the Justice Department in Washington to investigate wrongdoing in Louisiana. He became the bête noire of the election bad guys.

The most flagrant voting irregularities involved switching ballot boxes. With the majority of polling places in the garages and houses of people loyal to the machine, anyone could simply bring out a prestuffed ballot box and hide the authentic one if the opposing faction's people left the room for any reason or were not alert. Sometimes all the lights would go out, and the real box would be exchanged for one already stuffed with votes.

In another trick called the "endless chain," the machine's poll commissioner would fill out a ballot and hand it to the first like-minded voter who arrived. That voter would take a blank ballot, as usual, copy it from the ballot filled in by the commissioner, drop the commissioner's ballot into the box, and, on leaving, hand the newly marked ballot to the next person, who repeated the process. This ran up the vote total for all machine candidates.

We sent our women to the polls on election day armed with an awareness of the law and a thorough briefing on their duties. They took a powerful flashlight in case the lights went out, a long list of instructions for poll watchers that had the blessings of the Department of Justice, and a thermos of orange juice which was thought to lessen the likelihood of dehydration and of having to leave the room to go to the bathroom. Years later I heard the ultraconservative Senator Strom Thurmond give the same orange-juice advice to liberal Senator Ted Kennedy as a tactic for conducting a filibuster on the Senate floor.

Our women were well trained, honorable, and smart. The opposition, which had been used to handling only men, was thoroughly mystified. There was no way these women were a token opposition's "good ol' boys," whom they had tricked so often in the past.

The machine had a few women working at the polls, too, one of whom socked Mary Morrison, Cousin Jake's wife. Mary, who was slight of build, was explaining the law to an opposition worker when the woman got tired of listening and "pasted" her, as Mary described it, inflicting a black eye and a swollen lip.

At the same time, Aunt Rowena was having a scary experience in a rough riverfront precinct. As soon as the polls closed, ballots were to be removed from the boxes and counted, and a couple of days later the tallies were checked for accuracy. Well after dark when the vote still hadn't come in from Rowena's poll, a group of us went to see if she was okay. By law we couldn't go inside the polling place but we looked in. Rowena sat at a table with the opposition workers as they slowly counted the ballots. The Long people were hoping that she would leave and they could change the vote tally, but Aunt Rowena, trusty flashlight in hand, wasn't about to be moved.

The People's League was more successful than we had hoped in those 1939 elections, completely upsetting the Long crowd's apple cart. Sam Jones squeaked by Earl Long in the runoff and was elected governor, while Chep, Larry, and other league candidates won a majority of the seats in the state legislature.

Soon after he was inaugurated, Governor Jones asked Hale to prepare legislation for the new administration. Hale tried to persuade the governor that Louisiana should throw out its requirement that voters register every year and go for broke with permanent voter registration. The legislation was drafted, but huge arguments erupted over what could happen if poor, uneducated people of both races were taken to be registered by those wanting to control their votes. How would those blocs of voters ever be removed from the lists? asked critics of Hale's proposal. Not everyone was as reform minded as we were, and they wanted to keep the old system.

A compromise was reached, with a four-year registration period, but the four years expired in the middle of World War II, and rather than disenfranchise all the people off fighting for our country, it was extended another four years. By then everybody recognized that the system worked, and we've had permanent registration every since.

Hale also wrote the voting machine law that required the installation of machines in cities with one hundred thousand or more population, thereby assuring that the vote could be fairly counted and promptly promulgated. No more switching of ballot boxes, no more holding out results. Hale and I strongly believed that the freedom to register and to vote were inherent rights of all citizens of the United States, and that only through the exercise of those rights could true democracy operate.

Economic times were so hard that although many Jones supporters were looking for jobs, there were not enough state jobs to distribute, a situation that created a major political difficulty for the governor. He called Hale to the capitol and asked him to take over the patronage in New Orleans. Hale knew all the Jones people and what each one had done for the campaign. It was the last thing under the sun Hale wanted to undertake, but he took it on because Sam said it was the only way his administration could succeed.

What a daunting task! I remember one loyal Jones supporter who needed work, and Hale arranged for him to apply for a job. A few nights later, the man came by the house and confessed that he hadn't applied for the job and he wouldn't do so because it required that he be able to read and write. He was illiterate and he didn't want his children to know. Hale found another place for him.

The next year Hale at age twenty-six was the league's candidate for Congress in the Second District. After insistent urging from Hale and Larry Eustis, Governor Jones—without whose support he wouldn't have run—endorsed Hale, and various Democratic factions coalesced to support him. The Second District was composed of four parishes and half of another and included New Orleans and Romeville, the village in Saint James, where I had taught school. Hale was running against Paul Maloney, a popular and effective five-term incumbent who had gone to Congress in 1928 in a Long machine sweep, despite his personal distance from the machine's chicanery.

Mayor Robert Maestri of New Orleans was a major factor in the election, being a wealthy and powerful member of the same political faction as Maloney and very close to the Long faction. Hale was well acquainted with the people in Saint James Parish, and he had their solid backing. Jefferson Parish, a part of the district, had a strong factional organization under Sheriff Frank Clancy, who was more or less part of the old regime. In most parishes except the extremely urbanized ones, the sheriff was the tax collector and the parish executive officer and could legitimately deliver a large majority of votes.

Hale campaigned vigorously against Maloney's ties to the city and parish machine, using his oratorical gifts and training, which he would refine and utilize the rest of his life: a rich, sometimes booming voice, a mischievous sense of humor, good timing, and clear-eyed determination. Larry Eustis was his campaign chairman, and Larry's cousin Dave Eustis was the treasurer.

It was the year of *Mr. Smith Goes to Washington,* an enormously popular movie that starred Jimmy Stewart as a young senator fighting political corruption. Hale took as a slogan "Mr. Boggs Goes to Washington," and he had a picture taken with fifteen-month-old Barbara, labeling it "Hale Boggs and Boss," as a contrast to the political bosses backing his opponent.

Even though I was pregnant again, I was able to work vigorously in the campaign. Hale's campaigning partner was Nat Knight, our close friend who was running for public service commissioner in the district, which followed almost exactly the geographic lines of the Second Congressional District. Nat and his wife, Ada, lived across the Mississippi River in Gretna, and Ada and I kept clean shirts and pressed linen suits for our two special candidates on both riverbanks.

I used the daily laundry trek as the mile-long walk required by my obstetrician—our close friend, Dr. Conrad ("Connie") Collins—and I made it an outing for Barbara. As we pushed down Louisiana Avenue and onto Magazine Street, Barbara developed a delightful cadence to her recognition of the political posters: "Dere's my Daddy; Dere's Nat Knight." She knew a ticket early in life. The care of a toddler, proper health practices for my baby-to-be, and campaigning for Hale could, I discovered, be happily combined. We arranged our apartment to welcome many friends and to serve constant refreshments to our workers as they stuffed, sealed, and stamped the campaign mail. Close friends, "my three Charlies," Charlie Porpora, Charlie Ward, and Charlie Zutarain, composed themselves into a "line watch and protection group" to make certain that I walked.

Hale defeated Representative Maloney by eight thousand votes. In all, five candidates favorable to the reform movement were elected to Louisiana's eight-member congressional delegation: Hale, F. Edward ("Eddie") Hebert, James Domengeaux, Vance Plauché, and Jared ("J. Y.") Sanders Jr.

Thomas Hale Boggs Jr. was born eight days later in a difficult delivery. Tommy had a couple of health complications: breathing difficulties when he cried and weakness in his legs. I had told Barbara how much fun she was going to have with her new playmate, and as soon as Tommy came home from the hospital she was ready to play with him. She threw her ball into the bassinet and when he didn't throw it back, she immediately lost interest in this new creature.

Our pediatrician and friend, Roy de la Houssaye, told us that the failure of the thymus gland to shrink as it should have was to blame for Tommy's difficulties when he began breathing on his own. He recommended a new treatment procedure—radiation— to reduce the thymus. It was a difficult decision for Hale and me to make, but we took the chance with the hope of a normal life for Tommy.

We also were advised by the doctors not to put weight on Tommy's little legs until they developed more. I held him on my lap to feed him, and at night, he had to sleep in partial leg braces. (Fortunately two of my aunts had given me the use of a practical nurse for a month after I left the hospital, and she helped with the children.) For several months we protected Tommy's legs as best we could without depriving him of normal development, an exacting chore for our nurse Lucy Boutwell and me. One Saturday after he had gone to Congress, Hale was driving from Washington to Williamsburg, Virginia, to make a speech and I went along. We had left the children with Lucy, and it was so peaceful to be alone we decided to spend the night. I called home, and Lucy was in tears. Apprehensively I inquired, "What's wrong?" She answered, "Tommy just got up and walked across the room." So much for seven and a half months of special attention.

We had had the tremendous push for the People's League, the campaign for Sam Jones and the follow-through, with Hale helping his new administration and the state legislature, and then Hale's own campaign and election. With all that and the births of Barbara and Tommy, I was run-down and thin as a rail. I was in the process of getting the house ready to leave, packing to move to Washington, when, without warning, I suffered a severe attack of elevated tension in my left eye.

It was diagnosed as uveitis, which triggered the high tension, causing a false glaucoma, along with incumbent nausea, and temporary blindness. It was extremely painful and, worse, the doctors didn't know what caused it, so they put me through extended tests including those for tuberculosis and various allergies. My lungs were clear, but the tuberculin skin tests were always positive. They discovered that I was allergic to chocolate, which I loved, and to shrimp, spinach, ragweed, mold, and house dust. I avoided the foods and took shots for the other offenders. The doctors prescribed bed rest and the building up of my physical condition with vitamins and diet. If I hadn't had two babies, they probably would have sent me on a cruise!

As a result I missed Hale's swearing-in, which greatly diminished the joy of the occasion for both of us. It was a great moment in our lives. Hale called to tell me the thrill of standing in the historic House chamber and swearing to uphold and defend the Constitution he loved so well. At least we shared it that way, but I was sorry I hadn't been there. I could only console myself with the knowledge that my absence was unavoidable and that I had to get well for him and the children.

———

The children and I, accompanied by Lucy, went up on the train a couple of weeks later, arriving in time for Franklin D. Roosevelt's third inauguration. I'll never forget the sight of Barbara holding up her little leather-gloved hand to her daddy's big hand and marching down the freezing-cold ramp at Union Station. She had arrived in Washington.

Hale had leased an apartment on the top floor of a little hotel on Capitol Hill—"so I could hang diapers on the roof," he said— until we could find a more suitable place and have enough space for our family and our live-in nurse.

Paul Wooten, the *New Orleans Times-Picayune* Washington correspondent, who was a close friend, lived at Tilden Gardens on Connecticut Avenue, and he soon found an apartment which we could sublease in his building. Paul was prominent among the correspondents, having served as president of the National Press Club, the White House Correspondents Association, and the Gridiron Club, and he and his wife, Jewell, looked out for Hale and me and the babies in those first days as we began our new life.

I fell in love with the Capitol dome. It was the beacon leading me to pick Hale up in the evenings before I figured out Washington's peculiar traffic system. I was always pulling over and stopping, sometimes getting out of the car to look at it in different lights, pink as a wedding cake at sunset or shimmering bright white against a cobalt sky. Someone was standing next to me outside the Capitol one evening as I gazed at it.

"Isn't that the most beautiful sight in the world?" he asked. I turned and saw that it was "Mister Sam" Rayburn, the Speaker of the House. Whenever he was frustrated or fatigued, he'd go out to look at the dome and be reinspired.

I was impressed by the capital's public buildings and monuments, its avenues and parks. It was a leisurely Southern town, friendly and uncrowded, where none of the Congress members felt they really lived. The minute appropriations were in place at the end of June, everyone went home. Having lived in segregated communities, I found it interesting to discover that Washington was not as strictly segregated as I had expected. Public transportation and theaters were open equally to all and the government workforce and professional staffs were integrated. The city had a deep-rooted black community of well-educated and affluent citizens.

Hale and I were great admirers of FDR, and his ambitious New Deal programs, such as using public funds for relief and employing the jobless on public works projects, enchanted us. We had experienced the devastation of the agricultural economy, which had contributed to the loss of Brunswick and our friends' plantations; the pains of the stock market crash; and the Great Depression, with the closing of financial institutions that inflicted additional economic hardships on us and our parents. Hale's father had lost his job when the banks closed.

As the children of a war generation, we were against getting into another war, and we had railed against it at college, rejoicing in U.S. recognition of the Soviet Union and other international friendships. (We never suspected that those activities would come back to haunt us during the McCarthy era.)

Running for an unprecedented third consecutive term, President Roosevelt appealed to the isolationist mood of the country by promising parents, "Your boys are not going to be sent into any foreign wars." He was our hero and I believed him. Europe's wars would not be ours this time. We had worked in the campaign for his third-term presidency, and eight weeks later, our hopes remained high as he was inaugurated.

The inaugural parade was a terrible shock. I watched dumbfounded as huge amounts of military equipment slowly passed by and long columns of military personnel filled the broad avenue with the sound of their marching. I suddenly realized how close we were to war, and I was sick at heart, tears streaming down my face. Vance Plauché, one of Louisiana's new congressmen and a World War I veteran, was standing next to me, and he took my hand and said, "Oh, please don't take it so hard. The rest of your life you'll be finding that you say, 'If it wasn't for the war, such-and-such good wouldn't have happened.'" But that first impression stayed with me all of my life as I realized that everybody I knew was going to be involved in the war.

Within nine months President Roosevelt forced through the Congress the first peacetime extension of the military draft in our history, extending the limit on military service from twelve to eighteen months. It passed in the House of Representatives by the narrowest of margins, 203–202. Hale voted for it, believing by then that our involvement in the European war was inevitable and that we ought to support the president and be ready when the time came.

Although we read the newspaper accounts of Adolf Hitler's rise to power in Germany; his conquest of Poland; neutral Denmark, Norway, and the Low Countries; and the fall of France, we were unaware of the extent of his brutality against the Jews. We didn't know the proportions of the crimes. The New Orleans Jewish community is very old, large, and distinguished, and as family members arrived from Europe—some from the camps, others smuggled to safety—the horrors of the Holocaust began to unfold and everyone was sickened.

My major insight into the seriousness of this overwhelming destruction of life and liberty came later, through Philip Hannan, the young pastor of Saint Patrick's Church in downtown Washington, which was the "parish away from home" for members of Congress. He was sociable, gregarious, and highly motivated toward ecumenism long before it became so popular.

He was a "flying padre," a paratrooper in the 82nd Airborne Division of the Air Corps, which landed behind enemy lines and helped to liberate several of the camps. His descriptions of the horrible human degradation that he found were so overwhelming that our first wide view of the Holocaust came through the eyes of this remarkable cleric. It made a tremendous impression on us, and years later, on many of the members of the Jewish community when Father Hannan became archbishop of New Orleans. (After the war Hale and I reinforced our usual politically affirmative stand with support for the foundation of the state of Israel.)

The first meeting our mostly new congressional delegation had with the president was during a White House reception at which the guests were assembled in the East Room and ushered, a few at a time, into the Green Room to be received by him and his wife, Eleanor. Although crippled by polio, the president refused to greet guests from a sitting position, and he was assisted in standing by a strong military aide on one side and one of his tall sons on the other. Obviously guests were moved quickly with no time for even limited conversation.

Just as our delegation reached the door of the Green Room, it was closed, making us the first of the next group to enter. When the door was reopened, we were escorted in and rushed past the president at such a fast pace that Eddie Hebert, our congressman from the First District, called back to us, "Impressed with our views, wasn't he?"

Eleanor Roosevelt was an integral part of the presidency, serving as a collector of data and early observer of political trends for her husband. She was an innovator and leader in civil and women's rights and on the front line in the campaign for human rights around the world. She remains the woman for whom I've had the most admiration throughout the years—my heroine, a great political activist.

She appeared at many public events in Washington, and I had met her in receiving lines, but when I was invited to a White House garden party she was giving in honor of the Supreme Court justices' wives, I was thrilled by the opportunity to talk with her and to meet the other ladies.

You were not supposed to be one minute late for a White House party, but Tommy decided to cut his first tooth that day. He screamed and yelled and was in such horrible pain I couldn't leave him right away, and by the time when I finally calmed him and was able to leave him with Lucy, I was running very late.

Even so, I decided I couldn't miss the rare opportunity to attend such a special event. I thought Mrs. Roosevelt would understand why I was late, and I knew she would forgive me—a bold decision for a 24-year-old. As I arrived, she was leaving the receiving line to return to the White House, and we met halfway across the garden. I poured out my problem to her, telling her I knew it was rude and a breach of protocol to arrive late, but I couldn't resist the opportunity to see her again.

She said, "I can't believe you have a child who is cutting a tooth. Now come and meet these ladies," and she linked her arm in mine and took me through the receiving line. "Can you believe that this child has a baby old enough to be cutting a tooth and she couldn't come until now? I'm glad someone has her priorities straight!"

Washington was a gracious, close-knit kind of society, a great deal of it dominated by embassy parties and formal parties at the White House and at various clubs. The Congress and the diplomatic corps were imposed on the city's natural ambience, but compliance with the established protocol created a set of manners to which everyone could repair regardless of which state, town, country, or position they came from.

A rigid calling system required that, as a newcomer, you call at the home of everyone senior to your husband and leave a calling card. Monday was Supreme Court day, Tuesday was House of Representatives, Wednesday was cabinet, Thursday was Senate,

Friday was diplomatic. You did no calling on Saturday, and on Sunday you returned calls if accompanied by your husband. Anyone who knew Hale knows we never did any calling on Sunday. When your husband was a freshman congressman, you determined who was senior to him in the freshman class by the date of your state's entrance into the Union. Fortunately Louisiana was the eighteenth state.

Once a year you were expected actually to be at home and to invite people who had called on you and others who had entertained you to come to your "payback" tea. The rest of the year everyone appreciated very much if you were not "at home," so they could simply leave their cards and accomplish more calls that day.

Most people lived in Washington, where there was no parking on many streets between four and six in the afternoon, the calling hours. To get around that one woman would drive and the others would go to the door and pray nobody was "at home." If you did happen to be physically in the house, you could still say that you were not at home to the callers. My part-time housekeeper, who was completely honest and wouldn't tell even "white lies," had a difficult time being persuaded that I could be physically present and still not be at home.

Lady Bird Johnson, Pauline Gore, and Nancy Kefauver were young congressional wives when they came to see me, the first to pay an official call. They weren't required to come protocol-wise, but they did, and we became close friends from that day forward. Ultimately Lyndon Johnson became vice president and president, Senator Estes Kefauver the Democratic vice presidential nominee in 1956, and Senator Albert Gore Sr., the father of Vice President Al Gore.

Washington imposed other social rules as well, which were taught quickly to new wives by the senior members of the Congressional Club. Dinner party guests were seated according to rank to the right and left of the hosts. In this way you knew at a glance how important everyone was, or how relatively unimportant. You couldn't leave a formal social event until everyone who outranked you had left, which made this young wife long for the old folks to make a hasty departure so I could go home to my babies. By the time I retired from Congress, I found myself wondering why everyone left parties so early when we were having such fun.

The white glove question formed the big social test: whether to keep on both gloves, remove one, or remove both of them when going down a receiving line. The only way to divine the correct answer was to position yourself where you could see the hostess and the other women in the line to determine what they were doing, but by the time you had a clear view, you were usually already shaking hands and it was too late.

Hostesses had to plan their large parties well ahead of time because Washington had only a limited number of large silver chafing dishes, trays, candelabra, and gold-and-white china available to rent. Moreover, the Waiters' Union was the *real* "Four Hundred" of Washington society. With entertaining of sizable proportions limited to the six- or seven-month congressional sessions, waiters protected their jobs during the lean months by limiting their membership to four hundred men. Not until after World War II—when there began to be many big parties and the management of the Wardman Park Hotel, now the Washington Sheraton, hired and trained women to serve its private parties—was that exclusivity broken.

The first time Hale and I were invited to a party at the White House, I was asked by a *Washington Times-Herald* society reporter what I was going to wear. This had happened to me in New Orleans, but it was the first time in Washington, and I was so pleased at being asked that I described everything in detail. I had my dress laid out on the bed, but Tommy was on the bed and he stained it with grubby little hands and I had to wear something else. I was afraid it would seem that I had given inaccurate information to the press, an unacceptable action for me. I actually called to tell the society editor I had changed my outfit. Naive as that now may seem, it started my lifelong rapport with members of the Washington press corps.

Hale and I were fortunate in having the sponsorship of people like Jewell and Paul Wooten and to enjoy introductions to old-time Washington residents, known as "Cave Dwellers," by a distant cousin of mine, Buzzy Hewes, whom we knew through his niece, Ellen Floweree, from New Orleans. Ruth Overton, the daughter of Senator John H. Overton, and Helen Ellender, the wife of Senator Allen J. Ellender, were among our Louisiana friends who helped us learn our way around. Helen was active in the Congressional Club and the Woman's National Democratic Club, both of which I joined.

Another acquaintance was Ann Bullitt, whose father, Bill Bullitt, had been our ambassador to the Soviet Union. At a small dinner party given by Bill and his daughter and also attended by Congressman (later Senator) J. William Fulbright of Arkansas, his wife, Betty, and his mother, Hale and I heard a revealing account of what diplomatic service in Moscow was like.

Ambassador Bullitt, who served in Moscow from 1933 until 1936, had warned his successor, Joseph E. Davies—who was married to Marjorie Merriweather Post, a large contributor to Roosevelt's campaigns—that he believed the Russians were spying on him and that the embassy residence was probably equipped with eavesdropping devices. Davies refused to believe him, saying that the Russians might eavesdrop on the embassy but never on the official residence. Imagine the Davieses' surprise, Bill said, when a plumber they had called discovered microphones hidden, in sand used as insulation in the attic, where the pipes to their personal bathroom were located and where the Russians had listened, according to Bill, "to the sweet nothings from their nuptial couch."

We became close friends with Betty and Alan McCall-Judson, who were with the British Embassy, where he was First Secretary. The British Embassy lawn party was one of the important social events of the year, and the one at which ladies always wore their most beautiful hats. I had chosen to wear a brown chiffon dress with beige dots that was summery yet sophisticated, but I didn't have a hat to match it. There wasn't time to purchase one, so I plucked daisies from our dining room bouquet to put in my hair and went to the party.

I was enjoying talking with a group which included Thurmond Arnold, a rather rumpled intellectual and one of the New Deal brain trusters, when along came a woman looking extraordinarily stylish in a peach-colored chiffon dress and a lovely hat made of the same material. She glanced at me and said, "My dear, I thought the purpose of a hat was to frame one's face."

Thurmond won my everlasting devotion when he spoke up: "If you were as pretty and as smart as this girl, you wouldn't have to wear a hat either." From then on I didn't worry excessively about what I wore to the big parties.

Small "salons" were another form of entertaining, and two of the most prominent hostesses were Mrs. J. Borden Harriman, a well-known Democrat, and Mrs. Robert Lowe Bacon, a revered Republican. When you were invited for supper, you were advised of the topic of discussion and you were expected to arrive prepared to participate. The guest of honor was always pertinent to the subject, but one night several years later, we went to a salon at Daisy Harriman's for which no subject had been announced.

We were all trying to figure out what the subject was going to be, when Secretary of State Dean Acheson arrived. Dean had been in the Treasury and State Departments for President Roosevelt before President Truman appointed him to head State. As usual for anyone in that position, the secretary had great admirers but also virulent detractors for a variety of reasons: He had tried to dissociate the United States from the Chinese Nationalist regime, and he refused to see the Cold War in terms of "good" and "evil" but rather as a long-term situation; he sought to strengthen Europe's military capabilities through a North Atlantic Treaty Organization (NATO); and many people thought that he wasn't being sufficiently hard on possible Communists in our government.

That night, despite the fact that we were all Democrats, Dean became the target of several sharp rounds of criticism, and Hale came to his eloquent defense. From then on, we felt a special relationship with Dean and with Alice, his talented, beautiful wife, who remains my friend as do their children, with whom I have enjoyed many interesting associations.

The Walter Lippmanns had a salon in which we were included even though Hale and I were younger and less important than most of their guests. A highly influential newspaper columnist, Lippmann had been an ardent early supporter of Roosevelt's New Deal but had moved to a more moderate political position. Surrounded by bright minds from the press, politics, and government, we felt as though all of our heroes had come to life—as they had. It was there that we met James ("Scotty") Reston, the incomparable *New York Times* columnist, who in later years in Washington would come to play a very important part in our family's life.

At the Capitol the Lend-Lease hearings ended, having proved once again that Americans have to be pulled kicking and screaming into international situations. Opponents argued that the Monroe Doctrine was the predominant foreign policy and that U.S. involvement in other countries' fights was something we had always been against, but the threat of another world war was too strong for doctrinal debate. Congress passed the bill, and Hale voted with the majority.

Soon afterward Kendall Cram, a dear friend who had been in

our wedding, was killed when German submarines sank his ship filled with Lend-Lease supplies on the Murmansk run. Hale felt that he had voted the only way he could on the bill, but Kendall's death was a tragic blow to both of us.

Responding to the wartime mood, Hale sponsored a bill banning Communists, Fascists, and German Bund members from labor unions and defense work because their possible loyalty to Adolf Hitler made them potential security risks, and he supported legalization of FBI wiretaps in cases of suspected sabotage or other national security situations. In just twelve months our isolationist mood had vanished. Everything else in our lives was about to change as well.

CHAPTER SIX

ᴄᴦᴣᴼᴦᴠ

O N THE FIRST Sunday in December 1941, I bundled up
my children to take them out for a walk. I'd put it off all week
until the weather warmed up and Hale was available to help me.
The capital had been preoccupied with a visiting Japanese peace
mission, and I was unnaturally suspicious of it. I couldn't explain
why I didn't believe its members had good intentions, but I said to
Hale, "They're here only to allow them to maneuver wherever they
want to go while we are talking peace with them." He chided me
for being distrustful.

We were leaving when the phone rang and Hale answered it.
Paul Wooten said the Japanese had bombed Pearl Harbor. When
Hale told me, I didn't believe him. I said, "Oh, no, it must be
Manila! Pearl Harbor is halfway across the Pacific Ocean."

It was an amazing situation: We didn't believe the Japanese had
the capability of such a strike at such a distance, and they didn't
believe the United States had the will to fight.

Instead of going for a walk, we all got into the car and listened
to news reports on the radio as we drove slowly past the Japanese
Embassy, where clouds of smoke rose from the diplomatic papers
they were burning in the garden; past the German Embassy; and

then to the White House, where the president's advisers were converging. Finally, we drove down to spend a few minutes looking at the Capitol dome. A couple of days later its lights were extinguished for the duration of the war, but even darkened, the dome remained an inspiration to me. I knew that someday the lights would come on again to illumine the avenues to freedom throughout the world and to light our own way to justice for all our people.

The United States declared war on Japan and three days later, against Germany and Italy.

In New Orleans the German consul general, the charming and popular Edgar Freiherr Spiegel von und ni Peckelsheim, known as Baron von Spiegel, was always included in the socializing among residents and the diplomatic corps. He entertained beautifully at his house on Saint Charles Avenue for the top public officials and the city's leaders in industry, business, and society, and he was always among the first-nighters for the opera, ballet, and symphony. As soon as the United States entered the war and he went home, we learned that he had been in charge of German submarine activity for the entire Western Hemisphere.

We were shocked that he had been an important spy, but the revelation alerted us to the strategic importance of New Orleans and the entire Gulf of Mexico. Our armed forces became more alert about patrolling the Gulf and its shorelines for saboteurs or spies put ashore, and maintained close surveillance to prevent submarine activity in the Gulf, a part of the war that was generally unknown outside our region but was crucial to the defense of the United States.

Washington went on a wartime footing. Antiaircraft guns poked up from the roofs of the government buildings, and sandbags were stacked for protection around their foundations. We tried to bomb-proof the basement of the Woman's National Democratic Club with sandbags, and we stocked it as a bomb shelter with emergency food, water, and medical supplies. The club had been founded during President Woodrow Wilson's administration, largely as a result of women's suffrage, and Edith Wilson, a stalwart woman, was its first honorary president. We felt we owed it to her to protect the premises as best we could.

Public shelters were set up in basements, underground tunnels of buildings, and even in the Dupont Circle underpass, but the government's attitude was that private businesses and families should take personal responsibility for their safety in case of an air raid. We didn't build a bomb shelter at home, as many did, but I stored the same emergency supplies that we kept for hurricanes in Louisiana: water, food, flashlights, and blankets. Blackout curtains became the draperies of choice because of the threat of nighttime attacks; every block had its volunteer air-raid warden to make certain that no lights were visible.

Washington was full of military men and women, and out-of-work civilians from all over the country poured into the capital in search of government and war-supportive jobs. Gasoline and tires, shoes, butter, and sugar were rationed, and you didn't even think about steak or chocolate—they had been requisitioned for the military. (My feet still hurt every time I pass the Oyster School, where shoe ration stamps were dispensed. Barbara's and Tommy's little feet grew so fast I was always using my coupons for them. Aunt Frosty said, "Darling, what size shoe do you wear?" I said, "I wear 'thank-you' size." The shoes people gave me didn't always fit well, but they were very stylish and I was always happy to receive them.)

Whenever the Safeway store on Connecticut Avenue near Utah got a delivery of meat, everybody at that end of Washington converged on it. You took a number and waited your turn, and there would always be so many people that you had to wait a long, long time. I used precious gasoline coupons and drove to the store on those days because I was afraid my scheduled bus home would arrive before my meat number came up.

One day when, I went outside to leave, I found a parking ticket on my windshield. By inquiring around I discovered that the police waited until the store had a delivery of meat and then ticketed all the cars still parked after the four o'clock ban. The next time I went, I was number 111, and I stood there thinking, Oh dear, I'm going to get a ticket, but I couldn't help it. I stayed until I could purchase my meat, and when I arrived at my car, sure enough, all of them had been ticketed.

When I reached home I took my ticket in and told Hale what was happening. I said, "This is absolutely ridiculous." Hale said, "That's too bad, Lin."

I said, "You've got to do something about it."

He said, "I don't know what can be done about it. Maybe you should just go to the top." He was teasing me, of course. He planned to do something about it.

The next evening, when he came home, he said, "Give me that ticket. I'll see what I can do about it."

I said, "I sent it to the chief of police with a protest."

The chief of police wrote me back, apologizing for the unpatriotic actions of his officers. They got the word: There was never again a mass ticketing of cars on Safeway's meat day.

In the past we in the United States had thought we could escape direct participation in world events, but there was no way we could do so again. As the government began to determine its responsibilities in a world at war, Congress stayed in session all year. The presence of all those lawmakers, enduring the hot, muggy Washington August, may not have led directly to the accelerated development of air-conditioning, but it was around this time

Mother was a beauty," 1920.
(*Morrison Family Archives*)

Lindy's father, Roland
Claiborne, c. 1907.
(*Claiborne Family Archives*)

Lindy with an original
"Teddy" bear, c. 1918.
(*Claiborne Family Archives*)

The garden district houses on First Street, New Orleans.
(*Photo © 1994 George Long*)

Lindy at age three, 1919.
(*Claiborne Family Archives*)

LEFT: *Louis Bingham
Claiborne.* (*Claiborne
Family Archives*)

RIGHT: *Ferdinand
Claiborne ("Uncle
Daddy"), 1907.*
(*Claiborne Family Archives*)

Miss Corinne Claiborne, the lovely young daughter of Mr. and Mrs. George Keller of Pointe Coupee parish, who is spending a part of the winter here as a guest of her aunt, Mrs. S. M. Blackshear, and Dr. Blackshear. The picture is a copy of her portrait by Alfredo Galli.

ABOVE: *The young Lindy Claiborne.*
(Courtesy of the Times-Picayune)

RIGHT: *Lindy, a member of the Court at the Ball of the Harlequins, third from top left.*
(Courtesy of the Times-Picayune)

Miss Nenette Denegre, daughter of Mr. and Mrs. Thomas Bayne Denegre, who reigned as queen of the recent Ball of the Harlequins, is shown with several members of her court who played the roles of fireflies. They are, left to right, Misses Lilian Dameron, Peggy Poor, Corinne Claiborne and Brent Robertson.

Lindy with college friends, c. 1935. SEATED, LEFT TO RIGHT: *Halcyon Colomb, Jean Laidlaw, Nancy Reeves, Lindy.* STANDING, LEFT TO RIGHT: *Lynne Hecht, Cecile Kahn, Katherine Nolan, Katherine Colvin.* (Lindy Boggs Archives)

Visitors Are Entertained at Informal Affairs

Visitors continue to be the inspiration for many informal affairs. Pictured, Nancy Reeves (left) and her two visitors, Mary | Byrne and Lindy Claiborne of New Orleans, sat down for a moment on the steps of the Reeves home on Vance to plan for a busy day | yesterday. Mary (center) and Lindy stopped for a short visit with Nancy on their way home from Chicago, where they went to the fair.

Lindy with friends, 1934.
(Memphis Press-Scimitar)

Society

Hale-Claiborne Wedding, Carnival Ball of Caliphs, Attract Society

New Orleans Elite to Attend Ceremony at New Roads Today; Debutante House Party Also Is Scheduled; Another Gay Seasonal Dance Is Slated This Evening

A LARGE number of New Orleanians will trek to the country this forenoon to attend a wedding in which society here is much interested. And others will be trekking in another direction to be among the guests at a house party with a debutante as the guest of honor. And in town there will be delightful festivities that will keep all circles abroad.

The ball of the Caliphs of Cairo will be given this evening at the auditorium, interesting then.

Among private parties will be a buffet supper, at home, that Mr. and Mrs. W. Porcher Miles, Jr., and the former's sister, Miss May Miles, will give this evening for Misses Marjorie Hart and Martha Monrose.

Mr. and Mrs. Clarence Gelpi will be hosts this evening at a cocktail party at the family home on Calhoun street in honor of Mr. and Mrs. Louis B. Trenchard, Jr., of Phoenix, Ariz.

Among delightful events planned for over the week-end is the house party at which Mr. and Mrs. W. Horace Williams will be hosts, entertaining in honor of their daughter, Miss Eugenie Williams, at Cloche d'Or, their country home near Denham Springs, La.

Their guests, who will motor to the country today in various parties, will include Misses Dorothy Mary Brenchley, Marie Ella Gore, Georgiana Solari, Marion McCloskey, Augusta Pipes, Elizabeth McLellan, Messrs. Julian Humphrey, Thomas Thompson, Nolan Kammer, James Lea, Jr., and E. Shannon Livaudais.

No out-of-town wedding of the winter, in these parts, has claimed more attention here socially than that of Miss Corinne Morrison Claiborne of New Orleans and Pointe Coupee parish, daughter of Mr. and Mrs. George Keller of Pointe Coupee, to Mr. Thomas Hale Hoggs of New Orleans, son of Mr. and Mrs. William R. Hoggs of Long Beach, Miss., and New Orleans, to take place in New Roads, La., this forenoon.

A large number of society members here already have gone to the country to be among attendants on the bride and bridegroom-elect or just to attend the ceremony and reception following.

The wedding ceremony will be at 10 o'clock at St. Mary's Catholic Church in New Roads and a wedding reception will immediately follow at the home in New Roads of Mr. and Mrs. Ferdinand Claiborne, uncle and aunt of the bride-elect.

The attendants on the bride will be Miss Halcyon Colomb, maid of honor; Mrs. Haywood H. Hillyer, Jr., matron of honor; Misses Louise Tarlton, Betty Wheeler, Mary Byrne, Jane Buffington, Mary and Claire Boggs, sisters of the bridegroom-elect, all of New Orleans; Angelique Provosty of Alexandria, La., Katherine Kearney and Elizabeth Bouanchaud of New Roads; Vera Lee Hobgood of Torras, La.; Emily Samuel of Zachary, La.; and Ethel Dameron

of Port Allen, La., cousin of the bride-elect, as bridesmaids, and little Eustasia Bouanchaud of New Roads as junior bridesmaid.

Mr. Boggs will have as his best man his brother, Mr. William R. Boggs, Jr., of Jackson, Miss., and as his groomsmen, another brother, Mr. Archibald Boggs, Messrs. Adolph Jastram, Arthur de la Houssaye, Charles Seemann, Jacob H. Morrison, Stanley Morrison, Haywood H. Hillyer, Jr., Charles C. Bass, Jr., all of New Orleans; Marion Monk of Alexandria, La., John Lynch of Syracuse, N. Y., Marlin Hoge of Fort Smith, Ark.; Kendall Cram, Birmingham, Ala.; McVea Oliver, Monroe, La., and as his ushers, Messrs. de Lesseps Morrison of New Orleans, John H. Hobgood, Jr., of Torras, La., James Cleveland Roberts, Jr., New Roads, La., and Dr. Benjamin O. Morrison of Abbeville, La.

Among the many relatives and friends from New Orleans who will be at the wedding, besides those mentioned above, are Mrs. Edward Morrison, Mr. and Mrs. William R. Boggs, Mrs. Wiley R. Buffington, Mrs. S. M. Blackshear, Dr. Rufus C. Harris, president of Tulane, and Mrs. Harris, with their guests, Mr. and Mrs. B. V. Harris of Georgia; Mr. and Mrs. W. R. Boggs, Jr., Dr. Paul W. Brosman of Tulane and Mrs. Brosman, Mrs. Mortimer Robelot, Mr. and Mrs. William Drew, Mr. and Mrs. Marten ten Hoor, Mr. and Mrs. James Morrison.

Mr. and Mrs. J. H. Randolph Feltus, Mrs. Chlotilde Keller Cole, Mr. Stanley Morrison, Mrs. James Robin, Mrs. J. Hugues De La Vergne, Mrs. Robert McClure, Mr. and Mrs. A. B. Wheeler, Jr., Miss Betty Wheeler, Mrs. S. A. Fortier, Hiram Lee Brady and Graham Brady, Jr., Mr. and Mrs. Allen Ferries, Mr. and Mrs. Richard Shaw, Mr. Frank Percy, Miss Harriet Kostmayer, Mrs. Lewis Golden, Mr. Edward Seghers, Miss Louise Provosty, Mr. and Mrs. William Coats, Mr. and Mrs. Err

Mercer, Mr. and Mrs. James Menefee and a number of others.

Mr. Boggs and his bride will leave New Roads today on a short honeymoon and later will be at home in New Orleans.

Miss Claiborne is a graduate of Newcomb and a member of the Kappa Kappa Gamma Sorority. She is a lovely member of the younger set in society here, where she has taken an active part in the gayeties in younger circles. Her father was the late Mr. Roland Claiborne, son of the late Judge and Mrs. Louis Bingamin Claiborne of Pointe Coupee. Her mother was formerly Miss Corinne Morrison of Pointe Coupee.

Mr. Boggs is a graduate of both the academic and law schools of Tulane and a member of the Beta Theta Pi Fraternity. His mother was before her marriage Miss Claire Hale of Bay St. Louis.

BOGGS—CLAIBORNE

St. Mary's church, New Roads, was never more beautiful than on Saturday morning, January 22, 1938, when Miss Corinne Claiborne became the bride of Mr. Hale Boggs, at 10 o'clock with Rev. Father John Hoes performing the ceremony at nuptial high mass.

The altar was decorated with white camellias and greens over which the soft light of altar candles shed a mellow glow.

The pews reserved for the family were marked with white ribbons, white gladioli and ferns, while all other pews along the center aisle held standards of pink camellias, blue baby's breath and ferns.

When the organ under the skilled touch of Miss Celuta Jewell, pealed forth the happy strains of the wedding march, the ushers and groomsmen entered in double file, Messrs. Archibald Boggs, Adolph Jastram, Arthur de la Houssaye, Charles Seeman, Jake Morrison, Stanley Morrison, Haywood Hansell Hillyer, Jr., Marion Monk, John Lynch, Marlin Hoge, Kendall Cram, McVeigh Oliver, Charles C. Bass Jr., deLesseps Morrison, Jack Hobgood and Dr. Ben Morrison.

These were followed by the maids, walking alone; Misses Elizabeth Bouanchaud, Claire Boggs, Emily Samuel, Mary Boggs, Vera Lee Hobgood, Angelique Provosty, Ethel Dameron, Jane Buffington, Mary Byrne, Louise Tarleton, Katherine Kearney, and Betty Wheeler; Eustatia Bouanchaud, junior maid, Mrs. Haywood H. Hillyer, matron of honor and Miss Halcyon Colomb, maid of honor.

The maids were gowned exactly alike in blue tulle, over taffeta, fashioned with long, tight waist, square neck lines, short puffed sleeves, floor length skirts with swaying hoop skirt effect; pink slippers, matched the dainty flesh maline Juliet veil caught on top of their heads with tiny pink shell camellias; they carried old fashioned round bouquets of pink sweetpeas and blue delphiniums.

The matron and maids of honor wore pink costumes exactly like the maids with blue accessories. The dainty junior maid's dress was the same with the exception of a piquant pink hat instead of the veil.

The bride was queenly in white satin, modeled on long lines and falling in a long graceful train; the waist was square necked, filled in with tulle which formed a high collar and was also used for a rolled cuff at the end of leg-o-mutton sleeves. A long tulle veil was caught with white camellias to the hair forming a cap effect and flowed in billowy folds to the end of her train. Over this was worn a pointe d'alencon veil that was an heirloom of the Morrison family. Her bouquet was of white sweet peas and Valley lilies. She entered with her step-father... ge Keller and was met at ...l by the others.

groom and his best man Mr. William R. Boggs Jr.

Two of the maids and their attendants stood on either side of the chancel, while the bride and groom, best man and maids were facing the altar, the other maids and groomsmen stood in line at the foot of the chancel steps, and formed a most beautiful picture of beauty and happiness.

The choir was especially good, and Mrs. Robert M. Hunter sang Ave Maria, most beautifully.

Mendelsohn's Wedding March was played as they left the church.

Following the ceremony a reception was held at the residence of the bride's uncle and aunt Mr. and Mrs. Ferdinand C. Claiborne.

In the spacious parlor under an arch of evergreens and pink camellias the bride and her attendants greeted some three hundred guests from all parts of the parish and state and many from out of state.

Receiving with the bridal party were Mrs. George Keller, the bride's mother, Mrs. William R. Boggs, the groom's mother, and the bride's aunts, Mrs. R. Buffington.

Throughout the house—dining room, halls and galleries beautiful decorations of camellias and greens lent beauty to the scene. The beautiful bride's cake centered an exquisite lace covered table—in cutting the cake, Miss Angelique Provosty got the ring, but each eager maid received some token hidden neath the snowy icing.

The punch table was presided over by Mrs. Harry Wilson, of Baton Rouge and Mrs. Irving Dameron, of Port Allen.

The lovely tea girls were Misses Jeannette Gosserand, Bee Morgan, Joel Roberts, Estelle Schuermann, Dorothy Dameron, Netta Wilson, and Marie Elaine Gosserand.

The bride and groom left by motor on a two week's trip, after which they will be at home at 1727 Valence street, New Orleans. Her going away outfit consisted of a particularly smart rose wool tailored suit worn with a topcoat of grey caracul. Her black accessories matched the background of the printed silk blouse.

Some five hundred gifts of silver, crystal, English Spode and Haviland china, linen, bric a brac, paintings and useful household gifts testified to the popularity of the young bride and groom.

The large number of guests from out of the state and from almost every parish in the state makes it impossible to name all, but among these were Mr. and Mrs. W. R. Boggs Sr. of the Gulfport, Miss., Mr. and Mrs. W. R. Boggs, Jr., and little Eleanor Boggs of Jackson, Miss., Mr. and Mrs. Edward S. Morrison, Mrs. Anita Morrison, Dr. Rufus C. Harris president of Tulane and Mrs. Harris, Mr. and Mrs. B. V. Harris of Georgia, Dr. Paul Brosman, of Tulane and Mrs. Brosman, Mrs. Albin Provosty, Mrs. Nauman Scott, Mr. and Mrs. Ledoux Provosty, Mr. and Mrs. A. B. Wheeler, Mr. and Mrs. Robelot of New Orleans, great aunt and uncle of the groom, Mr. Edward Seghers, Mrs. S. M. Blackshear, Mr. and Mrs. Harry Wilson, Judge and Mrs. I. Dupont, Mrs. Chlotilde Keller Cole, Mr. and Mrs. William Coats, Mrs. J. C. Menefee, Miss Kate Hobgood, of Washington. D. C. Mrs. S. A. Fortier, Senator R. S. Wilds, Mr. and Mrs. Leon Landry, of New Iberia and many others.

Claiborne-Boggs wedding announcements, January 22, 1938.

(Courtesy of the Times-Picayune and the Point Coupee Banner)

RIGHT: *Mr. Boggs goes to Washington, December 1940.* (*AP/Wide World Photos*)

"BABY CONGRESSMAN" AND BABY
The father is T. Hale Boggs of New Orleans, pictured with Barbara Boggs, 19 months old. Congressman-Elect Boggs at 26 will represent the 2d Louisiana district. (Associated Press Photo)

Hale Boggs, 1940.
(*Boggs Family Archives*)

Mr. Boggs returns to Washington, 1947.
(*Boggs Family Archives*)

"The Four Corinnes," January 1947. IN WALL PICTURE: *Corinne Morrison (Lindy's great-aunt).* STANDING: *Corinne Morrison Claiborne (Lindy's mother).* SEATED: *Corinne ("Lindy") Morrison Claiborne Boggs, holding Corinne Morrison Claiborne Boggs ("Cokie" Roberts).*
(*Boggs Family Archives*)

Lindy stands in front of the remants of the Boggs family's original home in Long Beach, Mississippi, destroyed by the 1947 hurricane. The home had been built in 1875 by Hale's grandfather, Robert Boggs. (*Boggs Family Archives*)

Hale running for governor, 1952.
LEFT TO RIGHT: *Senator Russell Long, Hale Boggs. Mayor Chep Morrison.* (Boggs Family Archives)

The Boggs family at the Capitol, 1950.
(Boggs Family Archives)

Barbara, Tommy, and Hale at
the annual family Christmas
show, 1946. (Boggs Family Archives)

Barbara, Lindy, Tommy,
Hale, and Cokie at home
at 1304 First Street,
New Orleans, 1952.
(Boggs Family Archives)

Hale campaigning, 1952. (*Boggs Family Archives*)

Lindy, Hale, Tommy, Barbara, and Cokie in a campaign photo, January 1952.
(*Courtesy of the* Times-Picayune)

Lindy and Hale, c. 1958. *(Boggs Family Archives)*

Hale Boggs with President Kennedy at the 1960 Democratic Convention in Los Angeles. (AP/World Wide Photo)

Kennedy-Johnson Caravan, 1960 (Lindy third from right).
(Boggs Family Archives)

—Associated Press Wirephoto.
STRICTLY INFORMAL DISCUSSION WITH KENNEDY
. . . *Sen. Hale Boggs of Louisiana was on way from pool*

Senate Majority Leader Mike Mansfield, Senate Majority Whip Hubert Humphrey, House Majority Whip Hale Boggs, Vice President Lyndon Johnson, and House Speaker John McCormack at press conference with President Kennedy, 1963. (Official White House photograph)

that it became popular and, with television, would change Congress forever.

After the war, with air-conditioning, there was no longer a need for the long summer recess, leading many Congressional families to think about making their homes in or around Washington. With television, members of Congress could address their constituents, discuss national and international issues, and even run for office without being in their state or district. Before too many years we would all be using jet planes, WATS lines, computers, office copiers, direct mailings, cellular phones, pagers, fax machines, sound bites, and C-SPAN, and never again enjoy the slow-paced, small-town feeling of prewar Congress.

Knowing that eventually the owners of our place at Tilden Gardens would come back, I started looking for a home of our own. With Washington overrun, furnished houses and apartments to rent were extremely scarce; if you were lucky you might find a place that was unfurnished. I took Hale to a couple that I had found, but before we could say, "We'll take it," they had been rented to someone else. I calculated what we'd have to spend to rent and furnish a home, and I decided we might as well buy one. House prices and mortgage payments were modest compared to the rents, and many houses were for sale.

Hale was stunned. "Why would you want to buy a house in Washington?" he said. Washington was where he worked when he wasn't at home in New Orleans. He couldn't imagine ever making a home there.

I showed him several houses I had found that were for sale, but each had something wrong with it until we saw a two-story red-brick house on Stephenson Place, a quiet street in Chevy Chase, Maryland. It was so spotlessly, sparkling clean you could have eaten off the floors, and it was only a couple of years old, with a completely furnished kitchen. It had front and back yards, an alley that ran beside it, and a screened porch next to the kitchen that was a perfect playroom for the children. Hale was persuadeed that we should buy it and we moved in January 1942.

The only drawback appeared later, when a family with several children at the end of the alley began stealing Tommy's bicycles. They'd steal one and we'd buy him another, and they would steal that. After the first two we didn't bother the police anymore. We simply went to retrieve the bicycle at their house.

In the twelve months after Pearl Harbor, we had houseguests every night but one. All sorts of friends came to Washington, where they couldn't find hotel rooms or apartments or book passage back home because the military was using the trains. The only guest who genuinely disturbed me, however, was a British friend who left his shoes outside the bedroom door at night to be polished. (They were not.)

I discovered that the profession of congressional spouse is an extremely demanding and difficult one. When everyone began staying in Washington most of the year, the Congressional Club offered courses on protocol and appropriate entertaining, and it held programs on current events and issues so that the congressional spouses were knowledgeable about them. The club still hosts a series of annual parties for the president and vice president, the cabinet, heads of government agencies, and the diplomatic corps, in order that congressional wives and husbands can meet the important people everybody at home assumes they associate with every day.

Specialized courses were offered, one of the most popular explaining what goes on under the hood of your automobile and how to fix it. Mildred Pepper, an artist, whose husband, Claude, was a Florida senator and congressman, invited newcomers to the Capitol, where Howard Chandler Christy told us about his painting of the signing of the U.S. Constitution. (When I was teaching in

Romeville, the painting had toured the United States as part of the Sesquicentennial celebration of the Constitution.)

Portraits of a couple of the principals couldn't be found as guides but the artist resolved that problem by showing their backs or partially covering their faces. Mr. Christy said that he used live models to flesh out actual people. I said, "Oh my! Who is that handsome Alexander Hamilton?"

"You wouldn't be interested," he said. "He's a worker in the Navy Yard." Nevertheless, I enjoyed the knowledge that in this democratic society of ours, a laborer could portray the elegant Mr. Hamilton.

In the early years of our Republic, when the capital was being moved around, congressmen left their wives at home. When it appeared that the capital would be firmly established in Washington, and the wives felt they could live there, they were disappointed by the paucity of social or cultural outlets for women. A club for these purposes was proposed more than a hundred years later under a federal charter, in order that it would be seen as an official endeavor of the Congress, but the House minority leader, John Sharp Williams of Mississippi, was strongly opposed to it.

He happened to have a beautiful wife, who favored the club. On the day the proposal was to be acted on, she put on her prettiest gown and hat and her most alluring Paris perfume and invited her husband to lunch. While they were at lunch, the Congressional Club was chartered by unanimous consent, and it has been serving the spouses of Congress ever since.

Sam Rayburn liked to relax with friends over a drink when the day's work was done. Besides his older colleagues in the House, he occasionally invited a newcomer to join the informal group that comprised their "Board of Education" in a room below the Speaker's office in the Capitol Building. They lounged on a leather sofa or in big comfortable chairs scattered around Sam's desk, sipping bourbon and talking about legislation or world events or maybe listening to an impromptu but pertinent American history lesson from the Speaker.

Within the ranks of the freshmen, Sam looked for those with a potential that he might help develop for future positions of leadership. To be asked to join the board was the invitation most treasured by the House members. Maybe Sam liked Hale because he just liked smart Southerners. Whatever he saw in Hale, he invited him to join the select group, which included Congressmen John McCormack of Massachusetts and Wright Patman and the young Lyndon Johnson from Texas. (It was during one of their meetings, which he often attended, that Vice President Harry Truman was summoned by President Roosevelt's press secretary, Steve Early, to meet Mrs. Roosevelt at the White House. There, in the second-floor family quarters, she informed him that the president was dead.)

I will always be grateful that Mr. Sam came into our family's life. He stands out as one of my heroes, and he carries my everlasting affection and admiration. He understood that politics was the art of the possible, and he lived his life believing "If you tell the truth the first time, you don't have to remember what you said." That kind of honesty and integrity in government is the most enduring contribution one can make.

When Hale ran for reelection to the Second District, those who had been defeated by the People's League desperately wanted to get back in office. Governor Jones had less than two more years of his four-year term and could not run for reelection, a disadvantage to us because of the heavy reform vote he commanded. Forces that had been defeated were reconstituted behind Hale's original opponent, Paul Maloney, their longtime favorite whose greatest strength was in New Orleans. Hale had won some of those votes before, but the machine was determined to deliver a majority this time.

Many of our best campaign workers, including Chep, were away in the war, and Hale didn't feel that he could spend as much time campaigning as he had before because of wartime demands on the Congress. He knew that Maloney had been popular, but he didn't recognize how much opposition he was up against, a great deal of it orchestrated by the Long machine, until he began campaigning. The situation in New Orleans was more serious than he had realized, and Maloney stood a good chance of winning the election.

About ten days before the election, Hale asked me to join him, and when I arrived in New Orleans, I began to work in Jefferson Parish, trying to win Sheriff Clancy and his people to our side. Clancy was not part of the reform operation, but he was a strong and active and highly popular sheriff, and I felt I was helping to turn some votes around. One day he said to me, "Boggs should have gotten you down here earlier." The remark was an encouraging sign that we were making headway in the parish, but it implied that we had started too late to win. He and Hale ended up becoming best of friends, but not soon enough to help Hale in that election.

Hale lost to Paul Maloney by two thousand votes. It was a big disappointment, but looking back, I think it was better for Hale to lose and to share a wartime experience with his own generation. By being out of Congress and in the service, he became personally aware of the reams of government regulations with which most people have to deal. Had he always remained a member of the Congress devising those regulations, he would never have had that firsthand knowledge.

We rented out our house in Washington and moved back to New Orleans. Hale became an attorney for the state Department of Conservation and won a resounding victory for Louisiana before the United States Supreme Court in a crucial case upholding the state's oil and gas laws. He practiced law in New Orleans with Marion Epley Jr., who later became president of Texaco, and he resumed his patronage duties for Governor Jones.

Hale had always been interested in world trade, and when a special civic committee began studying the feasibility of establishing an international house and trade center in New Orleans, he was chosen as its executive secretary. His enthusiasm and knowledge, combined with his experience and contacts in New Orleans and Washington among state and federal officials, made Hale the natural choice. Everybody realized that nothing concrete could be done until the war was over, but this was the time to plan a for a peacetime future in which the high level of wartime trade activity through the port of New Orleans could be maintained and increased.

Rudolph Hecht, an internationally known financier and extraordinarily influential citizen, was among local leaders promoting the international house as a place to coordinate cultural, social, and commercial relationships among the people of the United States and those of other countries, especially our neighboring American republics. William Zetzman, owner of the company that produced 7Up, was an equally enthusiastic business and civic promoter.

Before Hale developed a formal proposal for the New Orleans International House, he talked to everyone who could make it a reality. We traveled to see similar centers in New York and Chicago, and he met with delegations from Washington and Baton Rouge to talk about agricultural products, manufactured goods, and foreign trading partners. Members of the New Orleans diplomatic corps were consulted on what their countries might offer to trade, and local businesses made their lists.

Hale became convinced that such a center was not only desirable but necessary. It would bring together exporters and importers and assist them with multilingual staffs of secretaries, banking consultants, and trade experts. Area universities pledged their participation by hosting conferences and speakers of international importance and creating educational programs for international executives and teachers.

The night before Hale's formal feasibility presentation to the International House Committee, he learned that his brother Billy was desperately ill and Hale hurried to the hospital. As the night wore on—one o'clock in the morning, two o'clock—I looked at the material that had to be pulled together by the next day. I thought it would be better to collate the material and to write an introduction than to leave it all for Hale. Whenever he came in, he would be able to correct it, but at least he would have an organized presentation.

When I finished I didn't know whether I had done it correctly—I had not done the research, nor had I directed the program—so I added a flyleaf on which I wrote, "Dedicated to World Trade, Peace and Understanding." It was an act of desperation of a young wife who was feeling inadequate to an unaccustomed task and it was done with a prayer. The project was accepted. New Orleans's International House was created, and when the building was dedicated, my motto was adopted and placed prominently on a wall of the entrance foyer.

Shortly afterward an effort was undertaken to open an International Trade Mart where U.S. manufacturers and producers could display their products to the foreign market and where U.S. investors could be encouraged to participate in joint ventures with Latin American businesses. It now occupies a handsome riverfront building designed by Edward Durell Stone.

I don't know exactly how many world trade centers there are in the world, but they all bear my motto.

Jimmie Davis was out campaigning for governor of Louisiana with a band that played "You Are My Sunshine," which he had written. He was the choice of the New Orleans reformers, and they and Davis's own backers asked Hale to run for lieutenant governor, but he declined. Hale felt that if he were going to have a career in national politics—and that was where he wanted to be—running for lieutenant governor of Louisiana was off the main track.

Hale had voted for the war, and now he felt it was his duty to serve his country in the military. Chep, who was a reserve officer, had already gone and Chep's half brother Jake Morrison, a revered attorney too old to be drafted, had volunteered for the army and was on his way. Hale was commissioned in the Naval Reserve and joked that he quickly went from being the youngest member of Congress to being the oldest ensign in the navy.

He was ordered to PT boat school in Quonset, Rhode Island, but on the train east, he met retired Admiral Telfair Knight, who had been called back to duty to take over the Maritime Commission. By the time Hale and the admiral had ridden together for twenty-four hours, Admiral Knight asked if Hale would consent to working for him at the Maritime Commission in Washington if Secretary of the Navy Frank Knox were in agreement. Hale accepted, becoming legal officer and legislative counsel with the dual task of handling the legal requirements to construct and open maritime training facilities across the country and of representing the Maritime Commission on Capitol Hill.

The children and I stayed in New Orleans. I was pregnant with our third child, and Barbara and Tommy were eagerly awaiting the baby's arrival. Every night when we would say our prayers, I would say, "And please, God, send us a healthy little baby," and Barbara would say "girl." Then she would punch Tommy and say, "Say 'girl,' " and Tommy would say "girl." It was Barbara's first lobbying effort. I was glad she was not disappointed.

Hale was able to come home for Christmas leave, which we hoped would coincide with the baby's birth, but as the days wore on, I think he was becoming apprehensive that he would miss the birth. Our baby girl was most obliging and arrived two days after Christmas with her sweet little face and the most beautiful almond-shaped eyes. We pleased family members from all sides when we named her Mary Martha Corinne Morrison Claiborne Boggs. When Tommy tried to say "Corinne," it came out "Cokie."

We stayed in New Orleans for a couple of months after Cokie was born. It was the first time Hale and I had been apart that long, and I missed him terribly. It wasn't so bad during the day, but from dinnertime on, I was lonesome. My eye problem was acting up again, although I was gaining weight and trying to rest. A practical nurse lived with us, and my father's sister, the suffragette of old, Aunt Celeste Claiborne Carruth helped me after the baby was born.

Our children took to politics from an early age. When a sound truck passed one day, Barbara, who was four and a half, said, "Now, I wonder who they want us to vote for? That doesn't sound like Mister Jimmie Davis's music." As the music continued, Tommy began marching around the house with a flag. Cokie was a strong child—she even turned over by herself when she was three weeks old. She was also a wonderfully good baby, who quickly developed her own personality. All these strengths stood her in good stead, because she had to withstand lively competition from Barbara and Tommy.

When we were all ready to go to Washington, Hale came down to help take the children back on the train and brought along Charlie Coulon, our Stephenson Place neighbor and a member of an old Louisiana family. We weren't accustomed to traveling with the baby, and while the rest of us finished our last-minute packing, Aunt Celeste held Cokie. We piled into the car to go to the station—Hale and I, Charlie, Barbara, and Tommy and all our luggage. We waved good-bye to Aunt Celeste and she waved good-bye to us. We were a couple of blocks away when suddenly somebody yelled, "The baby!" We dashed back to get her. Cokie almost missed her first Washington deadline.

I always wondered if Hale wasn't cheated out of a different kind of wartime experience by being stationed in Washington. It was the best thing for me and the children, but I think it was hard for him to remain behind within the bureaucracy in the States and not overseas where the action was. He said, "Lin, Washington is very different when seen from this side of the fence. Everyone has an entirely different attitude when you're in the Navy than when you're a member of Congress."

Even though he was in Washington, Hale remained the subject of political speculation in Louisiana. Paul Wooten suggested that he run in absentia for his old seat, and other writers hinted that he was being groomed for local political office. We heard that Governor Jones was promoting Hale for New Orleans mayor. Larry Eustis urged him to stay out of city politics and to run for Congress again, because the young men returning from the service would look to him for the leadership he had exerted throughout his academic and political careers. Chep, who was overseas, had already been reelected to the state legislature through the campaign efforts of his wife, Corinne.

As the war in Germany ended, many of Hale's friends were sent home. He was busy closing the maritime training bases that he had helped to open. Marion Epley Jr., returning from the service, found himself inundated with legal work for oil companies and independents, and he urged Hale to rejoin their practice. A group of people anxious to rid the New Orleans city government of the entrenched political machine went to Washington and asked Hale to run for mayor, but he declined.

The group then turned to Chep, who was homeward bound from Europe after restoring and reopening the German port of

Bremerhaven. Chep had no ambition to be mayor, but the group boarded his train in Atlanta, and by the time it rolled into the terminal on Canal Street, he had agreed to run. Women who had worked with the People's League and in the Sam Jones campaign became the "Broom Brigade," to sweep the old politicians out of City Hall and sweep in Chep and the reformers.

It promised to be an uphill battle. Chep's toughest opponent was the incumbent, Mayor Maestri. His backers had run the city for years; their beautiful clubhouse was diagonally across the street from City Hall so they could keep an eye on things. Chep pulled other Democratic organizations into a coalition he hoped would be strong enough to break the machine.

At last, we went home, arriving the day of Chep's final campaign rally. Hale put the children and me out of the car at our house, and he went off to join the rally crowd. At that moment, Mayor Maestri was riding in his car with his adviser and right-hand man, Mr. Parsons, and they were listening to the rally on the radio. They were feeling smugly confident of the machine's imminent victory, when suddenly they heard Hale's strong, distinctive voice booming through the air on behalf of Chep's candidacy.

The mayor turned to Mr. Parsons. "What's that boy doing talking like that? I've never done anything wrong to that boy. What's the matter with him, anyway?"

"But Mister Mayor," Mr. Parsons said, "Mister Morrison is Mrs. Boggs's cousin."

"Oh, that girl! She's got too many cousins," Mayor Maestri said. Chep won in an upset, and he was sworn in as mayor early in 1946.

Hale returned to his law practice with Marion Epley, and I hoped he would remain there for some time. In his short professional life, he'd had little experience of the outside world, and we talked seriously about whether he should stay out of politics for a few years. My feeling was he should establish a solid law practice and get back into politics several years down the road. Hale was doing well, earning more money than he made in the Navy or as a member of Congress, and we had three growing children.

I said, "We're very young. You're building your law practice, and I'm settling into my life. We can find areas of civic and philanthropic responsibility where we can make contributions. You can certainly continue to be an adviser to governors and mayors without holding a political office."

We talked back and forth, discussing our future, until Hale finally said No—that what he really wanted to do was to be a member of Congress. Despite his college nickname, he had no desire to be a senator. The House of Representatives, the people's chamber, was where the action was, he said. He felt that in the House he could best gratify his feelings for public service and participate in the aspects of national life in which he was interested. It was a tough decision, but once that decision was made we relaxed into it and built our lives accordingly.

When Chep went to City Hall, New Orleans was still very much "the City That Care Forgot," where business stopped for midmorning coffee, and rattling streetcars (including the line named "Desire") ran up Royal Street beneath Tennessee Williams's windows. The war had brought heightened activity to the port but little time or funds to maintain it or modernize the other infrastructure of the rapidly expanding city.

Chep became one of New Orleans's most popular mayors, steering it through thirteen years of growth, progress, and modernization without sacrificing its special charm. His big push was always Latin American trade, understanding, and friendship, and in later years, President Kennedy appointed him to be ambassador to the Organization of American States (OAS), a position he held with pride and with great effectiveness.

Chep was in City Hall, and Congressman Maloney had retired when Hale ran again in 1946 for the House seat from the Second District. He won easily over his most formidable opponent, Henry Vosbeim, and in the process the Vosbeims, Henry and his energetic, highly organized wife, Rae, became our friends.

We went back to Congress. With the war over, year-round sessions were no longer considered necessary and over the years we settled into a routine of packing up and moving twice a year, renting out the house we didn't happen to be living in at the time and sending the children to schools in Washington and New Orleans, depending on the congressional calendar. Right after Christmas we'd leave New Orleans and go up to Washington and come back in June. The only affordable way for all of us to go was by automobile, and Emma Cyprian, our live-in housekeeper, went with us.

If anyone ever needed persuading to become an integrationist, a long automobile trip with children and a black housekeeper would do it. Although Emma was a refined, educated, intelligent, polite, well-dressed woman, we could not take her with us into restaurants or into the motels or even into the restrooms at many of the gas stations along the highways of our route between Washington and New Orleans. It was insulting to this remarkable woman, who before coming to work for us had been a devoted and highly successful rural schoolteacher. The graduate of a normal school that granted certificates after two years of teacher training, she had elected to return from New Orleans to her country home in Folsom, Louisiana. When she started teaching, the neighborhood school was open only three months of the year. With her husband, a Tuskegee University graduate, she purchased a bus and with dogged determination brought the students to school for longer and longer sessions, until a full nine-month course was established. As the black movement gained strength, teachers with four-year college degrees replaced those with only two-year normal school certificates. Our children were the fortunate beneficiaries of that reform.

We had friends and relatives along the way with whom we would stay, and some old Southern resort hotels were accustomed to having families, children, and their nurses (they were also willing to take pet dogs and turtles!). But they were few and far between, and if a snowstorm came along, as occasionally happened at Christmastime, we had a difficult time finding lodging because we would not stay separately from Emma.

One place we all loved to stay was with Raburn and Rose Monroe, our friends from New Orleans, in their summerhouse at Highlands, North Carolina, in the Appalachian Mountains. The house had a long gallery, from which you could see five states. The children were in heaven.

The Monroes also had a cabin on a beautiful lake higher up in the mountains, where we went swimming and boating. One day when she was five, Cokie, Raburn, and Marsha, the Monroes' ten-year-old daughter, were in a canoe, and Hale and the other kids were in a flat-bottom boat. I was on the shore because our dog wouldn't go in the boat, so I was apprehensively watching everyone. Cokie turned around in the canoe to wave at the kids in Hale's boat, and suddenly the canoe tipped over.

Raburn came up, Marsha came up, but Cokie didn't come up. Hale dived in and joined Raburn in the search for her beneath the cold water. I was frantic, stuck on the shore and watching this—one of the most frightening experiences of my life. After a few moments that seemed forever, Marsha said, I later learned, "Why don't we flip the canoe over? She's probably under there."

They flipped the boat over, and there was Cokie. "I held the boat up," she said proudly. "I saved the boat." She had been in the air pocket, her head above water. A position it holds to this day in on-air and off discussions!

CHAPTER SEVEN

࿐

*H*ALE AND I did not deliberately decide to rear our children for lives of service, but they grew up with politics in their blood. That's what they knew, and it was served up at the dinner table with the likes of Mr. Sam, Lyndon Johnson, and John Kennedy raising their voices over plates of Emma's chicken. The conversations, usually about politics, were spirited and informative, with everyone trying to break in.

From the time they were tiny tots, the children were expected to meet and greet people. Barbara and Cokie loved it all and eagerly participated in parades and rallies. Tommy was less enthusiastic, but he, too, performed like a trouper.

We determined early on that since we couldn't prejudge how much they wanted to take part in political activities, the best procedure for us was to honor their interest. Fortunately this was before families were as exposed to the media as they are today, and many people thought that children shouldn't be "used politically." Hale took the lead in the matter, saying, "There's no way we can win an argument about our children's participation, so we shall allow them to participate according to their own desires."

I have always hoped that besides their genes, that attitude of honoring their wishes allowed our children to grow up self-confident and capable of maturing within their own personalities and their own lives.

Hale and I felt that keeping them in Washington for long periods of time deprived them of the privilege of knowing all the remarkable family members of older generations that we had known, but they spent many summers back home, surrounded by family and old friends. Because one grandmother lived on the Mississippi Gulf Coast and one in the country in Louisiana, the children were exposed to many of the same experiences and places that Hale and I had known. Cokie especially loved to spend the summers with her best friend and cousin, Josephine ("Jo Pepper") Morrison. They were just six months apart in age, and they would visit the relatives in New Roads and stay in Long Beach with Jo Pepper's parents, Claire and Stanley Morrison, always with a crowd of young people around.

Sometimes children react adversely to high-profile parents and want to live a more private life, but ours chose public service and public lives. When Cokie was barely in kindergarten, she took the stage on her own initiative at a big patriotic celebration at the Long Island, New York, home of my cousin Paul Seghers and his wife, Brounisha.

Brounisha, who was Polish, had been married to a Russian who was murdered by the Bolsheviks, shot dead before her eyes at their home in Moscow during the revolution. The servants rescued Brounisha and her baby son, passing them from one of their family members to another until she reached Germany, where she had a summer home. Sadly the infant didn't survive the journey. This tragedy inspired Brounisha to work with Herbert Hoover in France in his monumental effort to feed the starving children who were the victims of war. Paul, who had lost his French wife, met Brounisha through a mutual friend when he was visiting his daughter, who lived with her Parisian grandparents.

After they were married, the family settled on Long Island, where Brounisha became a patroness of the arts and an extremely patriotic U.S. citizen. She thought there should be an "I am an American" day, when people could celebrate the fact that they had become naturalized citizens, and she cajoled Hale into having it officially designated, which meant he was obliged to attend the celebration.

The Boy Scout who was to lead the Pledge of Allegiance was late, and our hostess was looking around for somebody else to fill in, when Cokie, who was not yet five, said, "I'll lead it!" She had put herself in kindergarten at Miss Aiken's Little School in New Orleans while Hale and I were on a trip abroad. Miss Edith Aiken was known as such an effective and excellent teacher we had no opportunity yet to judge how much Cokie had learned.

Before we could catch her, she was on the stage and a man on the organizing committee was proudly lifting her up to the microphone. We had no notion she knew the pledge to the flag, but she said it almost perfectly. She even improved on it: At the end she said, "With liberty and just nice for all." Then she scrambled down from the man's arms and ran to us.

I said, "Cokie, where did you learn the Pledge of Allegiance?"

"On *The Howdy Doody Show*," she replied matter-of-factly, as though everyone should have known that.

For years we broadcast a family radio show in New Orleans at Christmastime. Barbara would read "The Night Before Christmas," and the younger ones would participate as they could. When Tommy was eleven, we had our first Christmas television show. On the way to the studio I asked Hale if he had any special format in mind. "Oh, no," he said. "It will be the same family show."

Tommy spoke up from the backseat. "There's one thing I want you to avoid, Dad. Please don't ask me what I want Santa to bring. You'll embarrass me in front of my friends who are watching." We took along to the show Governor, the little cocker spaniel puppy we had recently been given.

The show was live, and everything was going smoothly until Cokie announced in her clear voice, "Governor just wet the floor." She was already showing signs of being an accurate reporter.

There was silence. Hale kind of smiled, crinkled his eyes, and looked at Tommy and said, "Tommy, what are you going to ask Santa to bring you this year?" Tommy glared at him, gritted his teeth, and began naming all the things he had wanted all year— every single thing that came to mind. We thought he'd never stop. At last Hale regained control of the show, but not before Tom had alerted all the people who did business with his dad to exactly what he wanted: early signs of the accomplished lobbyist he would become.

I probably knew Cokie was going to be a reporter one evening at the dinner table when Hale was talking about a White House dinner and she interrupted him to ask, "Daddy, what's a tuxedo?" He kept talking, someone else chimed in, and the conversation went along. Then Cokie raised her hand and kept it aloft until Hale stopped in midsentence and asked, "Yes, Corinne?" She said, "Getting back to the tuxedo—" She's been a persistent questioner ever since. She has said that it wasn't until she entered college that she met people whose fathers made things, like tape measures and furniture. That fascinated her, because in Washington nobody made anything but speeches, policy, and laws.

We tried to give our children a sense of discipline, not only to observe bedtime schedules and good eating habits but about their lives and their work. They were treated in an adult fashion, and they were expected to behave that way—to finish their tasks on time and to the best of their abilities.

Barbara and Cokie were lucky in that respect because they had the same order of nuns, Les Mesdames de Sacre Coeur, teaching them through elementary school and junior and senior high school in New Orleans and in Washington. The nuns felt a special commitment to instill a feeling of noblesse oblige in their students, and these educated, intelligent women demanded their best in a loving way. Barbara was one of those children who is perpetually elected president of her school class and president of every club she joins. Some years when we were living some six months in Washington and the other six in New Orleans, she was president of her class in both places.

Barbara Denechaud, the child of two of my dearest friends, Charlie and Mary Byrne Denechaud, and Tommy were childhood friends in New Orleans. When she was twelve she had rheumatic fever, and the summer when she was recovering, her family didn't want to go away for the Fourth of July, so they held a picnic at home. Hale was away at a convention and our Barbara was visiting friends in Florida, but Tommy, Cokie, and I went to the picnic. At about three o'clock in the afternoon, Tommy and Barbara Denechaud asked if they could walk to the Prytania neighborhood movie theater. That was their first "date." Even though they did go out with other people, they were "going steady" by the time they were in high school.

I've always been closer to my children than to anyone else in my family—so much so that I sometimes hope they don't feel as if I want them too close for their own comfort. Away from all the relatives as we were in Washington, we tried to compensate, giving our children the love, inspiration, and intellectual input the rest of the family would have provided. We were always happy when other people we admired took an interest in them, exposing them to different ideas and attitudes.

We were fortunate that, when we arrived, Washington was a rather small town and manageable for children, and we enjoyed the companionship of the extended family of our Louisiana delegation and a wider family among other Southerners in Congress. Hale and I came to know them all and loved to gather them for dinners and parties.

We were looking forward to our return to Washington when Hale was reelected to Congress in the fall of 1946. However, before our departure from New Orleans I experienced one of the most painful periods in my life. In December I had a baby boy we named William Robertson Boggs, for Hale's father. I had no trouble during my pregnancy, but I had a complicated delivery that required me to have several blood transfusions. Billy was hailed in the operating room as a fine, handsome baby, and he cried loudly. I thought he was the most beautiful creature I had ever seen, but within a few hours of his birth the doctors saw signs that his lungs were not getting rid of fluids. This was the same difficulty little Patrick Kennedy later experienced. (In 1963 President and Mrs. Kennedy's second son died thirty-nine hours after his birth of hyaline membrane disease.)

I don't know if medical techniques available now would have saved him, but two days later we lost Billy and I couldn't have any more children. It was a terrible time. I was so ill that Hale had to bury Billy in the lovely old Saint Mary's Cemetery in New Roads without me.

In February we were driving back to Washington when it began to snow. Hale looked at me and said, "Do I look yellow to you in this snow?"

I said, "No, why? Do I look yellow to you?"

He said, "I guess."

When we arrived at the house, I put the kids into their familiar Washington beds and then flopped, dead tired, into my own. In the middle of the night I awoke feeling nauseated, and when I stood up to look for some medicine, I passed out. Dr. Al Richwine, our close friend, was called, and he determined that I had contracted hepatitis from one of the transfusions I had received.

I was housebound for such a long time that Hale would bring people home to visit with me. One of them was John F. ("Jack") Kennedy, a freshman congressman from Massachusetts who had recently recovered from a bout with hepatitis. Hale thought it would cheer me up to talk with him, and it did. It also introduced me to a young man who would soon be joining our dinner table and would become one of Hale's most valued friends. It's an ill wind that blows no one any good.

President Truman was in the White House, but the Republicans controlled the House by a veto-proof majority of 248 to 188, and the Senate, 51 to 45. Representative Joe Martin of Massachusetts was the Speaker and Mr. Sam became the minority leader. Most members of Congress were ready to return to normalcy after the years of wartime shortages and high taxes, and they were becoming increasingly apprehensive about the Communist influence worldwide and in Washington.

Accordingly, the Republican-controlled Congress led by Senator Arthur Vandenberg, Chairman of the Senate Foreign Relations Committee, cooperated with Secretary of State General George C. Marshall to forge a bipartisan foreign policy aimed at rebuilding and strengthening our allies to contain Communist aggression.

In reaction to President Roosevelt's death, succession to the presidency was increased from only the Vice President to include the Speaker of the House and the President Pro-Tem of the Senate, and in response to Roosevelt's four terms, a constitutional amendment was passed limiting an individual to two terms as president.

The conservative attitude of the Republican Congress was obvious as it blocked or ignored legislation in education, housing, medical care, and social security while it passed the Taft-Hartley Act, limiting labor's powers, over a presidential veto, and the House Un-American Activities Committee was launched. Presidential budgets were reduced and taxes were lowered.

When I think of how enormous challenges sometimes make an individual rise to the occasion, I think of President Truman. Most people had no notion that he—or indeed anyone—could follow Roosevelt, but not only did he assume the presidency, he didn't let it change him. Harry S Truman never lost touch with his family members and friends from school, Army buddies, pals from politics, and members of both houses of Congress, where he served ten years as a senator from Missouri. His loyal friendship was a trait that contributed to his amazing success.

I knew the Trumans' only child, Margaret, through my New Orleans friend Ellen Floweree, and I was impressed by her lovingly respectful relations with her parents. The president and his wife, "Miss Bess," were warm, friendly people, well-read and fond of music. Although we were with them at official functions, we were not close personal friends; they were of an older generation and had their own Washington friends.

Mrs. Truman was admirable and gracious in ways the public never really knew. Not only would she lend her name and support to charitable and cultural women's organizations, but she would attend their special events, arriving ahead of time to admire the decorations, talk about the importance of what they were doing, and compliment members on their work. She was always friendly and loving, taking the time to do this despite her busy schedule.

But crowds seemed to stifle her, and the instant the first wave of people started through the receiving line, Miss Bess would become expressionless, shaking hands quickly as she passed each guest on to the next person with a minimum of contact. I always regretted that the general public didn't often see her as the affectionate and generous person that she was.

Hale was reassigned to the Banking and Currency Committee, and he quickly familiarized himself with the postwar outlook for newly urgent credit and housing needs, international trade, peacetime defense requirements, and the rebuilding of infrastructure, which had been generally ignored, except for emergency repairs, since the 1930s. Military and administration officials had realized during the war that there was no way of moving troops and war matériel by land across the United States, and one of the first bills introduced into the new Congress provided for the building of a national interstate highway system. When the project's affordability was in question, Hale introduced successful legislation dedicating a gasoline tax toward its construction and upkeep.

Those were the early days of the Cold War, and a bipartisan spirit prevailed in foreign affairs. Hale and Bill Fulbright responded by cosponsoring an historic congressional resolution proposing that the anti-Communist nations of Europe join together in a "United States of Europe," under the auspices of the United Nations. The idea behind it was that Western Europe should be united financially, politically, and diplomatically as a bulwark against the Soviet Union. The resolution received the unofficial approval of President Truman and it became a guiding light to the Marshall Plan and to a European mutual defense treaty against Russian aggression. It was a great source of satisfaction to Hale and Bill that Secretary Marshall credited their resolution as his inspiration for the Marshall Plan.

Hale voted with the majority to extend relief payments to weak nations, struggling to rebuild after the war and vulnerable to Communist takeovers, and to implement the "Truman Doctrine" by strengthening Greece and Turkey with emergency aid to enable them to counter Communist revolutionary movements.

Chep and Hale cooperated to give New Orleans a period of dramatic, unprecedented growth, which literally extended to every corner of the city, from modernizing the airport to moving downtown railroad tracks, upgrading the port, and developing whole new residential neighborhoods. I was aware of all that they were accomplishing, but I didn't realize that the voters saw it until one day when I was out campaigning for Chep and a thoughtful black woman assured me, "Don't you worry about your cousin's reelection. Folks vote with their eyes."

In 1947 a monstrous hurricane struck the Gulf Coast, taking the lives of Hale's Uncle Archie and Aunt Bessie Boggs. Water roared over the Long Beach seawall, destroying their cottage and, next door, the old family homestead built in 1875. Gentle artists and nature lovers, they had no children but they shared an idyllic situation with love for everything and everybody. Aunt Bessie was crippled, and when the water came she clung to a tree as long as she could but finally let go and was drowned. Six weeks later Uncle Archie died of pneumonia and a broken heart.

Because of Hale's personal tragedy, he was determined to develop a federal program to benefit hurricane victims, a labor of love that took him almost twenty years to accomplish. Archie and Bessie's insurance agents were hometown folks, and when they had sold their friends "comprehensive" policies, everybody thought that the coverage was for wind and water losses. Unfortunately it was not. Full hurricane insurance was expensive, beyond the financial reach of most residents, and the policies covered only wind damage. The 1947 hurricane had destroyed everything in its path, with great tidal waves roaring over the seawalls.

Hale promoted a national disaster relief bill combining affordable flood insurance with low-interest, government-guaranteed recovery loans for hurricane victims. He was still working for its passage in 1965, when Hurricane Betsy's disastrous visit to the same Gulf Coast area convinced Congress of the bill's importance and it was finally passed.

Returning veterans had encountered a critical housing shortage that alarmed President Truman and led him to set a national goal of clean, affordable, and safe housing to relieve the shortage and to improve building standards. In 1948 Democrats re-took the House and Hale headed the House committee charged with making that goal a reality, and in his early research he discovered that housing matters were scattered through more than a dozen different government departments and agencies, with little or no coordination among them.

He decided to take his committee to the people. At crowded public hearings in cities across the country, Hale and the committee members listened to experts in the housing field and ordinary home buyers and renters describe their frustrations and problems and suggest possible solutions to the crisis. As a result of the hearings and his study of the situation, Hale rewrote the nation's housing legislation and in 1949 for the first time, consolidated all housing matters into one bill.

Hale's housing counterpart in the Senate, freshman Senator Joseph McCarthy of Wisconsin, apparently felt no sense of urgency in conducting his hearings and developing a Senate bill. He seemed uninterested until a hearing he convened in Washington was covered by local television, and he quickly grasped the power of the new medium, stringing out his sessions before the lights and cameras.

The delay was annoying to Hale, who had no special connection to the new Republican senator and thus no way to prod him. But Senator McCarthy eventually recognized the need to have the housing legislation go forward and brought his bill to completion.

Their final compromise bill became the 1949 Housing Act, from which all future housing legislation emanated and which subsequently led to the creation of the Department of Housing and Urban Development during President Johnson's "Great Society" administration. Hale's belief that everyone deserved affordable, decent housing in a clean, safe neighborhood would lead him to take a far bolder step almost two decades later, but that was long after civil rights battles began to be won.

CHAPTER EIGHT

࿊

I ATTENDED my first national political convention in 1948 in Philadelphia. Although the Democrats were meeting in the City of Brotherly Love, there was little love in Convention Hall. A strong anti–civil rights movement pervaded many of the Southern delegations, intensified by President Truman's Civil Rights message to the Congress a few months before. He had asked for a federal anti-lynching law, the abolition of state poll taxes, voter protection laws, a commission to terminate racial discrimination by employers and unions, and an end to racial discrimination on interstate trains, planes, and buses.

So angry were some Democrats, fearing that the civil rights issue would mean their defeat at the polls, that they were ready to abandon President Truman in favor of another candidate. Up to the eve of the convention, party leaders including Hubert Humphrey, the mayor of Minneapolis; James Roosevelt, the eldest son of the late president; and Governor Strom Thurmond of South Carolina wanted to draft Dwight D. ("Ike") Eisenhower, the beloved World War II hero, as the Democratic presidential candidate. He was the president of Columbia University, and although no one seemed to know his politics or his position on any issue, he was enormously popular as the commander whose D-day plan had turned the tide of war and as the true diplomat who pulled all the Allied forces together.

This was the first national political convention to utilize air-conditioning and television. The television transmitted the country's first live convention coverage, but the air-conditioning did not meet the challenge. The hall was hot, humid, and uncomfortable, which only added to the feelings of frustration and anger that many of the delegates were experiencing over President Truman's insistence on a civil rights plank in the party's platform.

It was an unhappy social and physical climate. Hubert Humphrey, who was running for the Senate, made a speech in the middle of the night calling on Democrats to end their dedication to states' rights and instead to embrace human rights, meaning civil rights. I'll never forget the feeling as hundreds of delegates began rhythmically pounding their feet on the floor in protest. In that closed room they created an ominous sound of angrily beating drums.

Some Southern delegations picked up their state standards and walked out in protest against Humphrey's speech. I wasn't a delegate, but I was with Hale and Russell Long, who was running for the Senate, and both of them were Louisiana delegates. We walked out with the rest of our state's delegation and then we three brought the state standard back into the Convention Hall, where we remained to assure that Louisiana would be represented. When the rest of our delegation returned to the floor, they voted for Senator Richard Russell of Georgia as the party's presidential nominee.

Hale and Russell Long, a lawyer and a navy veteran, admired each other and held each other in affectionate regard. Russell had been sixteen when his father, Huey Long, was assassinated. A remarkable combination of his father's social populism and a fairly conservative economic perspective, he enjoyed the confidence and support of the Long machine, as well as of the Louisiana business community and political reformers, throughout his lengthy career.

President Truman was an underdog against the Republican nominee, Governor Thomas E. Dewey of New York, who had originally made his reputation as a tough prosecutor. The president had been weakened in the South by his civil rights advocacy and nationally by a split of the Democratic Party's votes among himself; Henry Wallace, the former vice president during Roosevelt's administration, who was nominated by the liberal Progressive Party; and Strom Thurmond, an uncompromising segregationist and the nominee of the newly organized states' rights parties, whose members were called Dixiecrats.

In the Confederate states and some border states, the official Democratic symbol on the ballot was the rooster rather than the donkey. Voters throughout the solidly Democratic South knew they had to "stamp the rooster"—mark the rooster symbol with a special eraser dipped in ink rather than mark the individual names or other ballot proposals—in order to vote the straight Democratic ticket endorsed by their state party organization.

The contest for the Democratic Central Committee's endorsement centered around the use of the rooster symbol, which Hale was fortunate in receiving. His favorable ties to the various Democratic factions in Saint James, Saint John, and Saint Charles Parishes were secure; his friendship with Sheriff Clancy in Jefferson was developing firmly; and in New Orleans, Chep as mayor had pulled the Democratic factions together into a cohesive campaign force.

Leander Perez, the ultraconservative political boss and district attorney of Louisiana's Plaquemines and Saint Bernard Parishes, who was a member of the state Central Democratic Committee, seized control of our state Democratic Party and gave Governor

Thurmond and his Dixiecrats the rooster. It appeared at the top of the ballot above Thurmond's name, which insured that he would win the majority of Louisiana's Democratic votes for president. President Truman was left completely off the ballot until Governor Earl Long (Huey's brother), the titular head of the state Democratic Party, ordered his inclusion, but Thurmond kept the rooster and easily carried the state.

Although the presidential race was extremely close, President Truman prevailed in a stupendous upset and was successful in helping to turn both the Senate and the House of Representatives back to Democratic majorities, which meant that Sam Rayburn was Speaker of the House again. Hale ran well and won his race. He returned to Congress, where unbounded personal and professional opportunities awaited him.

When President Truman and his vice-presidential choice, Kentucky's Senator Alben Barkley, returned to Washington after the election, the *Washington Post*, which had predicted a Dewey victory, greeted them with a sign portraying an enormous crow lying on its back and, beside it, a knife and fork. WELCOME FROM THE CROW-EATERS! it declared.

Hale and I made our first official voyage to Europe that fall. Hale was running for reelection but he had already won the Democratic primary which was tantamount to election since Republican opposition in the general election was rare in those days and always a losing effort.

I was accompanying Hale on this trip to participate in the second postwar meeting of the Inter-Parliamentary Union (IPU), an organization composed of lawmakers from many countries. Different members took turns hosting the meetings, and I was excited that ours was being held in Rome, a city I had longed to visit. Our plans included going via Interlaken, Switzerland, where Hale and

Bill Fulbright had been invited to discuss their United Europe proposal with the Western European parliamentary organization.

Before we left home we were told that anyone going to France
was allowed to take fifty pounds of foodstuffs into the country to
relieve the effects of rationing. We would dock in Le Havre and
spend a couple of days in Paris, so I asked the nuns at the Sacred
Heart Convent in New Orleans what would be appropriate to deliver to their sisters in Paris. I expected that they would want us to
deliver a little canned meat and a variety of longed-for commodi-
ties, but instead they requested fifty pounds of white flour.

We boarded the ship in New York with a fifty-pound sack of
flour. Senator Tom Connally of Texas and his wife, Lucile, were
aboard and Tom and Hale spent most of their time in the radio
room listening for reports of Lyndon Johnson's first race for the
Senate, which he finally won by the slimmest of margins. When
we docked at Le Havre and transferred to the boat train to Paris,
each passenger was allowed to take one satchel on board; all other
gear was to be sent ahead to the hotel. I planned to take a makeup
kit and blouse and fresh gloves to change into, but a member of the
ship's crew said, "Take the flour or you may never see it again."
My little niceties were replaced, and we lugged the sack of flour
onto the train.

We were met at the station in Paris by a friend of my cousin
Nancy Seghers. A six-foot-seven-inch-tall Britisher, Neville
Brazier-Crae was deeply involved in a one-world peace movement
in which Nancy was also active. Neville found a taxi and escorted
us to the Ritz Hotel, where he helped us check in. From that time
to this day, Neville has stayed in touch with us: He writes, he
calls, and sometimes visits unexpectedly.

I had never seen a more beautiful hotel suite than that one in
the Ritz, overlooking a garden filled with pink geraniums and with
a little antique clock delicately ticking away on the handsome

mantel in the sitting room. I thought I'd died and gone to heaven until Hale broke the spell: "We have to find the Sacred Heart nuns and deliver the flour," he said.

I knew the convent address, but I thought it would be rude to go without phoning first for an appointment. We searched the telephone directory for the telephone number: *Couvent, Ecole, Mesdames, Sacré-Coeur*—to no avail. Not even the hotel concierge could come up with it. I suggested to Hale that we send a note with a taxi driver, asking for an appointment, but he declared, "We're getting in the cab and we're delivering the flour. Don't worry, they'll be happy to receive us."

Our New Orleans nuns had written their Paris sisters that we were coming, so we weren't a complete surprise. When we reached the convent, we discovered that the nuns had taken in dozens of women and young girls, war refugees, who were still living there. I began apologizing for our sudden arrival, explaining why we had come without an appointment, when one of the nuns said, "We are women here all alone. We could not have our names in a public directory." We sensed by their excited glances at our sack that they couldn't wait to get their hands on the flour, so after several "politenesses," we left. That night at the Ritz we celebrated Hale's reelection, joined by two fellow congressmen-IPU delegates and their wives, Harold and Madeline Cooley of North Carolina and Bob and Frances Poage of Texas.

The meeting in Interlaken was filled with poignancy. People hadn't known whether their friends were alive or what the war had imposed on them and their families, and delegates embraced and wept with joy when they met. After years of severe food shortages and strict rationing, these erstwhile prominent people devoured all the food at the banquet tables at each of the sumptuous meals.

The United States of Europe proposal was received with great enthusiasm, especially in its intentions to preserve peace and to raise living standards throughout the region, and after Hale and Bill Fulbright discussed it with the delegates, some of its provisions were incorporated into a draft resolution for a European Union.

Kitty and Leon Macasse, Greek friends since their prewar visits to Washington, were in Interlaken and were going to the IPU meeting, so we decided to travel together. Leon was a longtime liberal senator and Kitty was effervescent, pretty, and formidable. We secured reservations to Rome, and on the day we left, we boarded the train and found a comfortable compartment to ourselves. We had a delightful time, visiting and laughing, until we reached Milan, where we had to change to the through train to Rome.

Kitty began to insist that we stay in Milan. "Rome through train?" she said. "How boring. If we stay here, there are many fine restaurants. We can have a delightful time. If we have to spend the night, I know a charming little hotel." Impractical as the notion was, it began to appeal to me.

Nevertheless, at the last minute we convinced her that we had to continue to Rome—an aide from the U.S. Embassy was meeting us there. We handed our suitcases through the open windows of the Rome train and clambered aboard a minute before it began to move. The only compartment we could find had only three vacant seats; a studious-looking Italian occupied the fourth. Kitty blamed Hale for making us leave Milan, and she assigned him to stand in the aisle, saying he could "walk all the way to Rome."

After a few minutes she spoke to our companion in rapid Italian and made a snapping gesture with her fingers. He suddenly stood up, fetched his hat and his briefcase, and bowed to us. As he left he motioned for Hale to take his seat.

I asked Kitty what frightening message she had given this poor man. "I told him that Hale was a very important person with the European recovery program and if he didn't give Hale his seat, Italy might be cut off just like that," and she snapped her fingers again.

The excitement of the Marshall Plan to rebuild Europe that had been adopted in April and the bold suggestions for what would become the development in 1949 of the North Atlantic Treaty Organization (NATO) as a shield against the Communists perfectly complemented our country's presence at the IPU session. The organization is dedicated to promoting the power of the world's people through their legislatures, congresses, and parliaments, with the underlying belief that countries should be able to get together on a parliamentary basis, despite animosities that may exist between heads of state.

Our delegation's presence was considered so important to the Truman administration that Senator Alben Barkley, then the Democratic vice presidential nominee, went as our chairman. With the Cold War under way, the U.S. delegation's agenda was in disagreement with the Communist bloc on most proposals; most of our efforts were vis-à-vis the agenda of the Communists, who were equal IPU members.

The people of Rome made a citywide celebration out of our meeting. For the first time since the war, an opera was performed at the Opera House, art museums reopened with important exhibitions, and the lights were on all over the city. We were able to do some touring, following the Appian Way, one of the routes of Saint Paul, and walking with flickering candles down into the catacombs, where the early Christians had been forced to hide and hold their services on the tombs of their martyrs.

We delegates were fortunate to have an audience with Pope Pius XII at his summer palace at Castel Gandolfo, near a beautiful little lake set like a blue sapphire among the gentle surrounding hills. My sophisticated husband was acting nonchalant about our imminent presentation to the pope until the Holy Father walked into the room, whereupon Hale jumped onto a chair and watched in wonder and respect as the papal delegation proceeded to the reception area. Later we all attended an emotional ceremony by the sea in which the remains of U.S. servicemen who had fallen at Anzio were being transferred for reburial in an English cemetery in Florence, where they would have perpetual care.

Always the thoughtful, gallant leader, Senator Barkley had canvassed the ladies among the U.S. delegation to ask if they wished to send any packages back to Washington with him on the President's plane, the *Sacred Cow*. Puzzled at my lack of response, he sought me out at a reception in a cavernous museum. Assuring me that I would not inconvenience him no matter the size of my shipment, I finally answered, "Well, I have an Italian doll and a French doll—" Quick as a wink, he replied: "Well, I don't know if I can get visas for them, but surely it will be a lot of fun!"

When we left Rome we headed for London via the ferry at Calais, and Hale and I shared a compartment with two very affable Scotsmen. People in Europe, where food was still rationed, were riding trains simply to be able to eat well in the dining car. When we reached the Swiss border, many diners were put off while a few Swiss passengers were allowed to board, the railroad's reason being the mountainous terrain ahead, which necessitated a lighter train that would nevertheless require all of the locomotive's force. Hale and the other men agreed to be deaf to anyone's pleas to join us, but then a beautiful Italian girl paused at our compartment door and asked if there was room. Our men immediately said, "Welcome, dear!" She came in, followed by five large relatives. We had to take turns sitting, but the Scotsmen had saved the damsel in distress.

The devastation of London seemed worse to me than any we had yet seen, because it was so identifiable. Painfully overlooking an area from the heights of Saint Paul's Cathedral, we could easily see where houses and shops had been and were no more, and take in at a glance the destruction of an entire block or neighborhood.

We stayed at Claridge's, where—even though rationing still prevailed in the dining room—all the prewar employees who could be found had been rehired in anticipation of better days. The breakfast menu advised us that our choices were juice, cereal, toast, and coffee or tea. Still, because there was a full staff, every meal was a production. One waiter would carefully place empty plates in front of us, then another would come to remove them. A third waiter would bring empty plates for the next course, and another would remove them. As the staff presented the plates, silverware, and crystal for various courses, we became hungry thinking about all the delicious food we were missing.

Everywhere we traveled we saw a true dedication to the belief that Communism was the most severe threat to a free society and that we had to challenge it and win, drawing our strength from our own system of freedom. In the IPU and beyond it, free countries were forming coalitions to outpace the Communists. It was in this context that the control of nuclear weapons became a paramount consideration.

Our belief and our national will were soon tested again. In June 1949 U.S. troops, which had occupied South Korea since the close of World War II, had been brought home, radically heightening the tensions between democratic South Korea and Communist North Korea, above the thirty-eighth parallel. Within one year, as Russia tested a hydrogen bomb, the world's new divisions between Communist and non-Communist territories were frighteningly obvious as North Korean armies invaded South Korea.

President Truman immediately ordered U.S. troops to join the UN forces in South Korea's defense, but our military and industrial forces weren't ready. We had reduced our military strength, retired our warplanes, and mothballed our fleets after World War II. Precious time and lives were lost while we prepared to go to war; in a three-month offensive the Communists overran most of

South Korea. A massive U.S. landing at Inchon led the counter-offensive that drove out the North Koreans and pushed them to the Chinese border, but suddenly thousands of Chinese troops joined the North Koreans, and the imagined horror of an atomic holocaust became a grim possibility.

Eventually, the thirty-eighth parallel was restablished as the boundary between South and North Korea. Cease-fire talks were held between the United States and China and North Korea and the fighting ended in July 1953. Although war had never been declared, the United States suffered more than 33,000 casualties.

Against this backdrop Senator Joseph McCarthy returned to television, demonstrating his skill with the medium to a much wider audience than had watched the housing hearings. In nationally televised hearings, he conducted a hunt for alleged Communist agents in the government, especially within the State Department. By the end of his hearings the term "McCarthyism" had entered our language.

I agreed with Hale's support of our country's involvement in Korea. We thought it was necessary to contain Communism and to reduce the threat of a global nuclear war by stopping Communist aggression before it could spread. The importance placed by government and the media on Senator McCarthy's hearings made us acknowledge the possibility that Communists might have infiltrated our government. But none of that prepared us for the drama that was about to be played out in Louisiana, where political opponents used Cold War suspicions and fears against Hale and affected our family's future.

CHAPTER NINE

*I*T APPEARED that Hale's Second District Congressional seat was secure for the foreseeable future. Mr. Sam appointed him to the Ways and Means Committee, which had the responsibility for Social Security and all tax and trade bills and which served the Democrats as the committee on committees, where assignments were made for Democratic House members. It was a prized assignment and although it required more work, it also bestowed more prestige and authority on Hale.

I had been around politics from my earliest years, and I always felt that I was meant to be involved, but never as the candidate. I enjoyed working in the office and as Hale's campaign coordinator—not campaign manager: How could anyone "manage" Hale Boggs?! I smoothed feathers among members of the campaign staff and among his constituents. A consensus builder by nature, probably from being an only child with all those relatives around me, I assumed the role of peacemaker.

Our life seemed to be predictably settled when, in 1951, Hale was asked to run for governor of Louisiana. Some of the people who had earlier sought his candidacy for mayor of New Orleans now felt that he could unite the state, pulling together city and country, Long and anti-Long, Catholic and non-Catholic, north and south Louisiana, healing the divisions and getting the state going on a progressive footing. According to the Louisiana Constitution, which then limited governors to one term, Governor Earl Long could not succeed himself, and we were told confidentially that Huey's son and political heir, our personable friend Senator Russell Long, would publicly favor Hale over the machine's candidate.

Being governor had never entered into Hale's plans. He did not wish to run, but to honor those friends who were urging the race on him he went to Louisiana to assess the situation. He traveled the southern part of the state, talking to ordinary people as well as to political allies, and then he called me to join him.

We started in the northernmost part of the state, branched out to the west and the south, and returned home to the east, meeting with political, business, civic, and religious leaders. Their message was always the same: "Run!" After our final stop at a rousing Ministerial Alliance meeting in Alexandria, we headed back to New Orleans.

When we reached the edge of the city, Hale pulled the car over and said, "Well, Lin, tell me. What do you think?"

I said, "I hate to tell you this, but I don't think you have any choice. I think you have to run."

"I don't want to run," he said, and he began to weep. He wanted to stay in the Congress, but with the support he was receiving and the hopes that were riding on him, he didn't see how he could avoid the governor's race and remain content with himself. He couldn't disappoint the people who believed so strongly in him.

I said, "I know you don't want to run, but you would do so much good for the people. There's strong resentment against Long's administration, and everyone's counting on you to heal old wounds and represent Louisiana to the rest of the nation in a positive way."

Thus his decision to run was based on the people of goodwill and those with political acumen and economic means who had confidence in him and felt that he was their great hope.

As we entered the race, it looked as though Hale probably could win, breaking an historic "jinx" against anyone from New Orleans being elected governor. We were buoyed by supporters on all sides. Even Bessie Rogers, my baby nurse (and the gift giver of the white mice), helped us. As the manager of the dining room of the Bentley Hotel in Alexandria, she arranged and supervised campaign parties for Hale. We were seeing great enthusiasm among the voters, and the campaign seemed to be moving steadily on the right track.

Then Hale was attacked by Leander Perez, who had persuaded the state Central Democratic Committee to leave President Truman off the state ballot in 1948. As leader in the Southern white supremacy movement, Judge Perez was very influential within the Louisiana Democratic Party faction that was segregationist, right wing, anti-Communist, and that appealed to a large segment of the people. He and his followers portrayed civil rights activities as being Communistic.

The Central Committee, of which he was a former chairman, was exceptionally powerful in the largely one-party state because it controlled the elections and interpreted the election laws. Judge Perez knew that he would have some very rough years if Hale, the politically moderate reform candidate, became governor.

He devised a campaign to stop Hale's candidacy, beginning with resolutions to the Democratic Central Committee. First he created a legal tangle, claiming that anyone holding a federal office, such as a seat in Congress, could not run for a state office without resigning the federal office. That gimmick brought the campaign to a screeching halt and tied up Hale, our time, and our money while everything was directed to a court battle.

Then he threw a bombshell. He said that anyone who had ever belonged to an organization proscribed by the House Un-American Activities Committee could not be qualified on the ballot as a Democratic candidate by the state Central Democratic Committee, and that Hale had belonged to such an organization. Hale had been a member of the American Student Union, he said, referring to a group Hale had once addressed at Tulane, and it was on the proscribed list—or Perez *thought* it should have been. The HUAC was one of many committees, panels, and boards, both in and outside the government, investigating and ruling on individual citizens' loyalty to the United States or their possible Communist connections.

Perez maintained that a newspaper picture of Hale wearing a mock-military uniform at a Tulane antiwar rally proved Hale was anti-American, and that by promoting international peace and the United Nations, Hale advocated doctrines harmful to the U.S. Constitution.

We were well aware that qualifying as a Democrat with the state Central Committee was essential to victory in the Democratic primary, and that the Democratic nomination was tantamount to election, there being few Republican challengers. (In my baby book my Daddy had written that he'd taken me to a cockfight when I was three weeks old so I'd learn how to "stamp the rooster" early in life and vote the straight Democratic ticket.)

Our first reaction was that Judge Perez had finally gone too far. Hale denounced the charges as false and accused the judge of using them as a smokescreen to obscure the fact that he would lose his political clout if Hale were elected governor. On the face of it, it was ridiculous that anyone would consider Hale a Communist, but this was during the Korean War, when everyone felt threatened to some degree by the possibility of a nuclear war with Russia or China, and Senator McCarthy was accusing many public figures of being Communists or Communist sympathizers.

Hale couldn't simply say, "I'm not a Communist" and have it stick, so we asked people who knew him well to say it for him. Probably the greatest enemy of the Communist movement was the Roman Catholic church, and the archbishop of New Orleans made a statement strongly denying the allegations about Hale. However, his support added fuel to another fire in a state divided between Catholics and Protestants.

Earl Long used it against us, traveling around Protestant northern Louisiana saying, "They say Hale Boggs is a Communist, but he isn't a Communist, he's a good Roman Catholic. You know, they say if Hale Boggs wins, the pope of Rome will come over here to run Louisiana. Now you know, the pope is a busy man, and those Catholics have a smart archbishop down in the big city of New Orleans where Hale Boggs comes from, and that archbishop and Hale Boggs are just like that," and he would hold up his hand and cross his fingers. Our campaign staff tried to keep Hale from hearing this speech, but our paths crossed one night in Alexandria and Hale heard it from the farthest periphery of the crowd. Although he recognized its potentially devastating effect, he roared with laughter.

I was concerned about our children's reaction to Judge Perez. The only positive step I felt I could take was to have them pray for him each night. One day, I came home unexpectedly and found these supposed little innocents, their fists punching the air, listening to the judge on a radio program.

Hale's first challenge took place before the Central Committee. Our contention that a congressman could run for governor without resigning from the Congress was passed on to the state court in Baton Rouge, which—after a tumultous hearing—decided in our favor. The accusation of membership in an un-American organization was dismissed by the committee, but it had to be formally answered in state court. When we won in Baton Rouge, Judge Perez took the case to the Louisiana Supreme Court.

During the opening arguments I received an urgent phone call from our friend Dr. Ambrose Stork, telling me that he had taken Tommy to Touro Hospital for an emergency appendectomy. I dashed out, feeling torn between abandoning Hale in the courtroom and being with my little son. Tom fared beautifully, and everything was resolved in our favor by the court, but it wasn't a happy period in our lives.

One night I came home late from working in the campaign, and as I was driving up to our home, I saw a light circling around it and shining into the windows. Instead of zooming off to call the neighborhood Garden District Patrol for help, I parked the car. I was sufficiently infuriated that someone was snooping around my house when my children were in there asleep that I went storming out of my car toward the light and confronted a man with a huge flashlight.

I began shouting at him: "What on earth do you think you are doing?! Don't you know my children are in that house?! What are you doing? You get away from here!"

I don't get mad very often, but I was very upset. I had no idea what he was looking for, whether he was a would-be thief just "casing the joint," or whether he thought he could get in, or whether he was working for an opposing candidate or faction.

He was so startled he didn't know what to make of me. "I'm Colonel Dooling," he said. "I'm a private investigator for your opposition."

I said, "Well, what are you doing?"

"I'm spying," he replied.

"You get out of here right now," I ordered him.

Backing away saying, "Yes, ma'am, yes, ma'am," he got in his car and drove off.

When I was running for Congress many years later, Colonel Dooling called on me at my campaign headquarters. He said, "Mrs. Boggs, you're the feistiest lady I ever met. I have a great deal of communications equipment and several radio cars, and I'll loan you a radio car if you can use it in your campaign." His CB radios were fairly unusual at the time. I accepted his offer, and we used the radio car almost constantly in coordinating my appearances at tightly scheduled campaign events, in communicating with head-quarters workers, and in alerting our young volunteers to reports of posters or yard signs being removed so that they could converge on the sites for the inevitable "poster wars" with the young people from other campaigns.

Still later Colonel Dooling's son came to see me for a recommendation to the State Police, and I was pleased to give it to him, a well-educated, well-mannered, and well-motivated young man.

The governor's race became one of the most confusing in the state's convoluted political history. Hale and Russell Long joined forces, but in addition to running against the influence of Earl Long, Hale had to campaign against the ghost of Huey Long to satisfy the anti-Long vote. He also needed the independents, the reformists, the political groups around former governor Sam Jones, and Chep's New Orleans organization.

Two weeks before the end of the campaign Earl Long began telling people that if they couldn't vote for his candidate, Judge Carlos Spaht of Baton Rouge, they should "vote for Boggs." This tactic made it appear that Hale was secretly a Long candidate and would do Earl's bidding. Nothing could have been further from the truth, but we had little time to counterattack. Hale received the endorsement of the *New Orleans Item*, while the *Times-Picayune* supported James McLemore of Alexandria, a strong conservative Democrat. Dudley LeBlanc, a patent-medicine salesman who invented a hugely popular tonic called Hadacol, was also in the Democratic race, along with Judge Robert Kennon of Webster Parish, who had anti-Long support; Perez's candidate, Lucille May Grace, the registrar of the State Land Office; and Lieutenant Governor William J. Dodd.

We were continually checking our areas of voting strength, and ten days before the first primary, I knew we could not win. Too much of our time and money had been dissipated in answering the Perez charges. I was especially disappointed because I knew that Hale's ability, his Washington experience and contacts, and his devotion to our nation's political system would diligently serve Louisiana and its people. I also abhorred the reality that untrue charges had been used to defeat him.

Spaht and Kennon finished first and second in the primary and went into the runoff. Hale ran a close third. He and I were preoccupied with consoling our valiant, supportive workers, who were passionate in their quest to unite the state and heartbroken when we didn't make the runoff. With all the anti-Long vote massed behind Kennon, who now received the *Times-Picayune* endorsement, he handily defeated Spaht for the governorship. Hale returned to his congressional job and was reelected in the next campaign.

An invigorated Republican Party, which had been developing in Louisiana, received a big boost from some of the moderates who had gathered behind Hale in the governor's race. They became so involved in politics that several of them formed a new Republican faction. Our close friend and neighbor, John Minor Wisdom, a lawyer who became a federal judge renowned for his leadership in the cause of civil rights, was a leader among those "new" Republicans who were seated at the Republican convention in 1952 as delegates for Eisenhower.

They made a substantial difference in his winning the nomination, and their success gave validity to being a Republican in Louisiana. Many people thought of Eisenhower as apolitical, and he was so popular it was not considered subversive, in his case, to vote Republican. During his two campaigns Louisianans began to vote Republican.

General Eisenhower chose as his running mate California Senator Richard M. Nixon. We had known Dick and his wife, Pat, since they first came to Congress in 1947, part of a lively group of mostly young Republicans who were elected that year. Nixon went on the House Un-American Activities Committee, where he made a lasting reputation for being hard on suspected Communists. Pat and I became friends, and I always admired her superior intelligence, her devotion to her husband, and her exquisite taste.

Because many friends who had worked in Hale's gubernatorial race were working for Eisenhower, Hale determined that he would not take a strong position in the presidential race. The Democratic nominee was Governor Adlai Stevenson of Illinois, a man of intelligence, charm, wit, and an international outlook. Although the governor hadn't wanted to run against the war hero and said he had no ambition to be president, the Democratic convention drafted him. He received some minimal criticism because he was divorced, but not enough to keep him from being the nominee. His family background—his grandfather had been vice president in President Grover Cleveland's second term and was William Jennings Bryan's running mate in 1900—added to his strength and his public appeal.

Stevenson called our home one morning when I knew him only as a political figure, not yet as a personal friend. Because I didn't know his voice well, and it was not yet five o'clock in the morning when he asked to speak to Hale, I replied that he was asleep.

Then he announced, "This is Adlai Stevenson."

"Good morning, Governor Stevenson. This is Eleanor Roosevelt," I replied, and hung up.

The phone rang again. "Lindy Boggs, this really *is* Adlai Stevenson!" he said. I quickly awakened Hale.

When he came to campaign in New Orleans, Adlai made a magnificent speech on the steps of City Hall. A few hours later I had a phone call from Hale to please send some warm clothes to Illinois because he was with Stevenson. He had gone down to the rally and become carried away, so enchanted by the articulate Adlai that he went off with him. He couldn't bear separation from active Democratic campaigning another second. The next time I saw Hale was at Takoma Park, Maryland, on the Stevenson campaign train.

Stevenson carried the Deep South, but most of the country was looking for relief, not eloquence, and voters elsewhere spurned him to find comfort with Ike—the retired general, the father figure, the man who met the mood of the nation. Eisenhower enjoyed such popularity that the Republicans didn't need to be concerned about the perception in some quarters that he wasn't a strongly partisan Republican. Conversely, Speaker Rayburn and Senate Democratic leader Lyndon Johnson, who became majority leader in 1954, could work smoothly with him and not be perceived as scalawags by the Democratic Party. Although the Republicans won the majority in the Congress in 1952, the Democrats gained control again in the 1954 election and the degree of cooperation with the Republican president proved to be unique.

With the governor's race and the election behind us, Hale and I determined we were in Washington to stay. I had to decide whether our children were going to stay in the same school all year or continue to go back and forth, a half year in Washington and the other half at home. Barbara and Cokie had few problems because the curriculum at their Sacred Heart Schools was the same in both places, but Tommy was going to be in seventh grade and he had been completely changing his schoolwork twice a year. Fortunately the Jesuit school Georgetown Prep began accepting day students from the seventh grade upward, and we sent him there for a classic Jesuit education.

Our little family, which had moved into the red brick house on Stephenson Place, now had three growing children and a move was sorely indicated. I knew from Aunt Frosty's real estate acumen that if an agent has to "sit on" a house on Sunday, that agent would be happy to see even a stray cat come in the door. I checked the news-papers, and on the weekends I would take the children with me to look at houses. After I had seen a few, I would take Hale back to any I thought were "fittin'," by Joe Trueblood's standards.

One cold day we went to see a house out on Bradley Boulevard in Bethesda, Maryland. I drove such a long distance that I felt I was on the other side of the planet, but the neighborhood was within striking distance of my children's schools. We found a pretty white brick house with Southern-looking columns across the front, set in a large, well-landscaped yard. Guarding its entrance were two enormous weeping willow trees; if you squinted, their branches resembled Spanish moss hanging from Southern live oak trees.

I went around inspecting the house and talking with the agent while the kids ran all over it. When I returned to the living room, there was Cokie, who was eight, still in her snowsuit sprawled in the middle of the floor. She announced, "I like it here. I feel at home here. I want to live in this house, Mamma."

I said, "But darling, it doesn't have a back stairway, and that's important when there are children in a house where there's going to be a lot of entertaining."

"I don't care."

"The bathrooms are much too small."

"I don't care."

"The dining room is small, too. It would be hard for us to have a big family meal, much less give a dinner party."

"I don't care."

"There isn't enough closet space for us."

"I don't care what you say, I love this house. I'm gonna tell my daddy to buy me this house!"

The enterprising agent called Hale in his office on Monday. "I have a house that your little daughter is dying to live in," he said.

Hale asked some questions, and that evening he said to me, "Why didn't you tell me about this house?"

I said, "Because it's inadequate for us. It's a pretty house, and it sits on about two-and-a-half well-tended acres, which would be nice for your garden and for the children, but it doesn't meet our family needs or our entertaining requirements either."

He said, "Well, the agent thinks I should look at it."

I said, "Inspect it if you must, but I want you to know it has these inadequacies."

He looked at it, and we got advice on some structural changes we had in mind. To make a long story short, we moved into that house and we lived there very happily. We eventually put the kitchen in the garage and doubled the size of the dining room. Right away it became a sort of home away from home for Tommy's boarder friends at Georgetown Prep. Nobody ever cared that it had no back stairway.

The previous owners had bought the surrounding property to protect themselves against any intrusive building. We bought it all with the exception of the lot directly behind us; the agent gave us the right of first refusal on that. With only five houses and no fences (except those of the people who kept horses) the neighborhood provided a parklike setting that all of us thoroughly enjoyed.

Some years later, we came home from a trip to Europe to discover that a violent storm had made a terrible mess of our yard, and we had already spent five hours picking up debris when the phone rang. It was the agent: Did we want to buy the lot behind us? There was a serious offer for it. Hale was exhausted and infuriated with himself for having so much property to take care of in the first place. "I don't want any more property," he said, and hung up. We wished many times in later years that we had bought it to ensure unencumbered access among the neighborhood houses where the children played, but that was the wrong day to ask.

Hale was a great gardener. He planted fruit trees, built a grape arbor, and coaxed some Jerusalem artichokes that I brought from New Roads to flourish like the huge sunflowers they were. Most of our table vegetables came from Hale's garden, and there were enough left over to supply Capitol staffers, family members, and friends. Whenever Rets visited she and Hale enjoyed their lovely companionship with gardening activities. On one such occasion Hale decided that he wanted to grow asparagus.

Canvassing the neighborhood, he determined that Jane Councilor had the best asparagus and chose a spot at our front gate with the same exposure and drainage as hers. Although I objected to the placement, I was overruled. Rets accompanied us to buy the asparagus corms, and she said to me, "My dear, you know the plant is so beautiful that its fern is sold by florists." What neither of them told me was that you had to build mounds eighteen inches high in order to plant the corms.

A variety of wildlife abounded in our neighborhood, and Hale had trouble with rabbits in his garden, so when he and Rets were ready to begin planting, they dismissed me by sending me to the hardware store to buy wire fencing to keep the rabbits out of the asparagus. When I came back I discovered the mounds at our front gate. I stuck my head out the car window and called, "Now we really are an old Southern plantation establishment. We have our own little cemetery in the front yard!"

One Saturday afternoon when Hale was working in the garden, General J. Lawton Collins, the U.S. Army Chief of Staff, came to call. The general's car pulled into the drive and stopped. "I say," his chauffeur called, "is Congressman Boggs at home?"

Hale said, "Just a minute, sir. I'll see." He ran around the house and went in the back door, splashed water on his face, ran a comb through his hair, opened the front door, and said, "Hello, General."

One of my favorite pictures was taken when I had to drag Hale out of his garden to pose for a book of photographs about Washington. We were scheduled to appear in colorful evening dress, but we forgot all about it, and when the Australian woman photographer arrived on Saturday afternoon, I couldn't get Hale into a tuxedo. I put on a lime-colored dress and a purple-and-gold gossamer scarf, and he put on a suit and tie and white shirt. The ensuing picture was used in the book, *The Evidence of Washington*. We were pleased that in it our graceful willow trees surrounded us with wistful beauty.

Hale and I entertained every year with Charlie and Jean Davis at a garden party, where we often happily hosted fifteen hundred people or more. Charlie and Hale were friends from the Ways and Means Committee, where Charlie was chief counsel, and the first party was an eightieth birthday celebration for Charlie's sponsor, Congressman Tom O'Brien of Illinois, a senior committee member. For five years we gave Mr. O'Brien a party on his birthday. The next year, when Mr. O'Brien retired to Illinois, we didn't feel obligated to give a party, but people phoned to say, "What's the matter? Are we off your list?" Then we realized that the parties were an annual event everyone looked forward to and that our friends had forgotten their initial purpose. We ended up having them for about fifteen years.

My responsibilities included making certain that there was plenty of food for everyone and getting it onto the tables. My neighbors would clear out their deep freezers for me weeks in advance, and I would have them all filled a month before the party. Everybody would say, "Aren't you frightened to death of what the weather's going to be like?" I always said, "No, I have nothing to do with that. I'm in charge of food, drink, decorations, and entertainment. Hale's the chairman in charge of the weather."

We enjoyed having guests—even one guest for dinner—and in that category Sam Rayburn was an all-time favorite. He would call Hale and say, "I'm really tired tonight. I don't feel like doing anything special, so I'm going to come to your house for dinner." No matter what we were doing, we dismissed all plans and were thrilled to have him. His marriage had been of short duration, and he had no children of his own, but among his friends' children he had favorites, usually the youngest one. Cokie was his pet in our family. She even lured him to help us bury Charlie Chicken.

Charlie Chicken was one of those poor little chickens that are dyed for Easter and on Easter Monday, they're sold for a dime. Tommy and Charlie Coulon, whose parents, Elizabeth and Charlie, were our friends, had bought this little chicken for Cokie, and they named him Charlie Chicken. My mother, who was staying with us, had a coop built for him. He developed a great personality, but Charlie's only expression of interplay with another animal was when our cocker spaniel would go out to round him up at night if he hadn't come in to roost.

Consequently Charlie Chicken wasn't afraid of dogs. The neighborhood dogs knew him and left him alone, but an itinerant dog came through one day and killed him. Emma Cyprian, who was no bigger than a minute, chased the dog and retrieved Charlie's carcass.

Cokie was so terribly upset that we decided the only way to appease her would be with a lovely funeral for Charlie. Tommy had a little woodworking shop where he made a nice cross, and Barbara put satin and lace in a shoebox coffin to lay Charlie Chicken to rest. We were waiting for Hale to come home to have the funeral, when he called and said he was bringing Mr. Sam and that Mr. Sam was very tired.

When they arrived Hale said that he and Sam wanted to have a quiet drink and then we would all have dinner together. I explained to the children that Mr. Sam was terribly fatigued and they would have to go ahead with the funeral without us.

Cokie went outside and suddenly began to cry. She ran into the den and climbed up on Mr. Sam's lap. "You've got to come out and see about Tommy Boggs," she said.

He asked, "What's the matter, darling?"

"He's being disrespectful to Charlie Chicken!"

Sam said, " 'Disrespectful to Charlie Chicken?' How's he being disrespectful to Charlie Chicken?"

"He's digging his grave, and when he puts the shovel in, he's humming that tune from *Dragnet*, Dum, da-dum-dum."

Sam said, "That's not very polite. Perhaps if I go out and see what's going on, do you think your father and mother would accompany me?"

We all went out, and Mr. Sam presided at Charlie Chicken's funeral. Imagine our thinking he was too tired to see the kids! Sam was a tough legislator, a very definite controller of his own emotions and of other peoples' destinies, but he loved little children.

The advent of a Republican presidency after twenty years of Democratic control of the White House prompted Katie Louchheim, the vice-chairman of the Democratic National Committee, to form the Democratic Congressional Wives Forum. It was a way in which we could pool our political knowledge and exchange experiences in order to be more helpful in campaigns and during our husbands' terms of office. Eisenhower was the first presidential candidate to campaign effectively on television, a talent we wives needed to develop for use in our spouses' behalf.

The lessons we learned and the media techniques we acquired were so effective that we forum members planned to launch an ambitious national station wagon tour, "Operation Crossroads," in the next election, teaming up with Young Democrats who would drive and help us distribute campaign paraphernalia.

A great deal of the action in the political, economic, and diplomatic spheres in Washington has always been carried on by women's organizations. When I became president of the Woman's National Democratic Club, my program cochairs—Regina McGranery, whose husband had been the attorney general during the Truman administration; Abigail McCarthy, the wife of Senator Eugene McCarthy; and Pauline Gore—and I enticed a long list of cultural, journalistic, intellectual, legal, political, and diplomatic figures to appear at our luncheons and press conferences.

Because Congress convened at noon, there was little other daytime activity that merited press coverage, so our programs were regularly written up in the women's pages. One good speaker led to the next, and people clamored to be on our agenda, turning it into a national showcase for the stars of the party—Eleanor Roosevelt, Daisy Harriman, and Perle Mesta joined President and Mrs. Truman, Adlai Stevenson, Estes Kefauver, Averell Harriman, Eugene McCarthy, William Fulbright, Paul Douglas, Albert Gore, Hubert Humphrey, Mike Mansfield, John Sparkman, Henry Jackson, Stuart Symington, Lyndon Johnson, and Dean Acheson as lecturers, panelists, book reviewers, debaters, honorees at receptions and luncheons and dinners.

The Club year commenced with the annual birthday party on January sixth in honor of Speaker Sam Rayburn, hosted by his fellow Texans, the vivacious Scooter Miller and her gracious, hospitable husband, Dale.

One of the outstanding star broadcast journalists on our schedule was Paul Niven, who had been expelled from Russia by Nikita Khrushchev. The date of his scheduled appearance at the Club coincided with his opportunity to cover Khrushchev's visit to California. When he asked permission to change his appearance at the Club, we suggested that his presentation would be especially timely and interesting to our membership. I have always been grateful that he accepted our demand.

For Mrs. Roosevelt's program, I invited her longtime social secretary to present her. The secretary demurred, asking, "What on earth can I say about Eleanor Roosevelt that everybody doesn't already know?"

"You'll think of something different," I assured her.

When the day arrived, Mrs. Roosevelt's aide, Edith Helms was so relaxed that I felt she must have been well prepared. Her moment arrived. She bowed slightly to the audience and proclaimed, "Ladies, 'she' is here!" It was the perfect introduction.

I was disturbed by the erosion of membership in many clubs that had chosen to integrate, and I was determined that we would integrate so successfully that we would not only not lose members but we would grow. The club's program series, featuring a nongovernment speaker or subject on Mondays and a speaker from Congress on Thursdays, became so popular that we had to limit access. There wasn't enough space for everyone who wanted to attend the programs, and we had to install closed-circuit television for the overflow press in the basement because there was room for only one press table upstairs. While all of this was happening, we quietly integrated amid greater popularity and success than we had ever known. Gladys Duncan, the charming wife of Todd Duncan, the renowned singing star of *Porgy and Bess*, was our first black member. She had been nominated by Daisy Harriman, one of our founding members.

Chapter Ten

༻⚜༺

I'VE ALWAYS BELIEVED that civil rights and human rights are intertwined. You can only exert your civil rights if your human rights are intact, but to be able to exercise human rights, you must have a government that will secure civil rights through a code of laws.

A demand for civil rights for all citizens swept over the United States like a wave in the 1950s. In the Congress civil rights initiatives involved dealing not only with issues but with individual attitudes. Holding the power over all legislation was the House Rules Committee, which decided whether a bill would live or die, and if it lived, in what form it could come to the floor.

Its chairman, Howard W. Smith, a conservative Democrat from Virginia, formed a coalition of like-minded Democrats and Republicans on the committee that blocked civil rights legislation or loaded it down with restrictive amendments that rendered it ineffective. Anti–civil rights demagoguery from some congressmen, from both the North and the South, so inflamed the public that when measures restrictive of civil rights were introduced, hardly any Southern members voted against them.

In 1952 the Republicans won a majority of the seats in

Congress, and Mr. Sam was replaced as Speaker by Joseph W. Martin Jr. of Massachusetts.

Hale was usually regarded as moderate on racial issues, and he always won the black vote in his district, but he and his moderate Southern colleagues faced a dilemma: They didn't like voting against civil rights legislation, but to vote their conscience meant certain defeat next time, and whoever defeated them would vote also against the liberal social and economic measures they supported.

Jackson Acox, the Reverend A. L. Davis, the Reverend Avery Alexander, and other black leaders in New Orleans implored Hale not to rock the boat. They were so afraid they would lose him to a conservative that they often advised him to vote against what they would have preferred for him to endorse.

On May 17, 1954, the U.S. Supreme Court struck down school segregation as unconstitutional, a pivotal decision that was to change the nation. The next day President Eisenhower informed District of Columbia officials that he wanted their school system to set a national example by desegregating before further orders were issued. The first steps toward the desegregation of other public facilities in the capital followed. Most Southern and border states had laws requiring segregation in elementary schools, and the pattern continued through secondary and higher educational facilities.

As a response to the court's school order, Southern legislators tried to draw the lines on what would be permissible in the way of civil rights legislation and what would not. They were looking for a position that could be supported by a majority and would end the blatant demagoguery. The result, popularly called the "Southern Manifesto," attacked the Supreme Court's order as an "encroachment on rights reserved to the states and to the people," while it reaffirmed "reliance on the Constitution as the fundamental law of the land." Written by a committee of Southern senators, headed by

Senator Strom Thurmond of South Carolina (elected in 1954), it was signed by nineteen senators and eighty-one House members, including Hale.

Hale didn't mean the manifeso to be strictly segregationist, but it was the best he and other Southern moderates could do under the circumstances. As Southerners they had to sign it. The public interpretation was that anybody who signed it was against civil rights, but that was not true.

So forceful was the Southern mood of the times, I had a question in my mind about when public rights may supercede private property rights. The South's strong feeling about property rights was exacerbated by the fact that almost everyone's property had been taken away from them during and after the Civil War.

When the federal government began insisting that all people, regardless of race, should be served in local, privately owned establishments, as strongly as I felt that there should be no discrimination, my feeling about the uses of private property made me wonder if that was not an invasion of the property owners' privacy. Although I felt that public properties, public facilities, public organizations, and tax-supported properties should be open to everyone, I began to recognize that the answer to the public use – private ownership dilemma resided in the court's decision that if anyone was operating in interstate commerce in any way, the public right took precedence. Despite any qualms I might have had, I recognized the validity of the direction in which the country was moving. When Congress convened in 1955 Hale assumed a position that would increase his already strong allegiance to the National Democratic Party and put him in some jeopardy in his native South.

Control of the Congress was again in the hands of the Democrats and Speaker Rayburn and House Majority Leader John McCormack selected Hale to be the deputy whip, an appointment that placed him firmly on the leadership ladder that ended with

Speaker of the House. The position of deputy whip was new; it had been created for him. His job was to help the whip, Carl Albert of Oklahoma, assess and line up votes for the "leadership"— the president, if he was a Democrat, and the party's elected officers in the House.

One of the minor bills that easily passed directed U.S. aid to the South Vietnamese government of Ngo Dinh Diem, an anti-Communist Catholic, to strengthen his country against attacks by the Communist guerrillas, the Vietcong. Several hundred U.S. military advisers sent by the Eisenhower administration were training the South Vietnamese army, and the aid totaled $216 million by year's end.

Hale and I made our first trip to that part of the world in 1956, when we went to Bangkok for an Inter-Parliamentary Union meeting. Among the U.S. delegation were Senator Albert Gore Sr., of Tennesse; his wife, Pauline; and their young son, Al Jr.

We made a stop in Taiwan, where refugees from Communist China were still living in shacks on the main streets of Taipei, the capital, where they had settled with their stacks of household goods and treasures when they had escaped from the Communist takeover in 1949. Not an inch of ground was unused; people even grew crops in the riverbed at low-water season. Under the leadership of Chiang Kai-shek, Taiwan had a more democratic system of government than that in force on the mainland, and the free enterprise system had already stimulated remarkable progress.

Although our body clocks had been completely reversed by the time zones, we attended a concert the night we arrived. The Chinese music was delightfully different to our ears, with strong percussion and cymbals, but Pauline and I were so sleepy that we kept dozing off, passing little Al from one pair of arms to the other. Albert teased us forever about how we tried to look dignified while sleeping through a Taiwanese concert.

(Years later, in 1989, I went to Antarctica as a member of Congress, and "Little Al," Senator Albert Gore Jr. of Tennessee, was on the trip. The South Pole is at an elevation of fourteen thousand feet; the temperature was fifty-five degrees below zero and the wind was blowing fiercely; it was not a place conducive to vigorous exercise. Al, who is a health-conscious jogger, was concerned about me in that climate and was taking good care of me, not knowing that high elevation agrees with me and peps me up. As we were climbing the steps of an observation tower, I could hear Al huffing and puffing behind me. I turned and said, "What do you want me to do, darling, carry you?")

From Taiwan our group went on to Thailand, where the foremost U.S. military presence was a military attaché at our embassy, Colonel Peters from Monroe, Louisiana. The colonel loved jazz and he invited us to a weekly improvised session with the king of Thailand, a fellow jazz buff and a mean saxophone player, which was arranged through the colonel's landlord and neighbors who were friends of the royal family.

Adlai Stevenson announced his candidacy for the Democratic presidential nomination again in the fall of 1955, and he campaigned hard against his chief rival, Senator Estes Kefauver of Tennessee. When Stevenson won the nomination the following summer, he threw the Chicago nominating convention into a turmoil when he refused to pick a running mate, leaving the choice to the delegates. Senators Kefauver and Albert Gore Sr. of Tennessee, Hubert Humphrey of Minnesota, and John Kennedy of Massachusetts all hoped to be chosen.

Hale was Stevenson's campaign manager in the South, and he thought Kennedy would be an asset. Comparatively young at thirty-nine, he was known nationally for his defeat of veteran Republican senator Henry Cabot Lodge four years earlier despite the

Eisenhower landslide, and for winning the Pulitzer Prize for *Profiles in Courage*, a collection of stories about U.S. political leaders who defied public opinion to vote their consciences.

Hale was also the unofficial liaison between Stevenson and Sam Rayburn, the convention's permanent chairman, and when Stevenson left the second place open, Mr. Sam surprised Hale by saying he would like it. Hale privately passed the word to Stevenson, thinking Sam might receive special consideration, but Stevenson reiterated his desire to leave the vice presidential choice completely open. Mr. Sam decided against entering the contest, and Senator Kefauver won the vice presidential nomination after a Kennedy groundswell was stopped.

Aside from the official convention, many of us were involved with *Jenny for President*, an entertaining show with a political theme produced by the Woman's National Democratic Club for the delegates' wives and other women at the convention. It was an original pretense at a nominating convention with speeches, music, "delegates," even a parade of state flags. Everyone paid her own way to Chicago, including the fifty flag bearers.

I was one of three cochairs with my two special friends Carrie Davis, the political activist wife of Memphis congressman Clifford Davis, and Florence Hoff, whose husband, Irvin, was chief administrative assistant to Senator Warren Magnuson of the State of Washington. The winner of our election for "Jenny," the perfect female presidential candidate, was Ann Chapman, a former president of the club and a native Louisianian whose husband, Oscar Chapman, was secretary of interior during the Truman administration.

Under the Chicago circumstances it wasn't easy being a theatrical producer. An electricians' strike halted the spotlight and sound equipment crews, and we had to meet with the union late one night up a long, dimly lighted stairway to beg for their cooperation, which they extended. The Musicians' Union informed us that for the size of our hall, we had to have a twenty-eight-piece orchestra. Our ladies would have been drowned out, so we negotiated for half that many musicians and paid for the whole orchestra. Men who had set the tables and chairs for the show didn't leave space for the parade of state flags. When I discovered this and asked the waiters to please move the tables a little, they said that their contract precluded such action. About twenty ladies were in the room, so I asked, "Is there anything in your contract that says you can't look the other way while we ladies move the tables?"

We also staged a fashion show with Carson Pirie Scott as our coordinating store, and we learned too late that the coordinator of our show and the orchestra leader did not like each other. Whenever the coordinator spoke, the orchestra tried to drown her out. Despite the hurdles *Jenny* was a tremendous hit. Through making arrangements for it, I became friendly with R. Sargent Shriver Jr., "Sarge," who was running the Chicago Trade Mart for Joseph P. Kennedy, its owner and the father of John and Robert Kennedy and of Sarge's wife, Eunice, who was the cochair of the convention host committee.

To counter the effectiveness of the wives of President Eisenhower's cabinet members, who were drawing crowds to their own campaign appearances, the Democratic Congressional Wives Forum initiated "Operation Crossroads" that fall, and for the first time, we spouses went out as a group to promote the national ticket. We hit the campaign trail in station wagons, concentrating on fourteen "swing" congressional districts where the voting sentiment was so evenly divided between Democrats and Republicans that the races could go either way. We staged rallies, made speeches, and gave interviews to the local media encouraging Democrats to go to the polls on election day. The Young Democrats driving us became the lead stars when we stopped on college campuses.

I appeared in a couple of television commercials for the Steven-son campaign. In one I was pushing my shopping cart through a supermarket, picking up various items and saying such things as, "Look at these prices. Inflation is out of control!" In the other one I said, "I'm Lindy Boggs. I have three children and I'm scared," about the possibility of nuclear war.

On election day, despite the expected Eisenhower presidential victory, Democrats carried twelve of the fourteen congressional dis-tricts in which we had campaigned in "Operation Crossroads." We were thrilled by the success of our first foray as a congressional team into national campaigning.

Each year the Congressional Club stages a "First Lady Lun-cheon," with the invitations, music, decorations, and program geared to some enthusiasm of the president's wife. In the last year of the Eisenhower presidency, the president and Mamie were pre-paring to move to a farm they had bought near the historic Civil War battlefield in Gettysburg, Pennsylvania, and the farm was cho-sen as the luncheon theme. The event is an annual favorite of the club, and former members and out-of-town members consider it a homecoming occasion. The committee members were quite upset when they were were advised that Mamie was ill and it appeared that she wouldn't attend.

When the phones began to ring at the clubhouse, I was asked as publicity chairman to field the inquiries: "If there is a story cir-culating that the first lady is ill, it will of course have to be checked out with the White House," I cautioned. None of us knew exactly what we would do if Mamie was unable to attend, but I felt that the ingenious members of the committee would work out some pos-itive solution.

"Miss Lucy" George, the wife of Senator Walter George of Georgia, took the bull by the horns and went to the White House to see the president. "Mister President, we wives are always representing you husbands when you are unable to attend events," she said, and he agreed. "This party is built around you and Mamie, and now she's sick and can't attend. You have to represent Mamie and appear in her place." Bless his dear heart, he agreed to be Mamie's stand-in, and the party was a tremendous success.

It is difficult to realize that anybody you know personally could be president of the United States. I've known eleven presidents, each of whom has had some influence on my life. Hale went to Congress when Franklin Roosevelt was in the White House, and I retired from Congress fifty years later, during the administration of George Bush. I first knew Bill Clinton when he was a Young Democrat, applauded his success as governor of Arkansas, and worked closely with him in the Democratic Leadership Council.

Seven major candidates for the Democratic presidential nomination in 1960 were close friends whom I loved and admired: Chester Bowles, Hubert Humphrey, Lyndon Johnson, John Kennedy, Robert Meyner, Adlai Stevenson, and Stuart Symington. Chet Bowles was a former governor of Connecticut, a member of Congress, and chairman of the convention platform committee; Bob Meyner was the governor of New Jersey; and Stu Symington was the Missouri senator who had been the first secretary of the air force.

It was very gratifying for me when I was appointed by the Democratic National Committee as chairman of the Presidential Campaign Kickoff Dinner, at which we hoped to raise sufficient funds to pay off a four-year-old, nine-hundred-thousand-dollar party debt. The challenge of filling a huge hall at the Washington Sheraton Hotel was dampened when my efforts were hampered by a feud between the chairman and the treasurer of the Democratic National Committee that severely limited early fund-raising among the state organizations: without the encouragement of the national chairman, the state party leaders were unenthusiastic about selling dinner tickets.

Our usual cadre of women volunteers worked diligently, often far into the night. The party treasurer came down from Philadelphia, and when he saw these elegant women putting aside their personal schedules and working the phones until ten o'clock at night, he was so embarrassed that he put aside his feelings. With the help of the legendary White House chief telephone operator, Louise ("Hacky") Hackmeier, he called the state chairmen and state and national committeemen and told them to sell tickets, send the money, and get the show on the road.

We advised the candidates' campaign staffs to gather a crowd of supporters to cheer at the dinner because we were going to have each candidate speak for seven minutes. We put the party notables at the head tables: former President Truman, Mrs. Roosevelt, and Sam Rayburn and all the congressional leaders. Ticket sales boomed, and in addition to the main ballroom we filled a big exhibition hall. So that the guests in each room would have the opportunity of seeing and hearing all the stars, each candidate spoke in one room and then in the other, and we swapped people at the head tables, letting them have their dinner in one room and dessert in the other.

Because I had worked so hard and so closely with the candidates and their staffs, I felt constrained in attending the convention where I would be tempted to show favoritism among them. Mr. Sam, who for years had been the convention permanent chairman, had announced that he didn't want to preside. He was hopeful that Hale would be elected in his place.

However, many Democratic leaders were so concerned about John Kennedy's Catholicism that they were apprehensive about electing Hale as chairman because he was a Catholic, as was Paul Butler, the chairman of the Democratic National Committee. Hale took his disappointment in stride and went to the convention in Los Angeles with 21-year-old Barbara as his eager companion.

I drove them to the airport in Baltimore, and as he got out of the car, Hale said, "The ticket's going to be Kennedy and Johnson."

"Lyndon would never accept that," I insisted. "You must mean the other way around."

He replied, "Lyndon's patriotic enough to do it."

Although Lyndon wanted to be president, he didn't enter the race until quite late, causing serious difficulties for his campaign. He had suffered a heart attack five years earlier, and at first he wasn't sure he wanted to run. Once he decided, he expected that the convention would deadlock on the first ballot and that—possibly by the third—he would be nominated.

As a skilled politician he knew he would have a strong chance, but a new style of campaigning was taking over. Candidates relied on polls, market research, and Madison Avenue packaging rather than on old-fashioned handshaking and the building of voting blocs and coalitions. Television was becoming the town square.

When Kennedy won the nomination on the first ballot and offered the second spot to Johnson, Johnson's friends begged him to reject it. He was more powerful as Senate majority leader than he would be as vice president, they said, and in 1968 he could win the nomination and the presidency. Everyone expected that Richard Nixon would be chosen as the Republican presidential candidate later that summer.

Hale had earlier suggested a Kennedy-Johnson or Johnson-Kennedy ticket to Mr. Sam, but the Speaker didn't seem to take him seriously. Hale knew that Sam had wanted the vice presidenial nomination four years earlier, and therefore that he considered it a worthy and important office. He said to Sam, "If you don't want Johnson to run, it means you'll elect Nixon." That did it. Sam persuaded Lyndon to accept the vice presidential nomination.

We were in Tokyo at the time of the first televised presidential debate between Kennedy and Nixon. After friends in the States called to tell us how Kennedy had outshone Nixon and how marvelous it was that things were looking up for the Democrats, Hale dashed out to pick up the English-language newspapers. One carried the text of the debate, and he read it when he came back to the hotel. He put the paper down with a puzzled expression. I said, "Tell me! Tell me!" Hale replied, "I'm not going to influence what you think. You read it."

I did, and I saw no reason for jubilation. Hale and I wondered why our friends said everyone was optimistic. The debate sounded rather tit for tat and fairly dull. We were baffled. We called the States and learned that the elation was caused by Jack's presence, his confident manner, and the healthy, energetic image he projected, and that Nixon had looked pasty and old and seemed defensive.

Later I heard that when Pat Nixon saw the debate on television, she called her husband, concerned because she thought he was ill. For the subsequent debates Nixon's people tried to present him in a better light, but irreparable damage had been done, and the first debate's huge television audience would not be repeated.

Tommy, who was studying economics at Georgetown University and was not yet old enough to vote (the voting age then was 21), went up to advance a Johnson campaign swing through New York. Johnson had first declined to go to New York City because he was worried that as a Texan he might hurt the ticket and cost it liberal votes, but Tommy thought that by campaigning on commuter trains the Johnson volunteers could reach many people in an informal way. The strategy paid off handsomely.

In the South the civil rights movement became a prominent issue in the presidential campaigns. The new Student Nonviolent Coordinating Committee (SNCC) was helping to stage black sit-ins at all-white lunch counters and restaurants, while the Reverend Martin Luther King Jr. and his Southern Christian Leadership Conference (SCLC) conducted marches and mass demonstrations for equality and "kneel-ins" at white churches. Other individuals, black and white, were registering black voters across the South.

When our children had reached high school age, we refurnished a basement recreation room so that it could serve as a boys' dormitory as well as party space, and this room now became such a haven for young civil rights marchers and workers—friends of our children and children of our friends—that we dubbed it our own "underground railroad."

Nixon's running mate, Henry Cabot Lodge, told a rally that the Nixon administration would appoint a black to the cabinet, prompting Kennedy to say that his administration would not consider race or religion in appointments, only an individual's qualifications. Both candidates wanted to appear concerned about civil rights without alienating the millions of Southern voters who opposed the movement.

Johnson decided to meet his fellow Southerners face-to-face, remind them of his Southern roots, and assure them it was all right for him to run with a liberal young Massachusetts Catholic. Like Hale he had a deep and genuine compassion for the poor and underprivileged, and he wanted to help them. He felt that a solution to the civil rights turmoil had to be found within the Constitution, while taking into account the feelings and way of life of the South. As the Senate majority leader, Johnson hadn't been asked to sign the Southern Manifesto; the other senators didn't want the document construed as an attempt to formulate senatorial or Democratic Party policy.

A month before the election, Johnson took a whistle-stop trip through the South to drum up support for the ticket. I was among the six Southern women chosen to make up an advance team that flew ahead to stir up local enthusiasm so that large crowds would meet the train. Johnson bet wisely that no Southern gentlemen would fail to receive us politely, regardless of how they might feel about JFK, LBJ, or civil rights.

Our group was composed of Johnson's doctor's wife, Mary Love Bailey, to say he was healthy enough to serve; and his minister's wife, Bea Barkley, to say it was all right for him to serve with a Catholic. Judy Moyers, the wife of Bill Moyers, who would later become one of Lyndon's presidential aides, came to us from the Campus Crusade for Christ; and Lorraine Gibbons carried our social service and cultural credentials as a member of the Junior League and a Dallas Symphony patron. And Carrie Davis and I were the politically experienced members of the team.

Never have I been so favorably impressed with a campaign team. Lorraine kept us all laughing. When we hit terrible weather and our little plane was bouncing all over the sky, Lorraine picked up the phone to say to the crew, "What's the matter up there in that cockpit? I can't put on my makeup with you all carryin' on like that!"

We wore patriotic costumes of blue blazers, white pleated skirts, white dickeys, and red hats, with prominent Kennedy-Johnson buttons. We were warm on the plane and those blazers were hot so as we flew from town to town, we would take turns going into the restroom, taking off our blazers, splashing water on ourselves, fanning a little bit, and going back out with our blazers on.

A young public relations specialist, George Dillman, accompanied us, and Lorraine finally said to him, "You're the only boy. You go sit in the john and we can all take off our blazers!" We were more comfortable after that. Despite that dreadful treatment, George has remained our dear friend throughout the years since our adventure.

The train was a grand political success, and we were received everywhere with warmth and kindness as we urged local Democratic officeholders to publicly endorse the Kennedy-Johnson ticket.

As the national campaign neared its end, Young Democrats wanted to conduct a final, limited "Operation Crossroads" for Kennedy. They asked me to go with them to western Pennsylvania, one of the regions with the strongest voter resentment of his Catholicism. Kennedy had calmed some religious fears with an eloquent endorsement, before Protestant clergymen in Houston, Texas, of "absolute separation of church and state," but voters in western Pennsylvania seemed to remain unconvinced.

I said to the Young Dems, "Don't you know I'm a Catholic?"

One of them replied, "With an Anglo-Saxon name from the South? They'll never suspect you."

We had a rewarding trip, but by the end I was exhausted. Our grand finale was a rally with Pennsylvania's Senator Joe Clark and Governor G. Mennen ("Soapy") Williams of Michigan, a nationally known figure who was our main speaker. The rally coincided with the end of the national campaign, and unfortunately it came on the weekend when Puerto Rican bishops issued a very pro-Catholic statement that was widely publicized. Anti-Catholic flyers warning against electing a president with a connection to the pope were under the windshield wipers of every car at our rally.

I was introduced early in the program, thankful that I didn't have to do anything but make my little bow, and then I sat on the stage sort of glassy-eyed and absolutely exhausted. After Joe and Soapy spoke, I heard vaguely out of one ear that "Lindy Boggs" was being introduced to speak. It was like winding up a doll. I must have given the same speech I had given everyplace else, but it was well received. When I sat down, I turned to the man next to me and asked, "What on earth did I say?"

He replied, "Lady, with a Southern accent like yours, you could've recited the ABCs and they'd have loved you."

I don't know how much our efforts had to do with it, but Democrats carried most of the South and Pennsylvania as Kennedy squeaked past Nixon into the White House.

As soon as the election was over, I was appointed cochairman, with Stanley Woodward, of the Kennedy inaugural ball. But first I had a more important event to attend. Tommy had awakened me early one morning some months previously to say he was going to get married. I said, "Why do you want to get married now, darling? He laughingly responded, "I'm tired of mowing the grass." Hale had him out pushing the mower across two-and-a-half acres every week.

He and Barbara Denechaud were married when they were only twenty, after they had gone to college around the calendar to finish in three years—Tom to Georgetown and Barbara to Manhattanville College in New York and then to Loyola in New Orleans. They planned to be married at Holy Name Church in New Orleans two days after Christmas 1960. Barbara chose all the music, and she and Tommy were satisfied that it would be a simple wedding ceremony with a Low Mass and as much privacy as they could maintain, considering the public nature of our family.

Among the older friends Tom asked to serve as ushers because they knew all of our family and friends, was Bob Ainsworth, an important presence in our lives. Time and again he had taken over to run Hale's campaigns when Hale couldn't get down from Washington, stepping in until he became a federal judge. He was married to Hale's smart and loveable cousin, Elizabeth Hiern. Bob, Hale, and their whole group had nicknames: Hale was the Butterine Kid, and Bob was the Mouthpiece.

Charlie Denechaud's father had been the attorney for the archbishop, and many priests, monsignors, and bishops who were close to his father always honored the family. Barbara Denechaud was so worried that they were all going to be at her wedding that she asked Hale's brother, Father Robbie Boggs, to marry them, thereby avoiding having to choose a priest from among the others. It would be Robbie's first wedding, but he was very fond of Tom and Barbara, and they assured him that it would be a simple ceremony.

The archbishop was out of town, but forty-four clerics, among whom were bishops, monsignori, and abbots, showed up, creating a sea of red cassocks in the front of the church. In order to make room for all of them, the wedding party had to be removed from the altar to the front pews. Besides that, it was Cokie's birthday, and she teased everyone that she had asked the organist to play "Happy Birthday" when she came in.

Robbie saw all that church hierarchy and decided he had better switch to a High Mass, a much more elaborate ceremony for the priest, his assistants, and the choir. Robbie wasn't at all sure of his procedure, but fortunately his experienced altar boys—Hale's nephew and godson Charlie Boggs; and George Tessier, the nephew of my chum Marie Louise—knew what to do. They brought out the requisite incense burners and clued Robbie at any time he faltered, and the choir and the organist quickly pealed forth with the proper music.

On graduation from Georgetown, Tom's first job was with Senator Paul Douglas of Illinois, who had been an economist on the faculty of the University of Chicago before he was elected. He headed the House-Senate Joint Economic Committee, of which Hale was a member, and Tom greatly admired him for his powerful intellect. The joint committee was seeking a promising economics graduate from a DC area college to work on its staff, and Paul requested a computer compilation of the qualifications of the colleges' economics students who might be available. Tommy's name was submitted by Georgetown University.

After interviewing "Thomas H. Boggs of Bethesda, Maryland," which was how his name was submitted, Senator Douglas, who had no way of discovering that he was our son, offered him the job. Tom, confessed to him, saying, "I admire you so much, I couldn't bear not to come and talk to you." Douglas replied, "You're the best-qualified person for this job. If taking it won't embarrass your dad, it won't embarrass me."

Hale, who felt Tommy had been offered the job without any influence, said, "If you can stand the heat of criticism and Paul can stand the heat of criticism, who am I to say I can't stand it?" We were all criticized that the job was a patronage perk, but Tommy compiled an excellent record there. His respect for the senator prompted him and Barbara to name their second son Douglas, in his honor; I was elated by their close relationship, in part because of my admiration for Paul's wife, Emily Taft Douglas, the only woman who ever preceded her husband in Congress.

Traditionally a presidential inaugural ball is a great and glamorous conclusion to the inaugural day festivities. My committee and I were provided with everything to make it such an occasion, including the huge organization required by every presidential inauguration to handle and coordinate secretarial work, accounting, transportation, printing, phone calls, mail, seating, dignitaries, invitations, tickets, security, and any unusual circumstance that may arise.

Only the expenses of the official swearing-in ceremony at the Capitol were paid for by the government. The expenses for the other inaugural activities were guaranteed by a citizens' committee that put up the money to cover them. I discovered that the largest source of income for which the guarantors were reimbursed is the inaugural ball.

The second Eisenhower inaugural had lost money, which made us doubly determined that we Democrats couldn't look as though we were fiscally irresponsible. Republican friends cautioned us against having more than one ball because the committee could not satisfy the demands for tickets and the multiple balls were so costly that they were unable fully to pay back the guarantors; they had engaged additional ballrooms at Washington hotels for a great deal of money.

We determined that we would have one ball at the National Guard Armory, the traditional site. We ordered a huge tented pavilion to be built adjacent to it with tables, chairs, music, and refreshments to siphon off some of the crowd and give them room to dance. But President-elect Kennedy was so popular, the early demand for tickets so heavy, and the hotels so insistent that we decided to have additional balls at the Mayflower, the Sheraton Park, the Shoreham, and the Capitol Hilton hotels. A formal inaugural gala, hosted by Frank Sinatra, was planned for the night before the inauguration at the armory.

That was the night of a surprise blizzard, a freak storm that arrived unpredicted and dropped tons of snow on the capital. When it began to snow hard that afternoon, everybody in the government was let off work at the same time, creating a traffic jam so monstrous that people ran out of gas waiting for the cars ahead of them to move.

I was caught at our inaugural headquarters, overlooking the Tidal Basin, where I could look out of my windows and see gridlock everywhere on the streets as well as the bridges across the Potomac. I was confined to the building. What concerned me more than the fact I couldn't get to the gala was that our committee staff was holding tickets to the balls to be picked up for state party chairmen, good friends, and Democratic contributors. We even held box-seat tickets for members of the Lyndon Johnson party, but no one could reach my office that night.

About two o'clock in the morning, I was able to mush out to the Mayflower Hotel with the Johnson tickets, then slide back to headquarters. The next day Hale brought the suit I planned to wear for the swearing-in and other daytime activities, and my inaugural ball gown and all the trappings to wear that evening. I had worked hard through the campaign, and I looked forward to being present when John F. Kennedy was sworn in, but it was not to be.

From the moment we opened the doors that morning, my office was besieged by people screaming for their tickets. I couldn't get away. We had a television set on, and a few minutes before the ceremony was to begin, I called for attention and said, "The inaugural ceremonies that we all came to Washington to celebrate are on television. Do you think we could be quiet to listen to the president being sworn in?" Sheepishly they quieted down and watched as Jack Kennedy, our young hero, became president of the United States.

The minute the ceremony was over, the yelling and screaming again commenced.

I dressed for the inaugural balls in my little office, and I made up my face in a spatula, the only thing I could find that was big and shiny enough in which to see my face. I was reminded of Aunt Paule Parlange in New Roads, who had declined to have her old family mirrors resilvered because, she said, when she looked at her reflection before going out, she was always "a vision of shimmering loveliness." There I was in my spatula, "a vision of shimmering loveliness," and, like Aunt Paule, I went forth knowing I would have the best time of anyone at the party.

The first ball the president attended was at the Mayflower Hotel. I had planned a grand march at each one, as we do at the Mardi Gras balls, with the president, the vice president, the cabinet designees, and military leaders presented to the crowd so the television programs would have something to show instead of snippets of people dancing or talking. Hale had tried to discourage me from staging the marches, but after we had made the rounds of the balls, he admitted I had been right. Dignitaries rode from one ball to the next in "VIP chariots"—decorated luxury buses stocked with food and drink. It was a magical night. Everybody was happy and optimistic. The real world seemed far away.

CHAPTER ELEVEN

*H*ALE AND I were overjoyed when our daughter Barbara went to work in the Kennedy White House. It was the perfect place for her capabilities. She was idealistic yet practical in her application of her ideals, an insightful politician who knew that you must have a budget before you can accomplish any social goals.

She had majored in political science at Manhattanville College, and after graduation she and a classmate joined Father John Sullivan in visiting Catholic colleges to recruit student leaders to go to Latin America in an apostolate to the poor, especially those in remote regions. Barbara's missionary fervor was evident in her earnest desire to improve the meager lives of the people and to have basic services brought to them in the name of the Church.

Throughout her college years she had been active in political pursuits and student organizations. Through these she met Paul Sigmund, a political science professor at Princeton University, who shared her liberal Democratic activism and her deep interest in Latin America. She also met Allard Lowenstein, an activist in the National Students Association (NSA) and among the Young Democrats who had worked with me on "Operation Crossroads." He was an enchanting person, a fervent Democrat and believer in human rights. He and Barbara found that they shared similar interests, and for a brief time they were engaged.

Working in the White House was glamorous and the best place to be if you were young, bright, attractive, and wrapped up in politics. Barbara wrote presidential holiday proclamations and other congratulatory messages while bestowing her special sparkling zest for life on everything she did and everyone she knew, as she always had.

Every Tuesday the House and Senate leadership attended a White House breakfast with President Kennedy, Vice President Johnson, and their congressional liaison assistants. It was a working session to plan what legislation would be moved forward toward passage in the coming week. One morning they discussed economic legislation the president wanted passed, but they agreed to postpone any public announcement about it. When the meeting ended a group of reporters, knowing that Hale always made good copy, converged on him and asked what had happened.

"I couldn't tell you that," he said, "but I do want to tell you about the terrible, bland breakfasts they have at this White House. They have awful old Boston eggs without any Tabasco and a dishwatery coffee with no chicory. No grits . . ." He went on like this, the Southerner making fun of the Massachusetts president's menu, deliberately diverting the reporters' attention from the real business of the meeting. The breakfast story was picked up by the wire services and went all over the world. We were called by people we hadn't heard from in years.

The next week President Kennedy secretly ordered a Southern breakfast. Barbara was his mastermind, borrowing my silver demitasse spoons, Tabasco holder, a small pot, and several small trays. I couldn't understand why the White House needed my silver, but I sent it at her request.

When the group was assembled as usual in the Private Dining Room and Barbara was strategically placed behind a screen, the first silver tray, bearing a small silver pot of coffee, a demitasse cup, and a silver sugar bowl containing Louisiana sugar, was carried through the door. Everyone inhaled the aroma of fresh chicory as the tray was placed not in front of the president but in front of Hale. Next came a bigger tray and a silver bowl filled with grits and steaming red-eye gravy in a silver gravy boat. A smaller tray followed, bearing a bottle of Tabasco in its own silver holder, and finally, a silver tray with hot biscuits. Everyone enjoyed Hale's breakfast, President Kennedy most of all.

It is often difficult for the first lady and the vice president's wife to select major commitments that don't interfere with their husbands' political paths. The day Jackie Kennedy discovered an old French Empire marble-top table being used as a worktable by White House flower arrangers in the basement, she began her commitment to restoring and refurbishing the historic presidential mansion.

She felt the White House had been a living, breathing place through many decades and style changes and that all of them should be represented. Original antiques were located and restored; others were acquired—either donated, loaned, or bought—and new pieces were made to resemble the early furnishings.

I took pride in the fact that some members of Jackie's father's family, the Bouviers, originally French, were from Louisiana, and I greatly admired her beautiful mother. I was pleased that Jackie was daring enough to be the "inquiring photographer" for the Washington *Times-Herald*. She and Jack Kennedy had met in 1952, and Hale and I were very happy the next year when they decided to be married. Only a long-standing commitment in New Orleans prevented us from attending their wedding.

I was aware of Lady Bird Johnson's special feeling for the natural beauty of this country long before that was a popular position to take. As the vice president's wife, she began making her interest known to a national audience, and one day I received a call from India Edwards, the former vice-chairman of the Democratic Party, whom I loved and respected. "We have to get Lady Bird off this environmental kick," she told me. "Many of our people in business and labor are not in favor of it." I said something polite but I was thinking, Thank God this country has a Lady Bird Johnson on an environmental kick!

Despite Johnson's position as vice president, we knew that his heart was with the Congress. He had a grand friendship and working partnership with Mr. Sam, and as Senate majority leader under President Eisenhower, he had come to respect and like Ike and they had worked well together. Johnson often said it was not necessarily the job of the opposition party to oppose; its job was to get along with the president and to consider whether what he was proposing was good for the country. If it was good, help the president, he said, but you had to stick up for your own party's principles and philosophy when you thought its proposals were better.

Because the government did not then provide a vice presidential residence, the Johnsons bought Perle Mesta's magnificent home, "Les Ormes," to accommodate the entertaining that was required, renaming it "the Elms." It had been built specifically for entertaining great numbers of people and had a swimming pool, a large terrace, and lovely gardens, yet it contained many pockets of privacy. Soon after they moved in, Lyndon and Lady Bird gave a birthday party for me there, and I was honored and touched by their thoughtfulness.

When Congress convened in January 1961, Hale and others in the leadership were optimistic about the Democratic administration. They were concerned about the economy, which was suffering under the dual burdens of inflation and unemployment, and they were aware that it's a great deal easier to push a social agenda in good economic times, when people are more willing to share the largesse, than in tough ones.

Congress worked gingerly with President Kennedy. A member of the House for three terms, he had served one term in the Senate and immediately upon his reelection there had begun running for president. He was forty-three years old, making it natural that some of the congressional leaders felt that they knew more about the government than did the president. Personally, however, he was extremely popular.

Because of his insights and wisdom, Hale worked well with President Kennedy. Hale was prescient all his life, and much of what he foresaw and was committed to as being the proper path for the United States turned out to be correct. He would be the greatest authority in the country today on the kinds of outreach and leadership we should extend toward the emerging democracies of the world, particularly those in Eastern Europe.

His foresight in suggesting a European Union and a Common Market was completely up to date. His understanding of history and his knowledge of various cultures and governments through the ages gave him the background to see what the United States would need in a more peaceful future world. This was an overriding interest, and he brought his expertise and thoughtfulness to his roles as chairman of the foreign economic policy subcommittee of the House-Senate Joint Economic Committee and chairman of the trade subcommittee of Ways and Means.

Five reciprocal trade agreement amendments that were about to lapse needed to be extended, but with Congress in a protectionist mood, Hale anticipated a terrible battle. He advised the president, "You're going to have as much trouble extending these five bills as you would passing a new omnibus trade bill. Why don't we try to write a new bill in light of the world's current and anticipated situations, such as the Far East markets, north-south trade, and Western European Market?"

President Kennedy was doubtful that such a comprehensive bill could be passed, but he agreed that Hale should proceed. Hale enlisted two respected and prominent internationalists, former Secretary of State Christian Herter, a Republican, and former World Bank official William Clayton, a Democrat, to explain and promote the proposal to members of Congress, government officials, members of the business and international communities, and the public. When the hearings they held around the county had ended, Hale and his committee wrote a House bill, while their counterparts created a Senate version.

The passage of the Omnibus Trade Bill the following year was what Hale called one of the most significant events of the twentieth century. It became the basis for continued U.S. participation in the General Agreement on Tariffs and Trade (GATT), and in all international trade treaties and organizations.

At the same time, increased world travel and trade had prompted the construction of Dulles International Airport out in rural Virginia. Commercial airline fleets were rapidly being converted from propeller planes to the popular new jets, whose need for longer runways threatened to render Washington's urban National Airport obsolete.

Designed by the esteemed Finnish architect Eero Saarinen with extended runways, people-mover mobile lounges to and from planes, a state-of-the-art control tower, and attractive shops and restaurants, Dulles was envisioned as Washington's airport of the future. Work was proceeding smoothly until a terrible snag developed.

The liquor code in Virginia prohibited the serving of alcoholic beverages in restaurants. In order to have Dulles built in Virginia, the state legislature had amended the liquor code to allow beer and wine to be served in the airport restaurant to make it more appealing to travelers. Because the rest of Virginia lived with state package stores and private clubs, it also meant that the airport restaurant could become a popular destination for Virginia residents of the greater metropolitan area as well.

This caused great competition for the restaurant rights, which finally were won by Henry Garfinkel of New York, the owner of Union News and American News newsstands in most rail, air, and bus terminals, and a major presence in the food business with the Savarin chain and the Top of the Sixes restaurant in New York City. He hired a famous chef and began planning the details of what would be a very swank restaurant, to be called Portals.

One night at a White House party several people said to me, "The president's looking for you." I thought he probably had a project that needed the attention of volunteers, so I kept ducking him. When I spotted him in the Blue Room, I'd retreat to the Green Room; in the Red Room to the Main Dining Hall. Before I encountered him, someone else said, "Jeeb Halaby is looking for you." Najeeb Halaby was head of the Federal Aviation Administration, and I came upon the two of them together.

President Kennedy told me that the Virginia legislature had reneged on the liquor license for the restaurant at Dulles and consequently the pace of work toward completion of the airport had drastically slowed. Garfinkel was no longer interested in opening the restaurant, Portals. Construction of the fast-food shops had fallen behind schedule. Exhibitors from exclusive stores that were to occupy a display area coordinated under the genius of Stanley Marcus were grumbling and didn't want to finish. Even the airlines were reluctant to complete their elegant clubs. Everybody was resistant to spending any more money.

On the other hand, he recounted, twenty-three nonprofit organizations wanted to hold their major fund-raising party of the year at Dulles as soon as possible. The president and Halaby agreed that the fund-raiser was a perfect way to announce to the public the completion of the new airport. The president asked me to be the chairman of the benefit party, and I couldn't refuse. My only requirement was that he put in a brief appearance at the event, to which he readily agreed. The next day I went to the White House to work out plans with his staff.

Clearly Travelers Aid was the most likely recipient of the party's honor and funds. Anticipating that the airport would be finished the following year, its officers had not budgeted current funds to open a Travelers Aid facility there. The organization had an admirable record for getting the most out of its money to help the traveling public, and it deserved the honor.

I went to New York to see Mr. Garfinkel to persuade him to alter his decision. I felt he was the key to a way out of our predicament; if he went ahead with Portals, everyone else would resume work and the airport would be finished. I told him about the charity event to help Travelers Aid and that there wouldn't be a party unless his restaurant was open.

Fortuitously Mr. Garfinkel was a great admirer of the work of Travelers Aid and proud to be among its regular major contributors. As we talked, he mentioned that he was a friend of the Newhouse publishing family, which had recently purchased the *Times-Picayune*, my hometown paper. They didn't want to upset its successful operation or its top management and editorial board, so our close friend Ashton Phelps remained as president and publisher. Norman and Donald Newhouse, sons of S. I. Newhouse, came down from New York to become part of the *Times-Picayune* family and of the city's philanthropic and cultural life.

With our Newhouse common thread, my meeting with Mr. Garfinkel became a warm and pleasant visit, and before I left he promised to complete his restaurant and to underwrite the party's expenses.

The gala Travelers Aid Ball was a dinner dance with Meyer Davis's popular orchestra providing the dance music. As a bonus we offered airport sightseeing "cruises" aboard the mobile lounges with the inimitable Charlie Byrd providing the entertainment aboard them. To operate within the liquor laws, each table bore a beautifully decorated basket filled with little individual bottles of liquor, my solution to the original problem. The miniature bottles were supplied by volunteer "rumrunners," friends who happily collected them and delivered them to the airport for a good cause.

Unhappily, the date of the ball coincided with the death of his newborn son Patrick, which precluded President Kennedy's participation. However, he graciously received the Garfinkels and other sponsors in the White House on the following day.

On November 16, 1961, Sam Rayburn died. Hale had suffered with his friend and mentor through his last illness, feeling as close to Mr. Sam as he did to many members of his own family. A month earlier Hale had written a letter of heartfelt tribute to Sam from London, where we were visiting.

> Whenever I am privileged to meet the leaders of other countries, I admire them, respect the fact that they've risen to the top in their countries' own circumstances and wish some of them well and hope they will grow in wisdom and goodness.
>
> And then I am always grateful that the United States has had you, an already mature and good man, to stabilize our government, administration in, administration out, to lead our leaders and to inspire our youth.

Sam had been Speaker of the House of Representatives longer than anyone in history, beginning in 1940 and handing over the gavel to the Republicans for only two terms. The voters of his beloved Bonham, Texas, had sent him to Congress in 1913, and they never called him home. It had taken cancer to do that.

As the year ended the Vietcong were increasing their attacks on South Vietnam, and Hale was persuaded with others in the leadership that the United States had to send troops or risk losing the entire region to the Communists. President Kennedy sent two United States helicopter companies, comprising four hundred men and thirty-three helicopters, for noncombat missions; and in a drastic policy reversal he told our two thousand military advisers in South Vietnam that if they were fired on, they could fire back.

When Congress convened in January 1962, John McCormack of Massachusetts became the Speaker, Carl Albert of Oklahoma moved to majority leader, and Hale became majority whip. Besides helping the leadership by finding and holding needed votes, Hale was the conduit between House Democratic members and the leadership, relaying the mood of the members to the leaders and the desires of the leadership to the members.

When a vote on an important issue was pending, the whip office called eighteen geographical zone whips' offices to rally the members. Each of them talked to the members of Congress from that area and reported back to Hale's office on the status of the vote for or against the leadership position. I kept looseleaf notebooks to track the passage of each piece of important legislation through the Congress and tallied the votes at every step of the process. Hale's devoted staff members had to do all the phoning manually, and all the tallying had to be done by hand as well. When it was time to vote, the whip's office alerted everyone to proceed to the House floor.

Once a week Hale met with his zone whips and with Speaker McCormack, Majority Leader Albert, and their staffs to decide on the strategy and scheduling of legislation for the following week. I discovered he was having these whip meetings without serving anything to eat or drink, so I would get up at five o'clock in the morning to bake coffee cakes, muffins, and sweet rolls and send them down to him accompanied by big jars of juice and milk.

As whip and later as majority leader, Hale sometimes became discouraged when he was overwhelmed with too much work, frustrated that he couldn't accomplish all of it to the best of his abilities. The Ways and Means Committee was heavy going because besides handling tax duties, including Social Security, its Democratic members made the committee assignments for House Democrats. In some ways that was helpful in his whip work, because he could lean fairly heavily on members who wanted to get appointed to their committees of choice.

There were sometimes difficult days and it was an enormous load, but Hale wouldn't have been a leader worthy of Mr. Sam's confidence if he hadn't tried to accomplish as much as he did, or had backed off from the intensity of battles.

I tried to relieve the tension as much as possible, especially in supervising his spontaneous parties. During the times of the year when the corn in his garden was ripe, Hale had a tendency to invite scores of people out to the house. He always assumed he had much more corn than he did, so I would have to dash out to the Farm Women's Market in Bethesda and buy the same species as his, picked that morning, and get home to cook it before he realized what I was doing. In cooperating with his tendency to dispensing generous hospitality, I learned to relax and enjoy it.

In October 1962 the Cuban missile crisis presented itself as a frightening test of President Kennedy's determination and his nerve. For several days our country was near the brink of nuclear war with Russia.

Russian freighters bound for Cuba were believed to be carrying missiles for installation by Castro, and our high-altitude photos showed missile bases on the island. President Kennedy summoned his top military and congressional advisers to the White House to decide on the proper U.S. response.

Hale was deep-sea fishing off the coast of Louisiana when a military helicopter appeared out of nowhere and began hovering overhead. It dropped a note advising him to call a Washington operator, after which the pilot led his fishing boat to the nearest oil rig. Hale was picked off the rig by the helicopter and flown to an air force base, put in the second seat of a fighter plane, and flown to Andrews Air Force Base in Washington. From there he was taken to the White House. It was a tense moment, and President Kennedy responded to it with valor.

The leadership group that had been summoned to the White House stayed in session ten days until the crisis was over. Although they were there as advisers, the congressional leadership would also have had to recommend a declaration of war if one appeared to be warranted. At last, on November 2, President Kennedy announced that the Soviet missile bases in Cuba were being dismantled. Hale came home and slept for hours.

On November 1, 1962, we celebrated the first birthday of Thomas Hale Boggs III, Tommy and Barbara's first child and our first grandchild. When little Hale was born, his parents were moving from an apartment in Old Town Alexandria to a house they had bought in Bethesda, and in the interim they stayed with us. When the baby was three days old, I put his cradle at the foot of my bed so I wouldn't have to get up with him at night; I could just rock his cradle with my foot until he went back to sleep. Our bonding, established then, has remained loving and strong.

Tom's sister insisted that we bring her nephew to the White House for his birthday, and the visit provided us with an unforgettable sight. Waddling through the hall was little one-year-old Hale, and coming from the opposite direction was John-John Kennedy, who was a year older. These two small creatures met in the hall and embraced. I suppose they'd never seen anybody else their size walking around in that cavernous place. We went on to the legislative liaison offices of Larry O'Brien and Kenny O'Donnell, where Barbara led the way in with little Hale, announcing, "I want to introduce all of you to the real Hale Boggs." Kenny responded, "No telling what will happen to a fellow scrunched down in a jet fighter for two hours."

To use government to good purposes was a tenet of Barbara's all the days of her life. In early 1963, she left the White House to establish a domestic volunteer corps that would teach people such basic living skills as good health; reading, writing, and speaking; child care; how to apply for a job; and carpentry, plumbing, and keeping a budget. With the help of college friends, she coordinated a Washington conference to promote this domestic version of the Peace Corps. Young people from throughout the country joined Barbara and her cochairs—publisher Malcolm Forbes and Ann Chapman, a past president of the Woman's National Democratic Club and the wife of Oscar Chapman, a former secretary of the interior—to inspire the meeting with energy and enthusiasm. The results exceeded all their expectations.

From that meeting emerged a national campaign for a volunteer corps to teach and train residents of the decaying urban areas of the United States, building their hope and confidence while giving them skills, and a program to encourage teachers to go beyond their traditional classrooms to help the least advantaged children in inner cities and remote rural corners.

Both proposals were eventually taken up by the government and became Volunteers in Service to America (VISTA) and the Teachers Corps. President Clinton's Americorps program, by which college students will be able to pay back their tuition with community service, is the newest proposal inspired by that conference.

The spirit of neighbors helping neighbors seemed almost tangible when Barbara organized her conference. The famous March on Washington that summer of 1963 showed that hundreds of thousands of people could peaceably assemble, and Martin Luther King's dream seemed possible. But, as we all know, that sense of possibility soon ended.

It's fair to say that any president may be under threat wherever he goes, but many people were excessively, even uncontrollably, angry at President Kennedy about civil rights at home and entangling alliances abroad. Such troublesome groups as the radical right and anti-civil-rights and anti–UN organizations were noisily active everywhere.

Before President Kennedy made a trip to New Orleans in 1962, I was interviewed by the Secret Service about a couple of people known to be agitators, and they were checked out. I didn't know who they were, but Hale was in close contact with the local authorities and federal agents, and he was comfortable about the visit. Some of the president's advisers suggested that he cancel the trip because of protesters, and the president mentioned that to Hale.

Hale said, "Mister President, when the time comes that you, as the president of the United States, can't go to an American city, then something's got to be wrong." The agitators were rounded up and quieted down, and the president received a warm, friendly reception.

When President Kennedy was planning his trip to Texas in November 1963, Hale suggested that he stay away because of a bitter factional fight among the state's Democrats. Hale advised him that he could get into political trouble, but the president laughed and said, "Well, that makes it more interesting."

The last time I saw President Kennedy, my mamma and Hale's mamma were visiting us, and I wanted them to see what beautiful things Jackie had accomplished in the White House. I of course didn't impose our plans upon the president but he found out that we were there and he sent for us. He told the two mothers what wonderful children they had, bantering with them as affectionately as he did with his own mother.

He asked me to step out onto the portico with him, and as we stood near the Rose Garden, he said, "I wanted you to see what Jackie and Bunny Mellon and their people have accomplished in this garden." Jackie had supervised changes undertaken at the president's request, and chrysanthemums and dahlias and marigolds were blooming.

"I can't tell you what serenity this has provided for me. When I'm feeling overwhelmed, I come out here and the loveliness of the garden puts everything back into proper perspective.

"How long do the chrysanthemums bloom?" he asked.

I said, "Until the first frost, Mister President." He replied, "I hope the first frost is very late this year."

When we went back into the Oval Office, he said, "This place is usually swarming with photographers, often when I don't want them. Here I am with three beautiful ladies and no photographer, but I'll fix that. Watch this." He put his head out the door: "Where are the photographers?" he called. A mob of them came running into the office with their cameras. Ten days later President Kennedy, my precious friend, was dead.

Only a few members of the cabinet and Congress were in Washington the day the president was killed. Congress, which had been in constant session, was finally in recess, and several cabinet members were on a trip abroad, leaving in town only Defense Secretary Robert McNamara and the president's brother, Attorney General Robert Kennedy. The Speaker, the majority leader, and Hale all were away from the Hill.

Hale was running errands downtown, and I was in the whip office with some of his staff members, when someone from the

Speaker's office apprised us of the news from Dallas and we turned on the television. I dropped to my knees and began praying that the president was not fatally wounded. There was such disbelief. We were all in shock. It was an eerie feeling, as though everything were out of context—the time, the city, the government. Secret Service agents moved in to secure the Capitol building because there was no certainty that there wasn't a plot to overthrow the government. Police manned all the doors and made people identify themselves going in and out, an unheard-of precaution at the time. When Hale returned to the office, he was shaken and upset. He had heard the dreadful news.

By midafternoon everybody began to converge back into the capital. Hale and Speaker McCormack went to Andrews Air Force Base to meet the newly sworn-in President Johnson and Mrs. Johnson, with Mrs. Kennedy. That evening President Johnson held a meeting in the vice president's office, at which he asked the leaders of the House and the Senate to work together in the transition.

Hale with the other Congressional leaders attended the funeral, and at Mary Albert's suggestion, the leadership wives gave up our seats so that other members of Congress who had been especially close to the president could attend.

Jackie Kennedy emerged as a national heroine with her plans for an occasion of grace, pomp, and meaningful beauty. Her dignified and charming reception of heads of state from all over the world and from many divergent political persuasions was matched only by the poignancy of the unforgettable sight of her with little Caroline and tiny John-John waving his American flag in a final salute.

As I said in a tribute to President Kennedy that I was privileged to deliver in ceremonies at the Woman's National Democratic Club, Jackie had given our nation "beauty for ashes, the oil of joy for mourning, the garment of praise for the spirit of heaviness," a blessing spelled out by President Kennedy's favorite prophet, Isaiah.

As soon as the funeral was over, Congress went back to work and didn't adjourn until Christmas Eve.

As sad as we all were, there was work to be done helping the new president, our old friend, get settled. A group of us helped Lady Bird prepare for the move and answer the mountain of mail she and the president had received. We were working on the third floor of the Elms when we took a lunch break. Sitting up on packing boxes with her shoes off, eating a hamburger, Bird wiggled her feet and said, "I sort of hate to leave this house. I had almost tamed it."

After they were settled in the White House, at Jackie's request one of President Johnson's first official acts was to create a federal commission to preserve and enhance the White House. Lady Bird continued the refurbishment of the residence and the establishment of a companion garden to the Rose Garden on the west side of the White House that she wished to name the Jacqueline Kennedy Garden, but Jackie demurred. It became known instead as the First Lady Garden until years later, when Jackie finally accepted the honor.

Less than a week after President Johnson took office, he appointed Hale to serve on a special commission to investigate the assassination of President Kennedy. Hale had thought a blue-ribbon panel was needed, and he had already broached the subject with the president. Chief Justice Earl Warren was the chairman, and the other members were Republican Representative Gerald Ford of Michigan; senators Richard Russell, a Democrat of Georgia, and Chairman of the Senate Armed Services Committee, and John Sherman Cooper, a Republican of Kentucky; Allen Dulles, a former head of the Central Intelligence Agency

(CIA); and John J. McCloy, U.S. High Commissioner for Germany.

Chief Justice Warren never failed to tell me that if it hadn't been for Hale's precise language in the commission's report, the report could not have been unanimous. It said that "according to the testimony presented to this commission," the committee "found no evidence" that anyone assisted Lee Harvey Oswald in planning or carrying out the assassination. The many allegations, suspicions, and rumors were never presented as testimony, nor was irrefutable evidence presented proving the existence of a conspiracy.

Hale always let the report and its accompanying documents speak for themselves; he never discussed them or the commission's work, and the children and I abided by his example.

Various other theories were expounded. New Orleans District Attorney Jim Garrison had his own conspiracy theory, and unlike other theorists he had the authority to empanel grand juries. Several New Orleans people who might have disagreed with the Warren Commission report never forgave Garrison for his prosecution of Clay Shaw, the respected director of the International Trade Mart. Shaw was acquitted of charges of conspiracy in the assassination, but his reputation and his health were ruined by the experience.

I had an unusual relationship with Jim Garrison. Hale's campaign organization always held a big New Orleans rally with flags, a band, and plenty of food when Hale ran every two years, and all the high officials would sit on a platform for everyone to see them. In 1968, we had some difficult problems with our constituents, who were divided over the widening war in Vietnam and the civil rights movement, in which Hale had supported the president.

It was a touchy situation and we weren't sure how many officials would show up for Hale, so we moved the rally to the WDSU-TV studio, transforming it into a rally platform, and invited everyone to come and be on television, an opportunity that was difficult for them to resist. When I called Garrison and explained the situation, he said, "What do you want me to do? What would help you more? Do you want me to be for Hale or against him?"

I said, "I want you to come down to the studio and be for him." He said, "I'll be there, Lindy."

After the sadness of the president's death, we were glad for some personal happiness in our own family. Barbara and her old friend Paul Sigmund decided to be married on January 25, 1964, in Blessed Sacrament Church in Chevy Chase, our original Washington parish church, with the reception immediately following at our home. Father Robbie Boggs was asked to perform the service, as he had done for Tommy and his Barbara. President Johnson and his family were invited, but the president felt that if he came to the church he would upstage the bride and groom, so Lady Bird and their daughters, Lynda and Luci, came to the church, and he agreed to meet them at the reception. We tented and heated the patio, and I began preparing weeks in advance for the expected crowd at the reception.

All the grocery stores had big sales on Thursdays, and we would watch for their ads in the newspapers. One Thursday Hale and I went to the Giant Food Store for a big sale on hams. We chose several hams and picked up a few turkeys, and as we were going to the check-out line, Hale said, "You know, it's going to be really cold. Why don't we have a couple of those hams chopped up and serve some red beans and rice?" (It's a traditional New Orleans dish, enjoyed regularly by both the humble and the mighty.)

I went searching through the store, and I finally came up with eleven one-pound bags of red beans. Between us we arrived at the check-out counter with five double baskets. The young clerk who was totaling our bill finally paused, pushed back his cap, and said, "Mister, I think I understand the hams and the turkeys, but would you please tell me what on earth you're gonna do with all those beans?"

Our friend Jim Pitts, who was a vice president of South Central Bell, was an amateur photographer of great talent, and Barbara agreed that he could take some wedding pictures. He took all the pictures at the rehearsal, and then he worked with the sexton at the church so he could unobtrusively photograph the wedding. Barbara didn't want a photographer detracting from the solemnity of the wedding or holding up the receiving line, so she arranged for everyone to come to the house before the wedding to have the formal photographs taken.

When the wedding was over, the reception began and everything started smoothly. Then President Johnson arrived, trailing an entourage of aides, Secret Service agents, and many, many photographers. The president went straight to the receiving line to embrace Barbara and give her a kiss, and all the White House photographers crowded in around them.

Our friend, who had enjoyed exclusive photo rights until then, suddenly yelled, "Get outta my way! I've got to shoot the president!"

He and his camera hit the floor at the same time, buried by Secret Service agents before he could utter another word.

CHAPTER TWELVE

ᷢᷢᷢᷢ

*P*RESIDENT JOHNSON was having a hard time making up his mind whether to run for his own full term as president, and the election campaign had come to a screeching halt. He wasn't sure that his imperfect heart would carry him through four more years of the extraordinary energy, drive, and attention to detail he knew the presidency required. Ever since he had suffered a heart attack in 1955, his doctors had warned him that another one could be fatal.

Hale and I encouraged him to do whatever his doctors required in order to run and serve. We didn't want him to endanger his life, but we hoped he could realize the ambitious social and economic programs for the War on Poverty and the Great Society, which he envisioned and which we enthusiastically supported. With the cooperation of Congress he had already pushed through the most contentious of all proposals, a tax cut desired by President Kennedy.

Until Johnson decided to run, he wouldn't permit aggressive campaigning by the Democratic National Committee. This left national campaign plans in disarray and gave rise to all kinds of other organizations to promote his candidacy.

I was the chairman of one of these, a national voter registration drive called 4 FOR '64, in which we signed up volunteers to work at least four hours a week registering voters. Those who did so received a pin; volunteers giving more time received a certificate. We studied the itineraries of party "stars"—administration luminaries, officeholders, and other Democrats who were nationally known—and coordinated our awards presentations with their visits to the towns and cities of our volunteers. Before the ceremony dates we sent publicity on the volunteers and their photos to the local newspapers and broadcasters.

My chief volunteer assistants were Scotty Lanahan, a talented journalist and social activist who was Zelda and F. Scott Fitzgerald's daughter, and Ceci Carusi, a civic activist and socialite who once, on losing a bet, had the gumption to join the circus for a year as a bareback rider. Both women lived in Washington and knew their way around national Democratic politics. We shared office space in an old Washington building on Fifteenth Street with Scientists and Engineers for Johnson, Senior Citizens for Johnson, Farmers for Johnson, and Teen "Dems" for Johnson—all created because the national committee was restrained in mounting a national campaign.

Whenever anybody in the building got hold of a "significant" volunteer who might be a potential star, they'd send the person to me for special placement. Meanwhile Scotty and Ceci worked with a large map to bring together the officials and our awards presentations and the media opportunities along the way.

It seemed that every time the three of us would be in a hard-hitting session in my room, I would have to break away to deal with a significant volunteer. Scotty and Ceci finally became so frustrated with these interruptions that they said, "We need forty-five minutes of your undivided attention. If you don't give it to us, we're going to quit."

I said, "Okay. You figure out some way in which we won't be interrupted."

They left. When they returned a few minutes later, they closed the door and said, "We're ready."

We updated our map, sticking all the colored pins in the right places, and finished a backlog of work without any interruptions. I was amazed that not a soul had come to the door. I said, "How did you keep everyone away?"

They suggested, "Go look on your door."

Stuck on my door was a horrible caricature they had drawn of an overweight, slovenly, dreadful-looking man and woman. Beneath it they had written: "Middle-Aged Citizens for Johnson."

By the time the president decided to run, our voter registration drive was a national success.

Under steady pressure and insistence from President Johnson, Congress passed the most comprehensive civil rights bill in history that summer, the Omnibus Civil Rights Act of 1964. It banned discrimination for reasons of color, race, religion, sex, or national origin in restaurants, theaters, gas stations, hotels, and motels—all places of public accommodation involved in interstate commerce—and in labor unions and by private employers of more than twenty-five persons.

Hale publicly opposed it, as he had opposed President Truman's Fair Employment Practices Commission and federal anti-poll-tax bills. He was trying to reconcile the states' rights over education and private property with the federal government's increasing incursions into those areas through court decisions and administrative procedures. Of course as a Southerner himself President Johnson understood Hale's position and because Hale didn't actively work against the legislation, his vote did not affect his leadership role in Congress.

Immediately after the president signed the civil rights bill into law, he and Lady Bird heard from many friends who said, "You've turned your back on your fellow Southerners. Our votes don't count." President Johnson knew that their votes did count and that he would need them in the fall election.

Republicans were experiencing similar difficulties. New York's moderate Republican governor, Nelson Rockefeller, was loudly booed when he tried to address fellow Republicans at the convention in San Francisco that summer. It had been a long time since something like that had occurred, and it revealed a turning point in the modern Republican Party. A newly resurgent conservative mood controlled the convention delegates and found its voice in Senator Barry Goldwater of Arizona, a retired air force general who became the Republican presidential nominee. Straight-talking and combative, Goldwater campaigned against the Civil Rights Bill, the Kennedy legacy, and President Johnson's social programs and tax bills.

With the president running, the Democratic National Convention in Atlantic City where I served on the arrangements committee was relatively uneventful. A film on John Kennedy's thousand days in the presidency evoked a surge of emotion among delegates and inspired some interest in the candidacy of Robert Kennedy, but the president had won the nomination by then, and he chose Senator Hubert Humphrey of Minnesota, the Democratic whip, as his running mate.

The only noteworthy thing that happened to me was the result of an act of God. I was part of a group of women volunteers lined up at the airport in our red-white-and-blue outfits, waiting for Humphrey's plane to land, when we were drenched by a sudden shower and our skirts shrank at an embarrassingly rapid rate.

Early in August the government had announced the attack by North Vietnamese PT boats thirty miles off the North Vietnamese coast in the Gulf of Tonkin on a U.S. destroyer and President Johnson's order for U.S. bombers to attack North Vietnam in reprisal raids. Within a week Congress unanimously passed a Gulf of Tonkin Resolution, prepared by the administration and strongly supported by the leadership, which empowered the president to order U.S. military action in response to any armed attack, to prevent further aggression, and to support our Southeast Asia allies militarily if they so requested.

In the absence of a declaration of war, this resolution became the constitutional basis for all further United States actions in Southeast Asia.

Although these momentous changes began to precipitate concerted action by groups opposing the Vietnam action, the most pressing issue that President Johnson had to address was the Civil Rights Bill.

President Johnson knew he had to win back voters who were upset and angry with him over the civil rights bill and give courage to Southern Democratic officials to support the ticket, but he wasn't sure how he should do it. Liz Carpenter, Mrs. Johnson's chief of staff, who had worked as Johnson's press secretary when he was the vice president, had the solution: "The Lady Bird Special."

Liz, who had organized the vice presidential whistle-stop in 1960, was a believer in whistle-stop campaigns in order for candidates to see and be seen by thousands of people who might otherwise be missed, and to give the press a lively story and exposure to the candidate. "The Lady Bird Special" would mark the first time a first lady went out on her own campaign train. It wouldn't be an easy trip: twelve hundred miles through the Deep South a month before the election.

Lady Bird and the president honored me by assigning me as the coorganizer and cochair of this exciting enterprise with Virginia Russell, the energic, charming wife of South Carolina governor Donald Russell. We worked at the White House with Lady Bird and Liz, preparing and double-checking the details. Tommy led one of the advance teams that organized women's campaign groups at every stop along the way. Lyndon knew that women would work the phones, spread enthusiasm, and bring out big crowds.

The train had an extra locomotive and a diner and carried special cars for staff, the press, Lady Bird's quarters—which contained the only bathtub—an office, a reception car for visiting dignitaries, and a red-white-and-blue caboose with a speaking platform. More than two hundred newspeople signed on and from the first whistle, we were in the papers and on the radio every day and on television every night.

Although Lady Bird was born and raised in Texas, her mother and father were from Alabama, and she had gone back to visit every summer until she was married. She and the president had a strong affinity for the South, and they wanted Southerners to know it. The president saw us off in Alexandria, Virginia, and Lady Bird spoke to the festive crowd. "The United States is a nation of laws, not men," she said quietly, "and our greatness lies in our ability to adjust to the national consensus." The Civil Rights Act had been passed by a majority of the Congress, she added.

During the next four days and nights, we held rallies in almost fifty trackside towns and great cities of the South, winding through Virginia, North Carolina, South Carolina, Georgia, Florida, Alabama, Mississippi, and Louisiana. The Johnson daughters Lynda and Luci and Virginia Russell and I were the official hostesses, while Hale and Secretary of Commerce Luther Hodges warmed up the crowds.

I was a greeter in the reception car, which local dignitaries boarded a stop or two before the train reached their towns. We introduced them to everyone and tried to make them feel welcome and comfortable so that when they went onto the platform as the train rolled into their hometown, they were already having a good time. I don't remember spending many miles sitting down.

Hale's campaigning skills and style were such that he was our master of ceremonies with a speech that had every crowd yelling for more. "You know what we had to eat on this train this morning?" he would ask. "We had grits! And at noon we're gonna start servin' turnip greens and black-eyed peas and some good ol' Southern ham with red-eye gravy. Tonight we're gonna sit down to crayfish bisque and Creole gumbo, and you know that on Monday we'll all be eatin' our red beans and rice."

He went on like this until he had the crowd cheering. "Now, you're not going to turn your back on the first Southern-born president in a hundred years?" he'd ask, and they would roar back at him and applaud like mad.

A local dignitary would introduce Lady Bird, and she would speak of the coming election as a test of whether we would move forward as a nation "in common trust and faith" or move backward toward denial of each other's needs in a national climate of fear, distrust, and dislike. She didn't mention any names; there was no need for it.

We knew we would face hecklers, and the first ones were in Columbia, South Carolina, Virginia Russell's capital city. They were led by a man with a crutch. The hecklers waited until Lady Bird got up to speak, and when the man raised his crutch in the air, it was the cue for an organized group of younger people, who were supposed to look like individual spectators, to surge forward, chanting and waving placards. Lady Bird said to them, "Now, you've had your say. All these people have come to hear what I have to say, so I hope you will give me that opportunity."

She handled the hecklers without raising her voice. She was a formidable foe, and the sympathy of the crowd was overwhelmingly in her favor, which gave her a much more commanding position than that of the local officials. They seemed embarrassed by these ugly displays toward the first lady and tried to calm the situation, but they simply shouted as loudly as the demonstrators, which was perfectly natural but didn't deter those bent on creating the disturbance.

The heckling was repeated elsewhere in South Carolina and in Savannah, Georgia, where we saw numerous Goldwater posters. We were never certain what the hecklers were going to do when they began waving their placards within a foot of our faces. It was tense at times but we held our ground and kept our heads high. We weren't afraid, but the adrenaline flowed.

Most of the crowds were friendly, although the man with the crutch and his gang followed us for a while. In some places blacks would be cheering in front while little clumps of silent whites stood on the fringes. At one point Hale and our other men became so angry with what they considered the hecklers' disrespect for the first lady that they threatened to silence forcibly the next person who interrupted. Lady Bird prevailed on them to ignore the rabble-rousers.

We were glad to reach Florida and Alabama, where Lady Bird's relatives and their neighbors bolstered our spirits and kept would-be hecklers in line. She had a host of Alabama relatives—so many, in fact, that reporters on the train began to ask her, "Is this next stop going to be a one-cousin town or a four-cousin town?"

Patsy Derby, Lady Bird's niece, was among our enthusiastic young leaders who worked the crowds at the stations, giving out buttons, bumper stickers, and other campaign paraphernalia. One day as we approached the next college town, she proposed that our young personnel could herald our arrival from the cab of the extra engine that ran ahead of our train.

I couldn't reveal to her that the engine was being used as a dummy to intercept any explosive device that might have been placed on the tracks. We had special surveillance along the entire route, including the inspection of overpasses and bridges by law enforcement personnel on the ground, in boats, and in helicopters.

I simply told Patsy the railroad wouldn't allow passengers in the other locomotive.

When we reached New Orleans, President Johnson met us and we went to the Jung Hotel, where more than two thousand people waited to hear him speak. His address included this segment in reference to the Civil Rights Act:

> Whatever your views are, we have a Constitution and we have a Bill of Rights and we have the law of the land, and two-thirds of the Democrats in the Senate voted for it, and three-fourths of the Republicans.
>
> I signed it and I am going to enforce it and I am going to observe it, and I think any man that is worthy of the high office of president is going to do the same thing.

On Election Day President Johnson and Senator Humphrey won by a landslide, carrying forty-four states.

Emma Cyprian cooked a chicken dish that Lyndon Johnson loved. It was half-fricasseed, half-smothered, a delicious pièce de résistance in her array of recipes. Years before he became president, Lyndon Johnson began trying to get the recipe. "Give me your cook's recipe for that chicken," he'd say. We would relay the request to Emma but she would reply, "I am not a cook. I do not pretend to be a cook," and she kept the recipe to herself. Emma was just four feet eleven inches tall and weighed only eighty-eight pounds, but she was not easily intimidated.

Johnson's doctors had placed him on a restricted diet for his heart condition, but he somehow persuaded Lady Bird that Emma's chicken didn't have fat in it. When Lady Bird began asking for the recipe, Emma gave her one, but it wasn't correct. She had left something out on purpose. Lady Bird said the chicken didn't taste the same as it did at our house.

When Johnson became vice president, the standoff reached the status of a Washington cause célèbre. I said, "Now, Emma, you really have to give him the recipe. We can't send him the chicken because the Secret Service intercepts all the food that comes to their house."

"I don't understand the problem," Emma said. "I've given them the recipe."

Lady Bird called. "Lindy, do you think if I put Emma on the phone with Zephyr"—Zephyr Wright was their cook—"that they could work out this chicken thing? Lyndon is insisting on having this chicken."

Emma got on the phone with Zephyr, and I listened in because I wanted the recipe myself. Emma said, "First thing you do is get out your big black iron pot."

Zephyr said, "Where do you get a big black iron pot?"

Emma answered, "You don't get one. You inherit one." After that the conversation went from bad to worse. When I hung up, I was not convinced that the recipe Emma had given Zephyr was correct.

The next day Lady Bird called me. "That chicken was not right. It was worse than the other recipe she gave me."

Without declaring a formal truce, both sides rested until I said, "Emma, Mr. Johnson is now the president of the United States. You must give him the recipe for your chicken."

She answered me with her usual determination: "If he wants my chicken, he has to come to my kitchen to get it."

As the new year began, President Johnson met daily to talk about Vietnam with his military advisers and congressional leaders, but like the president, Congress was almost completely dependent on the military chiefs' evaluations and recommendations. They believed that victory in Vietnam was required to save all of Southeast Asia from the Communists—the "domino theory": if one country fell, all would fall—and victory could be achieved if enough troops and firepower were used. Within a few months the United States began massive bombings of North Vietnam and landed its first combat troops—3,500 marines—at the port of Da Nang, South Vietnam.

At the same time violent confrontations between blacks and whites were occurring in the South. At Selma, Alabama, civil rights demonstrators, many of whom had been arrested while trying to register to vote, began marching to Montgomery and were attacked by state police. The television scenes of unarmed black men, women, and children being beaten by the authorities were extremely upsetting to many moderate Southerners and pushed them into support of the civil rights movement.

President Johnson met with Alabama governor George Wallace to resolve the conflict, but the governor insisted that he was unable to protect the mostly black crowd. Before the demonstrators resumed their march, the president sent three thousand federalized National Guard troops and military police to protect them.

With all this trouble at home and abroad, we began to worry that the president's great plans—his antipoverty program—would go down the tubes. And we were eager to see them enacted. Even so, when Lady Bird invited me to attend a White House conference on the Head Start program in 1965, I thought that perhaps I was already too busy. I was on the board of Washington Family and Child Services, which had forty-four social service organizations under its auspices, and I was active in other civic, political, and cultural organizations. I worked at the whip's office, and I was involved in Hale's political campaigns, all of which, as it turned out, prepared me for rendering service to Head Start.

I'm glad that I decided to go. In all my years in Washington that White House meeting was one of the most exciting I ever attended. Everyone tossed out ideas until we were buoyed by the exhilaration of dreams coming true: that we could be part of the solution to one of our country's oldest and saddest tragedies, the loss to society of the children who never make it through school. Head Start would provide a chance to change that.

To encourage the cooperation of talented social ladies who might not otherwise become involved, Mrs. Johnson elevated the program to a professional volunteerism project of the White House, and the wives of Southern governors and legislators seemed to outnumber those from the rest of the country.

Sarge Shriver, the director of the Office of Economic Opportunity (OEO), explained that the project hoped to give disadvantaged children a head start on their education, possibly helping as many as one hundred thousand children the first summer, before they entered first grade in the fall. The goal was to involve entire families in programs that would focus on health, social services, and education to rescue young children from becoming potential dropouts. For eight weeks the children would receive one good meal daily, basic teaching in vocabulary and manners, and a complete medical examination with screening for learning disabilities.

During a question-and-answer session, it became evident that in the few weeks since Head Start had been publicly proposed, queries and offers of help were becoming backed up. Someone from the American Association of University Women (AAUW) said, "We have many chapters and we'd like to help, but we wrote three weeks ago asking how you can use us and we have had no answer." Similar complaints were voiced by other organizations with thousands of members in their chapters nationwide who were ready to go to work. "What can we do?" they asked. "We wrote but we never received an answer."

When I was asked afterward by Lady Bird's niece Diana McArthur and Dr. Julius Richmond, the project development director, what I had gotten out of the conference, I replied that somehow I had to locate those letters, telephone messages, and other evidences of interest that the question-and-answer period had indicated needed immediate attention and get them properly answered.

The next morning I was given an office in a building on Fifteenth Street and asked what I needed to accomplish the task. I asked for seven tables, two desks, nine unrestricted telephone lines, and as much flexibility as possible in coordinating government and private agencies and volunteers.

I knew who worked well and had clout—cabinet wives, congressional wives, and Supreme Court justices' wives. I called them, signed them up, and they went eagerly to work. They took turns on the phones, organizing local volunteers to set up Head Start projects. The administration's antipoverty program was being criticized for not reaching the poorest people, so I asked Sarge to have his computers punch out for me the three hundred neediest counties in the United States. A great many of them were in the rural South.

Because our "Lady Bird Special" teams had conducted regional meetings, setting up volunteer groups to work for the Democratic ticket, Jan Sanders, the wife of President Johnson's congressional liaison, Harold Barefoot Sanders, suggested that those volunteers organize Head Start in their areas. Government agencies lent us a hundred young management interns, who went on a four-week barnstorming tour to explain the project and to help people fill out applications, reaching families in 240 of our target counties. Universities offered a one-week training program for Head Start teachers and aides, and hundreds enrolled.

Black churches pulled everything together, providing Sunday-school rooms, refectories, volunteers, buses, playgrounds. They got parents involved, widening the horizons for other children and family members. Sometimes our telephone volunteers would attend a regional meeting, and they'd come back to Washington reenergized. They would get on the phone and call a small-town organizer and say, "Now, Reverend, is anybody going to help those children cross the street to get to the classrooms?"

"Well, sure," the reverend would say, and volunteer Dorothy Goldberg, the wife of Associate Supreme Court Justice Arthur Goldberg, would write down the name of the chaperone.

"When they get inside, do you have anybody who's competent to look in their little throats and ears, check their health?"

"Oh, sure, sure. Miss Chaffee, she does that."

"If the children are invited to tour the courthouse, could anybody take them?"

"Well, yes. We've got the school bus, and we've got a good licensed driver. We couldn't get insurance if he wasn't licensed."

Dorothy would add "bus," "insurance," and "licensed driver" to the Head Start form she was filling out, and she would keep asking for details until all the blanks were filled.

In six weeks these remarkable women set up Head Start programs in 267 of the 300 neediest counties. Every state had at least one program, as more than five hundred thousand four- and-five-year-olds started the project.

President Johnson had always been insistent that women be brought into the government, not only as volunteers but with an equal right to jobs. He told one of his first cabinet meetings that he wanted fifty more women immediately appointed to government positions. When six weeks had gone by and only twenty had received appointments, he wondered what was going wrong. Thank goodness for his impatience. Areas of social responsibility and interest in which we spouses had been working for years were suddenly made national goals and passed into law during his administration.

Dorothy Goldberg was typical of these capable women, although she was the only community activist among them I've ever known for whom a civic celebration, "Dorothy Goldberg Day," was held in the city of Washington. She was honored when she and Arthur were leaving to go to the United Nations in New York, when he was appointed the new U.S. ambassador.

While Arthur was still an associate justice of the Supreme Court, Dorothy visited lower courts in the District of Columbia and discovered that the juvenile system's courtroom was utterly drab and forbidding, a terrible environment to which to bring children and their families. She saw the children becoming more and more apprehensive and angry as they waited for their cases to be processed. Dorothy, an accomplished artist with a great deal of practicality, gathered other women of the DC courts, and together they refurbished the courtroom, painting it bright colors and using attractive draperies and comfortable furniture. The beneficial effect on children and their parents was immediately obvious as they relaxed and talked quietly during their lengthy waits.

When Arthur Goldberg was appointed to the UN in 1965, succeeding the late Adlai Stevenson, President Johnson complimented me with the offer of a job in the economic division at the UN. I was sorry I couldn't take it because I was completely involved in helping at the whip's office, working with the Democratic party, and assisting Lady Bird or the president on special projects when they called on me.

I didn't feel I could turn down the UN assignment without meeting with the people with whom I would have been associated, and Dorothy wanted a good friend to help her get settled in New York, so we went together. When we walked into the Waldorf Towers apartment used by the U.S. ambassador to the UN, I was acutely aware for the first time that Adlai was truly gone. When a friend dies away from you and you don't see him, it's always hard to realize that he's truly dead, but the apartment had been stripped of everything that had made it personally his: the priceless paintings and artifacts that his friends Marietta Tree and Jane Dick, and his enchanting sister, Buffie Ives, had lent him, the exquisite mementos from his travels and his years of public service, the bookcases filled with well-worn books. Seeing it vacant made me very sad.

Dorothy had to start furnishing from scratch, and I said, "Let's think about what you need and where we can find it: New Jersey has porcelain, Rhode Island has silver, West Virginia has crystal and glassware, and the first thing you need to buy is a large freezer for all of the entertaining you're going to have to do."

As an artist well connected with the museum and gallery people in New York, she was able to select art to be placed on loan in the residence. When she learned that none of the spouses of the people working in our UN delegation had been to the ambassador's apartment, she initiated a series of social events to make the delegation family feel a part of a truly cohesive group. What an asset to our government she was!

It was quite a time for us. Our old and good friends were now at the pinnacle of government, Hale was in the leadership, and our children were growing up, getting married, and having children. For a time we thought Tommy might be moving to New York. He had attended Georgetown Law School at night, working days for the Joint Economic Committee, a heavy schedule that bothered Hale and me. Hale said to him, "We expected to send you to law school. Why don't you go to classes in the daytime and get a night job that won't interfere with your studying?" We didn't think it was fair to him or Barbara for him to have an intense, demanding job during the day and to attend law school at night.

Tom said, "The people in school with me are studying law in order to get out and be lawyers, and the competition is tough. Our faculty members are great. They come directly from the top law firms and from the courts to our classrooms. I think Barbara and I can handle it."

When he received his law degree in 1965, we encouraged him

to join one of the big law firms in New York or Washington. We thought it would give him an excellent background for his career, but he said he preferred to be in a small one and he joined Jim Patton, George Blow, Joe Brand, and Charles Verrill, who had established a growing practice in Washington. When Patton, Boggs & Blow was well on its way to becoming one of the big Washington legal firms, we kidded him about our earlier conversation.

Cokie had majored in political science and graduated from Wellesley College in Massachusetts in 1964. All the children excelled in the writing and speaking skills that are necessary to a political career. The only oddity was that Cokie became a reporter, but in some ways, that's the other side of the fence from politics, and Hale and I both loved journalism. After graduating Cokie went to work in television in Washington with Altman Productions, whose owner and president was Sophie Altman, the mother of one of her Wellesley classmates.

While she was at Wellesley Cokie had followed in Barbara's footsteps, becoming involved in students' political organizations. At one student convention she met Steven Roberts, an editor of the Harvard *Crimson*. They became friends, but they didn't become sweethearts until they both came to Washington for Barbara's Domestic Peace Corps conference. Barbara had volunteered our house for participants who needed a place to stay, and Steve took her up on it. He had a terrible cough and during the night I went to his room and administered a little restorative toddy and he now jokes that he never left after that.

In fact he came to Washington to work as a clerk for our old friend James "Scotty" Reston at the *New York Times* and became part of a circle of young people that would gather on our patio and talk politics. It was on one of those summer nights that the voting rights bill became the subject of conversation hotter than the July temperature.

There are times in Congress when you vote with the predominant feelings and best interests of the people in your district. At other times issues transcend home district matters and you use your best judgment and vote your conscience. After all, you're not elected to simply go with the flow, you're elected to use your own judgment, to exert leadership, and to uphold the Constitution and the principles of your own conscience.

In 1965 a Voting Rights Act authorizing the presence of federal observers at polls to ensure equal voting rights was proposed to Congress as another of President Johnson's civil rights initiatives.

Hale's black advisers were telling him not to vote for it because they were afraid they would lose him to a conservative in the next election. We had been working on extending the voting franchise since the 1930s; Hale believed that all people should be able to vote on their form of government and the candidates of their choice, especially with so many Louisianan blacks being sent to Vietnam. He thought it was simple justice that they should be able to vote on wars in which they were going to fight. He thought that if you insured the right to vote, people would then have the power to achieve other rights.

We women in the family pushed him hard on civil rights. He led us, and then we pushed him. It wasn't just Cokie and Barbara and me, it was Hale's Mamma and my Mamma and Grandmother Rets—four generations of us. We were all having dinner out on the patio one evening. Cokie and Steve were engaged to be married, and some of their friends had joined us. The bill was coming up the next day, and everyone was urging Hale to vote for it.

I thought of Bessie Rogers, Emma Cyprian, Aunt Hannah Hall—black women who had raised me and had helped me raise my children, women who had been prevented from voting because of their color. Cokie reminded her father that she had been required to take a literacy test before she could register to vote, a test that could have disqualified anyone the registrars sought to discourage.

"I'm going to vote for voting rights," Hale said. "I've always believed that if you give people the right to vote, they can achieve the other rights themselves."

Cokie said, "But, Daddy, you have to speak for it, too. Think what a difference that would make, to have a leader from the Deep South speak for it."

I agreed with her. I said, "It wouldn't only make a difference in the legislation, it would make a difference in your career."

Hale said, "Well, it could mean I would lose my career." He thought a minute and then he said, "All right. Enough's enough. I am voting for it, but I won't speak on it. I can't push my black supporters that far. They're already apprehensive about my voting for it. Now, let's leave it alone."

The next day Hale went onto the House floor to listen to the debate. A Louisiana colleague and close friend, Joe D. Waggonner of Shreveport, was speaking against the bill. Anybody who wanted to vote in Louisiana was able to vote, he said, and nobody had trouble registering.

Hale knew there were already enough votes to pass the bill, but Waggonner's speech made something snap inside him. He stood up and off the top of his head, he gave a beautiful, impassioned speech, one of the best of his career. Those were the days before House proceedings were broadcast to the members' offices; if you wanted to hear what was happening, you had to go to the floor. Because Hale had a wonderful voice and a grasp of issues, when he spoke the House listened. Word sped through the offices and corridors, "Boggs is up," and the floor and galleries quickly filled and fell silent.

He had never intended to talk on this bill, he said, but he was compelled to do so because of his friend's remarks. Hale described

himself as a man of the South, and he told of illustrious ancestors—
a great-uncle who had surrendered the last Confederate Army in
the field six weeks after Robert E. Lee surrendered at Appomattox,
a grandfather who had served on Lee's staff throughout the War
Between the States.

"I wish I could stand here as a man who loves my state, born
and reared in the South, who has spent every year of his life in
Louisiana since he was five years old, and say there has not been
discrimination . . . but unfortunately, it is not so." In an area near
New Orleans with three thousand black American residents, "less
than one hundred are registered to vote as American citizens.

"There are other areas where less than two percent or three
percent of non-whites are registered to vote. Can we say there has
been no discrimination? Can we honestly say that from our hearts?

"I know what the problems have been," he continued. "I sym-
pathize with them. I have lived with them, and I know that in the
minds of many good, sincere people there has been a fear that if
we made suffrage universal, as it most properly should be, there
would be a decline in the caliber of our government. But that fear
has been dissipated by experience in counties all over the
South. . . ."

"I love my state. I love the South with every part of me, and
I love my country. I shall support this bill because I believe the
fundamental right to vote must be a part of this great experiment
in human progress under freedom which America is." He was one
of only twenty-two Southerners voting for the bill, which passed
the House 333 to 85, and did it make a difference in his career!

Hale's political stands had occasionally altered our social relationships, and after that speech he was so harassed at some gather-
ings that he felt it was uncomfortable for his hosts. He tried to
avoid occasions that he felt would attract the most bothersome
other guests, but then his friends would say, "My Lord, that's just
Hale," and objections against him would be dispelled.

A cross was burned on our lawn in New Orleans. Hale and I were in Paris attending a meeting when we were telephoned and told about it. I was concerned because Rets and Aunt Rowena lived next door, so I called Rets from France and asked her what had happened and how she was.

"Oh, darlin'," she said, "you missed all the excitement last night. I saw snooty neighbors we hadn't seen in months."

Judge John Minor Wisdom, a champion of civil and human rights, lived diagonally across the street. "Why didn't they put the cross in the intersection?" he wondered. "That way they could have taken care of both of us."

We had some help on the civil rights front from the Church. Father Philip Hannan, whom we had known well in Washington, was sent to New Orleans as archbishop that year, and Hale and I were pleased that we would be able to enjoy his company and counsel, even though he would no longer be in the capital. He wasted no time making a profound impact on New Orleans. Organized white resistance to integration and other rights initiatives in New Orleans had resulted in a great deal of anger and animosity between the races and Archbishop Hannan immediately became involved in efforts toward peaceful integration and outreach to all of the city's varied communities, as well as working to achieve better housing for the poor and for the elderly.

Soon we needed additional enlightened leadership from the Church.

When Cokie and Steven began planning their wedding, it took some doing because Cokie is a Catholic and Steven is Jewish. Each of them talked to the bishop in Washington, who assured them that they could be married in the Catholic parish church and that Steven's family rabbi could help to officiate. I was pleased that the rules of the church had relaxed and that a person could be married in church to someone of another faith and have their own minister or rabbi at the altar with the priest. As a proud Catholic, I was also pleased to be able to show others that the church was ecumenical, opening its loving doors.

One day Cokie asked, "Could we be married in Daddy's garden?"

I recounted my feelings about how wonderful it would be to show the people at the wedding that this great new ecumenical day had dawned.

She said, "All that's very nice, but Grandpa Abe wouldn't be caught dead in a Catholic church."

Later I asked Hale if he would talk to the archbishop about having the wedding at our house. Hale said, "No. If I talk to the archbishop, you'll always think that the decision was made by my persuasiveness. If the archbishop decides it for Cokie and Steve on their own, you'll think it was the working of the Holy Spirit."

Once the garden wedding was approved, we began working toward the big day, September 10, 1966. Steven's family rabbi couldn't come, and we weren't sure what to do until Steve's mother said, "The rabbi is really there just to give a blessing." That's true of the Catholic ceremony, too: The priest is there only to witness the sacrament between the bride and groom.

A revered Jewish leader would be as acceptable as a rabbi, an adviser in the Jewish faith agreed, and after consultations among Steven's family and ours, Arthur Goldberg was the unanimous choice. Cokie and Steve would be married to each other, witnessed by Father Robbie Boggs and UN Ambassador Arthur Goldberg.

It was an enchanted evening. Besides Cokie and Steve's friends and his family's guests, Hale had invited President Johnson and his family and many friends in Congress, the diplomatic corps, and the cabinet and the courts. He felt that so many people were coming anyway, what difference could a few dozen more make? We had a huge tent for the ceremonies, illuminated by chandeliers laden with cascades of garden flowers. After the ceremony the space was turned into a dance floor. Another tent was erected over the patio, where a buffet was served. Little Hale's younger sister, Elizabeth, who was almost four, was in the wedding, along with Barbara and Stacia Stouse, Cokie's goddaughter, my cousin Dinky's daughter. Cokie's friends were ribbon bearers, lining the aisles in their pretty white dresses. We built a beautiful little platform under the apple trees, and flowers were blooming over the trellis.

Little Hale, who was almost five, was the ring bearer. His mother had loosely tied the wedding rings to a satin pillow so that Cokie and Steve wouldn't have any problem releasing them. Little Hale had started down the aisle with the pillow when the ribbons slipped out and the rings fell to the ground. The poor little fellow was horrified. Steve's mother, Dorothy, and I were seated in the front, and we didn't know what was going on. We began to think that maybe the bride and groom had changed their minds until someone came and told us of the problem.

People offered their rings as substitutes for the service, but Cokie wouldn't be married with any other ring than Steve's. The wedding was held up while everyone searched. Finally one of President Johnson's Secret Service agents borrowed the little flashlight the president's doctor always carried, and he got down on all fours and crawled around, peering through the grass until he found the rings.

CHAPTER THIRTEEN

***

HALE AND I supported the administration's conduct of the Vietnam War, but Barbara and Cokie were noisily antiwar, and they argued vehemently with their father. I don't think anyone ever won the arguments, but both sides certainly made their positions known.

Tommy was not as noisy as the girls, but he, too, wished we were not involved and that we would get out of Vietnam as soon as possible. By the summer of 1967, he and Barbara had three children, Douglas having been born in February. Barbara and Paul had two sons: Paul IV, born in 1964, and David, fifteen months younger. Paul didn't feel as strongly antiwar as Steve did, nor was he as vulnerable to the draft, but he was philosophically against it. We all had friends or children of friends in the war.

Hale and I felt that the Johnson administration was trying its best to end the war in the most expeditious and honorable way. People had expected that if we went into Vietnam it was not going to take us very long to finish and come home, but we were restrained from doing heroic deeds there. We were facing the Soviet Union and China and the nuclear bomb. The Soviets were frightened of us and China, China was frightened of us and the Soviet Union, and we were frightened of the Soviet Union and China.

The antiwar movement grew along with the civil rights movement, and with the "black power" movement that had branched off from civil rights.

As the war intensified, so did draft evasion, protest, and urban black riots so violent that some were quelled only by paratroopers or National Guardsmen.

In 1967, 475,000 U.S. troops were in Vietnam, and we were routinely bombing North Vietnam and firing into Cambodia and demonstrations against the war were attracting hundreds of thousands at home. That fall Senator Eugene McCarthy, a Democrat from Minnesota, launched an antiwar campaign for the presidency.

At the end of January 1968 came the debacle of the Tet Offensive, with coordinated massive attacks by North Vietnam and the Vietcong against the South Vietnamese and our troops in Saigon and thirty other cities during the thirty-six hour cease-fire declared by the U.S. and Saigon in recognition of the Tet (Lunar New Year) religious observance. The ease and effectiveness with which the attack was carried out undermined the belief that the U.S. military was close to a victory in Vietnam.

In mid-March Senator McCarthy narrowly missed defeating President Johnson in the New Hampshire presidential primary — the first in the nation. A few days later Senator Robert Kennedy of New York announced his candidacy for the Democratic presidential nomination as an antiwar candidate. Both he and Senator McCarthy wanted U.S. troops to be withdrawn unilaterally from Vietnam and brought home.

Gene McCarthy and his wife, Abigail, were Bradley Boulevard neighbors and close friends; during the week Gene and I would often attend early Mass at Our Lady of Lourdes Church in Bethesda together. In addition to our many mutual political endeavors, Gene and Abigail hit many respondent chords with Hale and me philosophically, intellectually, and religiously. When Gene was in the House, he and Hale had collaborated on many programs that came before them on Ways and Means. Abigail and I worked together in the Mothers' Club at the Sacred Heart Convent School our daughters attended, at the Woman's National Democratic Club, and in a host of Washington philanthropic endeavors.

In a televised address to the nation two weeks later, President Johnson announced a reduction in the bombing of North Vietnam—a demand of the antiwar groups—and he invited North Vietnam to join the United States in actively seeking peace. He then shocked everyone by saying he would not seek or accept the Democratic nomination for another term as president.

Devastated when I first heard his announcement, I was then swept with dismay and disbelief. I was in Tennessee to address the state Democratic women, and they had come together, liberals and conservatives, in a resolution that backed President Johnson in his conduct of the war and his attempts to achieve peace. I was taking their resolution back to Washington to him, and I knew he would be pleased. It was then that I heard the news.

At first I was afraid that it meant his heart condition had worsened. He had endured so much already, pounded by the Vietnam protests and the defection of friends and cohorts like Senator McCarthy. He had weathered most of the storm and was on a course that would pull us out of Vietnam. I felt that all his programs still needed his guidance.

I liked Bobby Kennedy a great deal. I always felt that Bobby and I were in more or less similar positions with our "stars," my husband, Hale, and his brother Jack. We were their organizers, their buffers against criticism. Bobby was an excellent planner, organizer, and expediter.

Gene had been terribly disappointed when Johnson didn't choose him to be his vice presidential running mate in 1964, and his defection from the mainstream Democratic Party wrapped itself into the Vietnam War. Although I wasn't in agreement with his presidential campaign, I became the beneficiary of a welcome campaign gift from Abigail. At the conclusion of the grueling presidential race, in an effort to literally "wash [the whole thing] right out of her hair," Abigail changed her hair color and gave me an exquisite human-hair wig whose color exactly matched my own. It had been given to her by thoughtful hairdressers to accommodate the occasional "no hairdresser time" schedule of the campaign.

With President Johnson's support, Vice President Humphrey entered the presidential race as a clear alternative to the antiwar candidates.

A few days after the president's surprise announcement, the Reverend Martin Luther King Jr., was assassinated in Memphis, Tennessee, where he was helping to settle a garbagemen's strike. Dr. King had been a favorite of the older black ministers in New Orleans, who were proud that the organizers of the SCLC had met and elected him their chairman in the Reverend A. L. Davis's Mount Zion Church in New Orleans. Many members of the black community who were good friends of Hale's and mine were fond of Martin, as they always called him, and inclined to think of him as a bright star.

In the turbulent days following Dr. King's murder, our house was again filled with fervent young sympathizers, including some who had been arrested and released from jail through Hale's intercession. Those who were not totally discouraged by King's death became dedicated civil rights workers in Mississippi and throughout the South, and they continued to check in to our accommodations for their rest-and-recreation visits. Each time I heard reports of murders, beatings, and total property destruction in the South, I felt a lump in my throat and a tear at my heart. *What if it's one of ours this time?* I feared.

Washington was one of the one hundred U.S. cities affected by riots in the wake of Dr. King's death. The annual Cherry Blossom

Festival was under way, and Hale's niece Sally, the daughter of Archie and Sally Boggs, the Louisiana Cherry Blossom Princess, was staying at our house. Hale was off making a speech, and Sally and I were watching the television news. When they said Dr. King had been killed, I didn't want to believe it. All I could say was, "No! No! No!"

Although many festival activities were canceled, the next day we were on our way to a reception at the Congressional Club when a couple of teenagers carrying big bags of clothing ran across the street right through the traffic. We were two blocks from Fourteenth Street, the location of the most severe trouble, and with a shock I realized that those teenagers were looters. It was an awful situation. The police—unaccustomed to such vicious rioting—were horrified, not frightened but surprised, at the intensity of the mobs.

Once we were safely inside the Congressional Club and we were told of the rioting and looting, I was concerned about the young people with us. I was not unaware that serious riots, deliberately planned, could erupt near our clubhouse. We were fortunate that we suffered no serious consequences. We all stayed calm, and the rioters kept their distance.

A week after Dr. King's death, Congress passed a civil rights bill that opened the doors of housing to all races. Owners of apartments and houses were ordered to offer most of their rental and sale properties to everyone, regardless of race. As a longtime advocate of decent housing, Hale thought the Fair Housing Law was necessary for the nation to move forward. Although he expected voters to understand that it was a vote of his conscience if not of his constituency, many of them did not.

Voting rights had been a more abstract subject. Most people didn't think it would affect them directly if everyone could vote, but housing was personal. Private property was private enterprise, and people felt threatened by a law that said, "You are required to do this." (New Orleans had long had its own "open housing," especially in the French Quarter and the adjacent Tremé section, where blacks and whites lived harmoniously, but it had not been forced on anyone.)

In May Vietnam peace talks were convened in Paris, but no substantive talks could begin until delegates agreed on the shape of the conference table. Meanwhile the presidential campaign season heated up with Humphrey, Robert Kennedy, and McCarthy competing for Democratic primary votes. McCarthy was encouraged by a victory over Kennedy in Oregon, but then Kennedy began to win consistently. He collected more than 50 delegate votes in four primaries and swept to victory in early June in California, where he won 174 delegate votes. After celebrating the important victory with his cheering supporters, who filled a Los Angeles hotel ballroom, he was fatally shot minutes later.

I was horrified by his death. How much sorrow could the Kennedy family endure? I had trouble believing it, and I think all of us wondered when the awful acts of violence against our leaders would end. Bobby would have been a formidable candidate.

When the Democrats met to choose a president in August 1968 at the International Amphitheater in Chicago, Hale was the chairman of the platform committee of possibly the most contentious, disruptive political convention in modern times. It was not the ideal time nor place for keeping cool.

Telephone workers and bus drivers were on strike. Hundreds of radical young people were holding a "Festival of Life" in Lincoln Park. Demonstrators for Black Liberation, Students for a Democratic Society, and the Committee to End the War in Vietnam congregated in Grant Park. Police, soldiers, and National Guardsmen were on duty everywhere as Mayor Richard Daley's security forces tried to protect the delegates, officers of the convention, and the safety of demonstrators as well.

However, confrontations between law enforcement authorities and demonstrators outside the Hilton Hotel convention headquarters and in the parks became angry and muscular, while smaller clashes between security personnel and delegates or members of the media flared up at the convention hall and during demonstrations. I felt sorry for both groups—the young people protesting the war and those protecting the delegates and trying to impose order.

Even though the parks and the Hilton were miles from the convention site, many people watching on television thought that the demonstrators were in the amphitheater. Because of the communications strike, few television cameras were used; and whenever one was set up, crowds converged making it appear to viewers as though there was total bedlam in the hall.

Hale had held platform hearings in several cities prior to the convention, and a great deal of the attention focused on lowering the voting age from twenty-one to eighteen. Young people were being inducted into the armed services and sent to Vietnam, but they weren't yet able to vote. Hale didn't think it was fair; a majority of his committee's witnesses agreed.

The Reverend Jesse Jackson, an articulate and persuasive young black spokesman; Marion Barry, an attractive local youth leader, and the entertainers Sonny and Cher were among those testifying in Washington in favor of a lower voting age. Jackson, who brought a group of young people with him, had told those kids, "You have to register for the draft. We're going to give you the right to register to vote to give you power over where the army is going to send you."

I had known Marion Barry for several years, since the civil rights migration hit Washington in the late fifties. I was a board member of Family and Child Services, and we suddenly had to try to integrate thousands of people into a city that didn't have enough housing, public transportation, school systems, or utilities to accommodate them, and that lacked industrial opportunities for training unskilled, uneducated labor. None of the city's resources could absorb the huge numbers of people who came from other parts of the country, particularly from the South, thinking of the capital of the United States as Shangri-la.

Barry formed an organization of young people called Pride, Inc., and he taught them that the way to succeed was through honest work for a good wage commensurate with their skills, staying on the straight and narrow, and developing themselves educationally and athletically. His kids were impressive when they came to the hearing in their neat, white uniforms.

Secretary of State Dean Rusk testified on Vietnam, and he provided the most dramatic moment of the platform hearings in Washington when he was called from the witness table to receive a message from the White House notifying him that Russian troops and tanks had invaded Czechoslovakia. He cut short his testimony to hurry to a meeting with the president. We were stunned and upset by the news. The "Prague Spring" of liberalization had seemed to be a positive sign for the future of Czechoslovakia and other countries within the Communist sphere.

Hale held his last hearings in Chicago, where a group of welfare mothers and women from the housing projects testified. They were revved up to talk about various welfare and public housing reforms they wanted passed, and it appeared this was the first time most of them had ever participated in anything vaguely resembling a national hearing.

I'm sure some of the black women knew Hale was a Southerner, and when they came into the hearing room and saw him in his white linen suit reminiscent of the plantation owner's attire in the Old South, they were immediately confrontational. It was a fairly small room without enough places to sit until Hale told an aide that no one should stand and to find extra chairs for the ladies. That helped to eliminate the antagonistic feelings, and everything went smoothly.

The Chicago telephone strike limited Hale to one house phone and only one outside telephone line in our hotel suite, which made it almost impossible for him to conduct business in a normal way among the 110 members of his committee. Other officers of the convention were similarly restricted, and the convention center itself could provide only limited telephone communications. (This was before the present-day capabilities of computerization, cellular phones, and communications satellites.)

This lack of easy access to communications greatly inhibited the running of all phases of the convention and diminished the availability of comprehensive television coverage.

The biggest platform battle came over the Vietnam War and how the United States ought to end its participation. This was the major issue that had drawn the demonstrators to Chicago and caused Mayor Daley to call out the troops.

The delicate problem of trying to work out the party's Vietnam position was so critical in its implications that Hale felt that the only way to get a good compromise was to hold private sessions. At one of these Argyll Campbell, one of his longtime congressional aides, discovered a microphone hidden in the hearing room, an intolerable intrusion that engendered increased anger among the various committee members. Subsequently Hale's committee sued the television network responsible for planting it, but the suit was later withdrawn.

The question of how to end the war carved divisions within the party and between the presidential candidates. Vice President Humphrey rejected unilateral withdrawal and adopted the president's position that deescalation of the war was contingent on South Vietnam's ability to conduct more of the war itself. We would stop bombing North Vietnam only when doing so would not endanger the lives of our own troops, and taking into account the response from Hanoi, Humphrey said.

Senator McCarthy, who had picked up many followers of the late Senator Kennedy, demanded an unconditional halt to the bombings, to be followed by the withdrawal of all foreign troops from Vietnam. The war was costing billions of dollars that should be spent at home, he said, and it was causing irreparable damage to the country.

On the eve of the convention, Hale was summoned to the White House. Majority Leader Carl Albert, the permanent convention chairman, and Senator Jennings Randolph of West Virginia, a proadministration member of Hale's committee, also were called. President Johnson showed them a telegram from General Creighton Abrams Jr., U.S. commander in Vietnam, which said that halting the bombing of North Vietnam would help the enemy and that a Vietcong offensive might be imminent. The generals were also saying they couldn't make the sacrifices that were required in Vietnam unless they had strong backing from the government.

The convention fell behind its timetable, and not until after midnight on the second night did Hale begin the presentation of the platform. Each side would have one hour to speak on the Vietnam War plank, and he read the majority, proadministration position members of his committee had chosen over the doves' position by a vote of sixty-five to thirty-five.

I was on the podium near Chairman Albert, who was suffering with a bad cold and laryngitis, a high temperature, and stopped-up ears. An air-conditioning unit was humming loudly and blowing on him, further complicating his health problems and his ability to hear the delegates. The Illinois delegation, with Mayor Daley as its chairman, was seated directly in front of the podium, the customary place for the host delegation.

It was too late for prime-time television coverage, which the McCarthy people especially had wanted in order to gather more support, and delegates were worn out from the long day. Far back in the room was seated the strongly antiwar Wisconsin delegation, and after a while its chairman, Don Peterson, stood up and moved for adjournment. Albert denied the motion. Other delegates began yelling, "Cut off the debate! Cut it off!" and they began chanting, "Let's go home! Let's go home!"

Albert couldn't hear well, and he couldn't understand what they were saying. He looked down at Daley and asked, "What are they saying?" And Daley replied, "They're saying, 'Cut off debate.' " Television caught the picture of Mayor Daley giving Albert the cutoff sign, a lasting image but one that gave the wrong impression. He was not dictating the closing down of debate; he was interpreting the message that everybody thought it should be ended. The chairman cut it off, and the session was over.

Hale tried to do everything he could to bring about compromises between the McCarthy ranks and the administration position, but he failed. If there hadn't been a communications strike, he felt that positions could have been discussed informally over the phone and there wouldn't have been so many confrontations between the opposing views. His attempts at compromise might have succeeded if there had been more conversation, more discussion.

Three hours were given to the Vietnam debate the following afternoon, and just before the issue was put to the convention vote, Hale told the delegates of the telegram from General Abrams. Then he said that no compromise was permissible on the Vietnam War plank: Delegates would vote for the administration position or for the minority position. The administration side won.

The platform was one of the most liberal documents ever passed, especially in the areas of lowering the voting age to eighteen; universal health care; expansion of educational opportunities; protection of the environment, both natural and human-made; greater coverage of workers by the minimum-wage law and equitable pay scales in the workplace; the creation of a federal welfare system especially to benefit needy dependent children regardless of where they live; and assuring the civil rights of all persons under a government that is responsive and compassionate and committed to justice and the rule of law, but much of this went unnoticed as all attention was focused on Vietnam.

The convention chose Humphrey as its presidential nominee, and he selected Senator Edmund Muskie of Maine as his running mate. We had known Humphrey since he was a graduate student at LSU, and he and his wife, Muriel, were good friends of ours. He and Hale were in the congressional leadership together when Humphgrey was the Senate majority whip, and I served in many organizations with his sister, Frances Howard, who was extremely capable and hardworking and a prime mover behind the creation of the African Museum of Art in Washington.

As expected, Richard Nixon was the Republicans' candidate. George Wallace, the former Alabama governor, ran as the nominee of the American Independent Party, on a platform against school integration and for law and order.

I always had compassion for George Wallace, who started out with great concern for his people and strong ideas about economic progress. I think he was caught in a situation that was bigger than he was. If he hadn't been as relatively liberal as he was perceived to be when he started out, I don't think the disappointment in him would have been so strong, but some people felt that he was turning on his own beliefs when he became a strong segregationist.

At the end of October, President Johnson ordered an end to the bombing of North Vietnam as a step toward a peaceful settlement of the war. A week later Nixon won the presidency; Humphrey took fourteen states, while Wallace carried five.

I still think it's a shame that Humphrey didn't win that election. If McCarthy hadn't broken with him and Wallace hadn't run, he would have won easily. I always believed that he had the ability and the heart to have concluded the Vietnam War sooner—and in a different way. We never would have had Watergate and the fall of the president and the attitude of distaste they left behind about the federal government. The country's social services agenda would have been well advanced, and we would have had peaceful cooperation throughout much of the world.

On the other hand a Democratic administration might not have been able to reach out to China as Nixon later did. It was a great deal easier for a Republican, especially one who had been bitterly anti-Communist, to accomplish.

Any third-party candidacy plays havoc with the natural progression of the electoral process. This disturbed me, too, about the Ross Perot candidacy in 1992, when there was much speculation about what a strong third-party candidate would do to a close presidential election and what would happen if the election were thrown into the House of Representatives.

I cannot imagine the ramifications of a presidential vote going to the House these days. When the election of 1800 resulted in a tie between Thomas Jefferson and Aaron Burr, the House endured five days of balloting with a weekend intervening—you can surmise the maneuvering that would go on these days—and my ancestor, Congressman William Charles Cole Claiborne, held Tennessee for Jefferson.

President Jefferson rewarded him first by appointing him territorial governor of Mississippi and then by sending him to oversee the transfer of the Louisiana Purchase. He stayed on as territorial governor of Louisiana, and when Louisiana became a state, he was elected its first governor. Later, when he was forty-two years old, he was elected to the Senate from Louisiana but died before he could be seated. Thus the historic Jefferson-Burr electoral college tie for the presidency helped to establish the Claiborne family presence in Louisiana.

We returned home worn out by the Chicago convention. Hale had two months to campaign for reelection, and for the first time in twenty-six years he faced a very stiff race. His chairmanship of the platform committee, which supported the administration's Vietnam policy, had cost him the enthusiasm of the liberals who ordinarily would have been behind him, and his vote for open housing had provoked the ire of conservative supporters.

Not even his speech for the Voting Rights Act had stirred so much negative feeling in Louisiana as did his vote for the Fair Housing Law. Before he cast that vote, he had no viable opposition of any importance. Shortly thereafter both Democratic and Republican opponents came after him.

The Second District had become more conservative over the years, and Hale's politics were too liberal for suburbs like Metairie, where people had moved from other parts of the South, lured by space-industry jobs at the Michoud plant or at Kaiser Industries— installations Hale had been instrumental in establishing. We knew that non-native suburban voters tended to be more conservative than the locals on issues of health, education, and welfare.

To follow population shifts the legislature had reapportioned Hale's district in 1960 and again effective with the 1968 election. First we lost Saint James Parish, where I'd taught school and we always got 95 percent of the vote; then we lost Saint John the Baptist Parish. We were left with Saint Charles, Jefferson, and part of Orleans Parishes, and Hale won the Democratic primary.

One of the brightest spots of our personal year came in October, when Cokie and Steve's first child, Lee Harriss Roberts, was born. Then it was on to the general election, in which Hale faced his Republican opponent, Dave Treen, an intelligent and aggressive young lawyer from Metairie who had run against him twice before. During this presidential election year, Treen was well financed by the national Republican Party and well armed with attacks on Hale's support of administration spending and the Great Society program. Treen contrasted Hale's open housing vote with the "no" votes by the rest of the Louisiana delegation.

Hale's campaign was also well financed, and it was supported by most of the Democratic factions. Besides support from the black community, he counted on the strong backing of organized labor through the state AFL-CIO, which was led by Vic Bussie and his wife, Fran, outstanding advocates for the poor and the disadvantaged and among the first who organized to work with us when Hale went to Congress.

A longtime family friend of ours, Dr. Alton Oschner of the Oschner Foundation, was Treen's campaign chairman. Hale enjoyed telling rallies that he had obtained millions of dollars in federal grants for the Oschner Hospital and that he knew Dr. Oschner would continue to call on him for help after the election, and he would continue to deliver. The anecdote underlined his service through seniority: "Boggs Delivers" was his campaign slogan.

Hale was reelected—by the smallest margin of his career. He beat Treen by three thousand votes for a 51 percent majority. The vote was so close that I cautioned Hale against going to the television stations to claim victory until the returns from certain key precincts were announced. It had been a very tough year.

In late November we received welcome diversion from the grueling experiences of the convention and campaign by a trip we took with our close friends from Louisiana, Gillis Long, Hale's Congressional colleague, and his smart, interesting wife, Cathy, and Ham Richardson, a world-famous tennis player, and his beautiful wife, Ann. We stopped first in London for the Davis Cup Tournament and then intended going directly to Moscow. However, our flight was delayed by bad weather, so we added a stopover in Copenhagen to see our good friends Angie and Robin Duke. He was the U.S. Ambassador, and his chief of staff, Angie Novella, a longtime assistant to Bobby Kennedy.

Because we would be prohibited from changing dollars in Russia, we were required to buy coupons ahead of time in the United States to be used to pay for hotels, food, transportation—everything except purchases we might make in the private "dollar stores." And now that we were behind schedule, we had fewer days in Russia than we had anticipated, and we ended up with about four extra days of coupons.

We flew into Moscow from Copenhagen quite late at night, and the Russian bureaucrats at the end of their shift at the airport were not happy to see six Americans arriving. Gillis had a problem with his credentials, which delayed us, and we were glad when we reached the Europa, an elegant old hotel that had a faded glory—a seediness peculiar to old, beautiful places. Hale and I went to our suite, which was large and had a beautiful sitting room. We were feeling most fortunate to have such accommodations when Ham and Ann came knocking at our door. Ham said, "They mixed up our accommodations. We have your suite. Come see it and we'll switch."

Their living room was as big as a ballroom and filled with cherubs on the mirrors and wall scones, captured in stone statues and ornamenting the enormous chandelier. Hale took one look and said to Ham, "You better stay here. You can chase Ann around this big room a lot better than I could chase Lindy."

Early the next morning I heard someone walking around in our suite. I went into the living room, where I encountered a man setting the clock. He finished, passed me with a nod, and went out the door. At luncheon that day at the American Embassy, I told the story to the ambassador and he began laughing.

"He didn't come to fix the clock," he said. "He came to activate the microphone." That was good news to me. From then on I would say, "We've been waiting for our tea for an hour," and in ten minutes, a knocking at the door would announce its arrival. We also had people assigned to follow us who were so conspicuous that one day Hale pointed at the man on duty and said, "Couldn't we offer that poor guy a drink?"

I went to visit our son-in-law Steven Roberts's great-aunt in her Moscow apartment and our Intourist guide, a cultured woman, fluent in several languages, escorted us as far as the door. She must have checked out the family and been assured there wouldn't be anything subversive between the U.S. official and the Russian citizens because when we arrived, she refused to go in. I said, "You come too," but she said, "Oh, no, it's your family."

There were four apartments with a communal kitchen, but Steve's relatives also had a small space within their apartment for cooking. A bookcase and a piano were arranged to partition off the main room and create privacy in what was a very limited area.

French was the neutral language I used with the great-aunt, a lovely woman and the matriarch of a handsome family. Her grandchildren, a girl and a boy, came directly from school to the apartment and apparently spent a good deal of time there. They were bright and interesting; the little girl had won silver skates in ice-skating competition. When their aunt, the daughter-in-law, arrived she must have thought we were oldtime Southern politicians, because she defiantly started playing "The Battle Hymn of the Republic" on the piano. When I joined in, singing lustily, she was astonished. She was a scientist and a good Party member, but she relaxed and seemed to enjoy our visit.

Our last stop was Leningrad, since renamed Saint Petersburg again, where we caught the train to Helsinki. On boarding, we were required to give our passports and Russian exit documents to the top official in our rail car. Then, having an excess of coupons and nowhere else to spend them, we treated ourselves to a feast of caviar and champagne and went to bed.

In the middle of the night armed guards burst through the locked doors of our compartment. Hale was soundly asleep, looking very innocent in his baby blue pajamas. I awakened and said, "What's the problem?" but the guards insisted on waking Hale and talking to him. They kept waving an official-looking paper at us.

He reluctantly woke up, "Lin, what do these people want?" he asked somewhat testily.

I couldn't tell exactly, but I thought he had filled out something wrong on our official documents. I turned to the man who seemed to be in charge, and using sign language and English I asked him to show me what the problem was.

The minute he showed me, I realized what had happened. We were supposed to take only a limited amount of dollars into Russia, which we declared, and then they required that we declare how many dollars we were taking *out* of the country.

We had arrived in Russia with a thousand dollars, and we were leaving with five hundred, but Hale had made his dollar sign in a hurry and instead of two vertical lines down through the *S*, his second line was to the right of the dollar sign and it looked like a *1*. The result was that it appeared we were leaving with fifteen hundred whereas we'd only declared a thousand on entering. I showed the guards other specimens of his handwriting, and I drew the mistake for them. They said, "Oh, oh," and they left. I think the whole incident was just a way to let them assert authority over a U.S. official.

I went back to sleep, and when I awakened Hale wasn't there. I knew I couldn't have slept through the return of the guards, but I didn't know where on earth he was. I changed from my nightgown into a dress and went out searching. I didn't have far to go. He and the conductor were sitting at the end of the car with a big samovar of piping hot tea in front of them. They were drinking tea and yakking away, one in English, the other in Russian, having the best old time.

Despite the difficulties we never regretted the stands Hale took in the sixties. They were difficult years but proud ones—we felt we had accomplished something important borne out of personal commitment and experience.

A couple of years later Hale and I took our grandson Hale on a car trip out West, something neither of us had ever done. We went first to Winnetka, Illinois, for the wedding of Nancy Davis, the daughter of Jean and Charlie Davis, our annual garden party co-hosts, and then we continued across the country to Jackson Hole, Wyoming, to see the real West. We visited Cokie and Steve in California, where he was sent in 1969 as Los Angeles bureau chief for the *New York Times* and she was producing a children's television program, *Serendipity*. Then we headed down the Southern route to Texas and a visit with the Johnsons at their LBJ Ranch.

About six o'clock on the first morning, I heard a knock at the bedroom door. I answered and Lyndon said, "I knew you'd be awake and I knew Boggs wouldn't. Come on downstairs."

We ate breakfast by a window with a view of the ranch and the enormous Texas sky. He was proofreading the manuscript of his memoirs, and he shared with me a section on civil rights initiatives that he had put in personal terms, describing the problems that were presented to a white person driving through the South with children and a black nurse before the civil rights laws of the 1960s. All those years driving back and forth to Washington, the Johnsons had done the same things we had, suffering the same frustrations, disappointments, and anger for the ones with them who were being slighted. I was proud that he too had included the experiences he had known in that regard and that he had paid tribute to the influence of those women.

CHAPTER FOURTEEN

❦

WHEN PRESIDENT NIXON presented himself as the tax-
payers' defender against the Democratic Congress in a "war on inflation," he was following an old tradition.

Our presidents often depict themselves as trying to save the
people from Congress or the Supreme Court or both, as President
Nixon did with his vetoes of congressional bills and his support for
a constitutional amendment barring the busing of schoolchildren to
promote desegregation. The Founding Fathers deliberately created
tension between the three branches of government, giving them
separate powers but adding a system of checks and balances to
make them interdependent.

Each president has his own style of working with Congress.
President Kennedy had regular Tuesday breakfast meetings with
the leadership, while President Johnson—a longtime member of
the congressional leadership—had a much more hands-on connection with frequent meetings at the White House, not only with the
leadership but also with key committee members of both parties.
President Nixon met irregularly in more formal meetings, usually
only with the Speaker and House majority leader and the top two
leaders of the Senate; his meetings didn't extend to the whips or to
other officers.

Congress itself was changing: In January 1969 Shirley Chisholm, a New York Democrat who was an expert in early-childhood education, took her place as the first black woman elected to the House of Representatives, where she became an advocate for the urban poor. Senator Edward Brooke, a Republican from Massachusetts, which he had served as attorney general, was already two years into his term as the first black U.S. senator in eighty-five years.

Early in 1969 U.S. troop strength in Vietnam peaked at more than 540,000. While Hale continued to support the administration, we were both relieved when President Nixon began a gradual withdrawal of our forces, thereby initiating a "Vietnamization" of the war—turning over major participation to the South Vietnamese military. Nevertheless, antiwar demonstrations continued.

President Nixon turned out to be less conservative than people had generally assumed, and some of his programs were similar to those put forth by Democratic administrations. The most comprehensive tax reform ever undertaken and a tax reduction highlighted his first year in office, when Congress also passed, and he signed, a national environmental policy act that laid the groundwork for future standards and regulations, and a housing and urban development act that required that a new low-income dwelling be built for each one razed in urban renewal projects.

Hale was often the Democratic spokesman against the President's programs that were in opposition to the Democratic agenda, but he was also a leader in rallying Democratic support for those of the president's bills that he thought would help the nation, such as an income tax surcharge. This support left him open to criticism by disgruntled, more liberal colleagues, which he was willing to endure and to recognize that such liberal opposition could help him at home.

In 1970, as the antiwar mood spread, Congress repealed the Gulf of Tonkin resolution, and Senate resolutions were passed to limit future U.S. military action in Southeast Asia.

In any event, Hale sailed through the 1970 congressional election, defeating his Republican opponent with almost 75 percent of the votes. For a time it looked as though he might not be the only Boggs in the House of Representatives: In the same elections Tommy ran for Congress from Montgomery County, Maryland. I would have been the happiest, proudest person in the country if they could have served together.

Various Democratic factions encouraged Tom to run, telling him that he was the only person who could unite the party in his district. It was the same encouragement Hale had so often received, and I had recognized in Tom his father's ability to pull people together. In some ways Tom combined it with a sort of toughness, by being able to knock heads together when necessary as well as getting people to talk to one another and listen to reason.

The minute Tommy's hat was in the ring, the factions began to fight among one another and to remind voters not only that Tommy was not a Maryland native but that his father was a congressman from Louisiana. All things considered it was phenomenal that he won the Democratic nomination.

The incumbent Republican, Gil Gude, a dedicated public servant, won the election and he and his wife, Jane, became my stalwart friends. When Gude decided to retire, he invited Tom to lunch and told him that of all the people he had encountered, he believed Tom could best represent the district. By then Tom had established himself as a fine lawyer who was helping his partners build a respected firm, and he was no longer interested in running for Congress.

I'm proud that Tom is an effective lobbyist as well as a respected lawyer; both are honorable professions. From the beginning of Congress, lobbyists have done a special job in conveying the interests and needs of various areas of our economic, political, and social life, so much so they are registered with Congress. The information they bring and the clients they represent are an integral part of our national fabric.

Tom works hard through the week in Washington but enjoys his weekend at the Eastern Shore of Maryland, an area of low coastal plains and marshlands that greatly resembles southern Louisiana. The goose-hunting season ended one day when I was there and the deer season began the next day. Douglas, their youngest child, was not quite five years old. I was worried that he would get up early in the morning and wander outside where some eager deer hunters might not see him; so I set my alarm clock to be up at four-thirty.

I was awake and alert to any little sounds, and as the dawn arrived, I heard shooting begin. I looked out of my window and was surprised to see a flock of geese peacefully lolling on the water as though nothing unusual was happening. When Tommy awakened, I remarked: "That's the most amazing thing I've ever seen. Just yesterday they were being hunted and today those geese are completely undisturbed by the gunfire. How on earth do they know?"

"Oh, Mother, they read the 'Posted' signs for the deer season."

Speaker McCormack announced that he would retire from the Congress in January 1971, and almost immediately a group of liberal Congressmen decided to challenge Hale for majority leader. They were convinced—correctly—that Carl Albert would become Speaker. They thought, however, that since the majority leader had advanced to the Speakership over the last several decades, the way to derail this ascendancy and put themselves in power was to win the majority leadership. They believed sincerely that they were going to break into the line and win a Democratic caucus election.

A few unhappy colleagues wondered whether Hale had been under so much pressure as a Southern Democrat taking a national position on such hot issues as civil rights that it had affected his ability to lead. It's true that he had been exposed to tremendous stress, but he could certainly lead and, more important, for Congress and the country, he was a consensus builder who could bring together people from various sections of the country.

Hale could be very charming and helpful, but like many people who are sometimes driven, he could also be brusque. I think that as he grew older and became more intense about what needed to be done in the Congress and the country, he became less patient with what he saw as the unrealistic demands some people placed on his time and energy. There was no doubt in my mind that he would be majority leader and, after Albert retired, Speaker of the House. If he hadn't run, particularly with some people saying he couldn't win, he wouldn't have had any faith in himself.

He didn't think that the job of majority leader meant he had to be unwavering as the loyal opposition against the Republican president. His job was to move the legislative programs ahead, to cooperate with the president or to disagree when he thought he was wrong. "Opposition for opposition's sake is obstructionism," Hale said, "and we are not obstructionists."

But even that attitude was criticized as old-fashioned by some younger House members, who favored more divergence. Although Hale was required to leave the Ways and Means committee to become majority leader, he was able to postpone that departure until after the decisive Democratic caucus vote for majority leader on January 19, 1971.

Congressman Morris ("Mo") Udall of Arizona, the most prominent and popular opposing candidate, was backed by organized labor and had supported a system of automatic pay raises for Congress. Other challengers were Bernie Sisk of California, a moderate who had the support of the large California delegation and some Southerners; Jim O'Hara of Michigan, who was considered very liberal and a friend of big labor and who later became associated with Tommy's law firm and was like a big brother to him; and Wayne Hays of Ohio, a moderate who headed the House Administration Committee, which oversees all the committees of the House and allots office space and parking privileges to members.

I don't think there was anything personal against Hale in their efforts as much as there was a desire to break into the leadership. I remained friends with all of them, leaning heavily on dear Mo, who had lost an eye in early adolescence and became a mentor to Barbara when she lost her eye to cancer.

What all of them failed to realize was that the House is a multifaceted organization, composed of many other aspects than merely one's attitude toward liberalism or conservatism. One of the groups that made up a large majority was big-city voters, and the problems of big cities are much the same in every state. Hale had been "Mr. Housing" since the 1940s, and he had actively promoted urban development, urban renewal, and aid to the cities. He was on Ways and Means, which meant that Democratic congressmen from all sorts of factional preferences owed their committee assignments to him, and during Hale's nine years as whip, we had personally welcomed the new members of every Congress and I had worked closely with the wives, trying to help the new families as we had been helped when we first arrived in Washington.

When it was time to vote on majority leader, big new cans, which were always used as ballot boxes, were brought into the House chamber and Democratic members marked their choices and dropped them in. Hale won the first tally, but he didn't win a majority of the votes, so there was a runoff. The winner needed 123 votes, and Hale won with 144. Udall received 88 and Sisk 17.

Representative Ed Edmondson of Oklahoma slipped out of the meeting to call me with the news: "I'm not supposed to be telling you this, but you deserve to know it more than those of us in the room." I was forever grateful to Ed and he was especially helpful to me during all of the years of his Congressional service.

I'll never forget the scene on the first floor of the Capitol at the same time as Hale and Ted Kennedy walked down that long hall. Teddy had lost his bid for reelection as Senate whip after serving just two years and he turned to Hale and said, "Hale, how do you do it?"

"Ted, it's simple. You count. One, two, three."

Even after Hale's election as majority leader, some controversy surrounded him—particularly when he took on the FBI.

Our generation had grown up thinking that J. Edgar Hoover and his Federal Bureau of Investigation were heroic Americans, especially after Mr. O. John Rogge was sent from the Department of Justice to help us in the early days of the People's League. When Hale was accused of being a Communist, his admiration of the FBI and Hoover was brought out in the hearings and court cases.

(When we first went to Washington, Lansing ["Tut"] Mitchell, who, with his wife, Virginia ["Beanie"], were among our dearest friends, was already in residence as an FBI agent. Tut went on to a distinguished judicial career, culminating with his service on the bench of the U.S. District Court for the Eastern District of Louisiana, where he now sits in senior status.)

Hoover's first quest had been Prohibition racketeers, and then the bureau concentrated on Communism, but by 1971 Hoover, who had been FBI director since 1924, appeared to be veering from this perception of his agency and his own reputation. Dissatisfaction was felt within the agency, and criticism of the bureau and its director was heard among the public. It began to seem that the FBI was focusing its attention on officeholders who demonstrated opposition to the White House, the FBI, or Hoover himself.

Stories of infighting filtered out of the bureau, a few even reaching the press. Hale had good friends within the bureau and, as frequently happens, some of them complained to him and to their other friends in Congress.

In the midst of this we were told by another friend that our home telephone was being monitored; a trusted acquaintance verified that for us and said that the eavesdropping could be ordered only by certain government investigative agencies.

Following Hale's assertion on the House floor that our phones were being tapped, I received a phone call one day from a man asking that I go to a pay phone to call him back. When I did, he advised that Hale's terminology was incorrect, because monitoring methods other than installed devices were being used. Consequently, Mr. Hoover could deny that a tap had been installed on Hale's phone or the phones of other members of Congress.

It was a matter of semantics: They weren't "installing a tap"; they were listening from outside with electronic devices. The caller said that the best way to interrupt the eavesdropping was to put running water between myself and the phone. Though I never knew if he was telling me the truth, I nonetheless abided by his suggestion: from then on I'd run the water in the sink whenever I used the kitchen phone.

That summer our son-in-law Paul took a sabbatical from Princeton to Cuernavaca, Mexico, in which he was joined by Barbara and their three sons—six-year-old Paul, five-year-old David and two-year-old Stevie. They rented a house that came complete with palm trees, a swimming pool, and several servants. Despite the fact that she was relaxing in that tropical luxury, Barbara realized that she could not find satisfaction in such a life. When they returned to Princeton, she joined a group of women developing female candidates for public office.

The electorate was changing: new, younger activist candidates were running for office and winning. Congress had finally passed a constitutional amendment lowering the voting age to eighteen, and after the required ratification by thirty-eight states, it had become the Twenty-sixth Amendment to the Constitution.

Instead of promoting someone else, the group unanimously chose Barbara as its candidate for the Princeton Borough Council. Barbara said once that when she needed to do something directly and head-on, she thought of her father, and when she wanted to accomplish something indirectly, more subtly, she thought of me. She called me to ask what I thought about her running.

I said she had a lovely home and family, civic work she found gratifying, and an important job teaching school. "Why on earth would you want to change such an attractive way of life?" I asked.

At that point Hale grabbed the phone. "Run!" he said. She did and she won handsomely.

A factor that helped to motivate many women toward political activity was a proposed Equal Rights Amendment (ERA), taken up by Congress early in 1972, which banned discrimination against women on the job and elsewhere because of their sex. Representative Martha Griffiths of Michigan, a crackerjack attorney who was on Ways and Means with Hale, asked him to sign on as a cosponsor of the ERA bill to ensure that it would be brought before Congress in case the committee with jurisdiction failed to hold hearings on it. To circumvent that possibility, a majority of the House was required to sign on as cosponsors to release the bill and keep it alive.

Hale said, "When you get two hundred and seventeen members, come back and see me." A simple majority was 218.

A few weeks later she returned. "Hale, is it going to be you or Jerry Ford [the Republican leader] who will be my two-hundred-eighteenth congressman?" Hale signed on with alacrity.

Many women I respected opposed the ERA, and there was serious opposition to it in the Second District, especially among some well-organized women's groups. Under the Napoleonic Code in Louisiana, men are responsible for the support of their women, first as the father and then as the husband, and many women were afraid the ERA would remove those economic safeguards. The code also affirms the wife's ownership of half of the community property and her right of usufruct over the other half on the death of her spouse; on the death of both parents all male and female children inherit equally. Despite those questions, I was a firm supporter of the amendment. I would have had the ghost of my Aunt Celeste to deal with otherwise.

The ERA was passed in March 1972, and many states ratified the amendment almost immediately. Only three more states needed to vote "yes" in order to achieve the required approval of three-fourths of the states for ratification, but suddenly there was a big push against the ERA. Even some states that had already ratified it wanted to rescind their ratification.

It was a curiosity to me that within state legislatures, the debates over the ERA, which unveiled and investigated the unequal situation of women, produced some significant corrections within those states. The debates engendered by the ratification process for the amendment became at once the catalyst for change and one of the causes of it not going ahead. If the conditions have been corrected, went the argument, what was the need for the ERA?

Because Hale had signed on as a cosponsor, most of the ERA opponents did not fault me for later continuing his work with my favorable participation in the debate on the amendment.

In addition to the fight for women's rights, the world was changing in other ways as well. After almost a quarter century of isolation from the United States and much of the free world, China opened its doors to President Nixon in 1972. Under the prevailing anti-Communist attitude in the United States, only a Republican president with a strong reputation for anti-Communism could have accomplished the breakthrough. Soon after his visit the Senate leaders, Majority Leader Mike Mansfield and Minority Leader Hugh Scott, went there with their wives, Maureen and Lucille.

Within a few weeks Hale, as House majority leader, and I, with House Minority Leader Jerry Ford and his wife, Betty, were given the exciting opportunity of a ten-day official visit. Hale and Jerry received State Department briefings on the political situation in China and her neighbors and the proper protocol to observe.

Betty arranged a special State Department briefing for the two of us about our responsibilities and expected code of conduct. One of our instructors was Day O. Mount who had accompanied the first gift pair of pandas from China to the Washington National Zoo, Ching Ching and Ling Ling. In exchange for the pandas, the United States had sent China a pair of musk oxen, Mathilda and Milton.

It's a terrible pun, but "panda-monium" had broken out in this country: Everybody was wild about the pandas. The Friends of the National Zoo organization was selling panda T-shirts and coffee cups, cuddle toys, key rings, cigarettes, and postcards—panda-everything-under-the-sun. Betty and I went to the zoo shop, bought something of everything panda, and took it all with us to China.

Our group included Mr. Mount from the State Department, our son-in-law Paul Sigmund; and Harry Lee, the federal magistrate in New Orleans, who was a husky Chinese-American over six feet tall, both of whom went as aides to Hale. Hale said he was taking Lee, a longtime friend, as his interpreter. Harry wisely waited until we were over the ocean to tell us that the only Chinese he could speak was "a little Cajun Cantonese."

Gary Hymel, Hale's capable, affable administrative assistant, was in our delegation, as was Eugene Theroux, special counsel to the Joint Economic Committee and longtime family friend. Jerry Ford's group included as an aide, Bryce Harlow, a former counselor to the president; Robert T. Hartmann, legislative assistant; Frank Meyer, administrative assistant; and Paul Miltich as press secretary. Rounding out the delegation were Dr. Freeman H. Cary, assistant attending physician to Congress, and William A. Brown, deputy director of the Office of Asian Communist Affairs in the State Department.

Betty and I had sent word to the Beijing Zoo director that we wished to visit him, and when we reached our hotel, an appointment was made for our day at the zoo. Meanwhile Hale and Jerry were engaging in extensive discussions with Premier Chou En-lai, discussing an agenda that ranged from the Vietnam War to trade to seeking the means for a normalization of relations between the United States and China. The shortage of television equipment, which they were told was customary, limited the coverage of their meetings.

However, television crews appeared when Betty and I went to the zoo. The cameras whirred away as we presented all our panda gifts to the delighted zoo director and told him how the people of our country had taken the pandas to their hearts. We posed petting Mathilda and feeding a bottle of milk to poor little Milton, who was molting. It was the biggest TV coverage of the trip, much more than Hale and Jerry had with their vital, high-level talks.

Everywhere we went we stayed in official guest houses, usually former monasteries or convents, behind whose walls we were contained and protected. With few exceptions we were kept isolated from the people and everyday life. Deng Xiaoping was in exile, and because there was not yet official recognition between our governments, we were guests of the Chinese People's Institute of Foreign Affairs, a quasi-governmental enterprise fostered by Chou.

Jerry Ford, who, as a representative from Michigan, was familiar with heavy industry, asked to see a steel mill, and we were all flown to the Anshan Iron and Steel Works in the Manchurian city of Shenyang, near the border with the USSR. As is usual in every country, the farther away we got from the capital, the more independence we found among the people and, in this case, the more divergence from a strict Communist party line.

Russians had built the mill with materials and of a design compatible with those they had built in Siberia, and they had taught the Chinese to run it. When the equipment and the techniques failed and the Russians went home, the Chinese adapted both to their own needs and conditions. Jerry said it used the most basic technology, but he was impressed by the work ethic of the men and women who worked side by side six days a week for salaries that ranged from eighteen to fifty-five dollars monthly. Small government apartments were rented to the workers for from two to five dollars monthly; nurseries and child care were available for a nominal price, and the workers' medical care was free.

When we learned that rice was being grown nearby in that cold Manchurian climate, we went to see the rice commune. Because of China's huge population—we were told that that commune alone consisted of twenty thousand persons—few machines were needed in the cultivation and harvesting of rice. I was fascinated by the workers' relative democratic independence, totally removed from life as we had seen it in Beijing. Worker housing resembled the quarters provided for field hands on the Louisiana plantations of my youth—individual little houses in a row, each with a small yard in which to grow a garden. The workers were allowed to keep chickens, ducks, and pigs, which gave them a much more plentiful food supply than many Chinese enjoyed.

I saw the "company store," a general supply store just like the old days on the plantation, where they obtained their provisions all year and paid their bill at harvesttime. A loudspeaker was installed in the middle of the housing area for official announcements, and there was a common hall for meetings, schools, nurseries, and medical facilities.

Men and women worked in the paddies and fields from sunrise until sundown, with a long break for lunch and a rest, and everyone shared in the profits, which were distributed according to individual efficiency. Workers were divided into teams, with each team member graded by fellow members on each day's work. One would say, "So-and-so didn't produce much today, and her score should be lower." Someone else would say, "But do you realize that she was sick and she didn't want to let the team down?" They would go back and forth until a fair score was reached. Individual grades were combined as team grades, with enormous competition among the teams to be the best.

At harvesttime the government was given a fixed percentage of rice, the commune kept what it needed, and the remainder was sold to the government to earn revenue to buy whatever equipment was needed by the commune. Money left after those purchases was divided among the members according to their individual grades.

We were scheduled to fly on to Shanghai but bad weather intervened, and we flew back to Beijing for an unscheduled, eye-opening experience. Throughout our stay security had been perfect and tight everywhere: Authorities would clear streets before we reached them, with the result that we usually traveled down streets totally devoid of people. Having chaired presidential trips, balls, and convention events, I was amazed and awed by their crowd control.

But when we arrived unexpectedly in the capital on a Sunday, we saw the normal conditions. There were huge crowds wherever we looked, thousands of pedestrians filling the sidewalks, thousands of bicyclists whirring down the streets. I had never seen such immense crowds. We went into a store and it was bedlam, with people crowding around to see us and others trying to go on their regular way. We could understand why, with the tentative kind of relationship that then existed between the United States and China, the government would be apprehensive about having official visitors subjected to what was for them the everyday give-and-take of the crowds.

When our hosts-guides inquired about our shopping preferences, I asked to find some pretty service plates. We braved the crowd, and our guides led us through the store. As I searched for a dozen matching plates, I realized there was no possibility of finding twelve alike. Hale said, "Don't you think it would be more interesting to have twelve different plates?" So that's what I bought, and I've always been thankful. Each large, colorful plate is more interesting and more beautiful by being different from the others.

I was also eager to find something of art or crafts to bring back. In the spirit of a new motto, China Did It Once—China Can Do It Again, the government had brought master craftspeople and artists, called "veteran workers," out of retirement to teach younger artists such traditional decorative skills as jade cutting, sculpture, cloisonné, and porcelain. The older ones thought they were in heaven, being able to use their abilities again and having them recognized as worthwhile after years of banishment under the hard-line Communists.

We were told that there were artists who were producing attractive paintings and etchings of horses, which had been a Communist no-no, banned for many years as an "imperial symbol." We learned they were surreptitiously being sold up several flights of stairs in a nondescript building, so we went to see them. Perhaps it was all a tourist trap, but I bought some paintings that I still enjoy.

Throughout our trip we were entertained at luncheon and dinner parties with food of great variety; beautifully presented in eleven or twelve courses. Hale kept musing about the absence of

Peking Duck, but we were not served it until Premier Chou En-lai hosted a formal dinner party in our honor in Beijing. Then the duck appeared: duck feet, duck neck, duck innards, duck skin, pieces of duck meat—dish after dish and all deliciously prepared. At the end of our hours-long meal, the premier leaned forward, smiled broadly, and said to Hale, "Enough Peking Duck?"

From China, Hale and I flew to the Democratic convention in Miami, traveling all night and changing planes in New York. I was relieved that I didn't have any responsibilities for the convention and, for a change, could attend as an interested observer. George McGovern, in his second term as senator from South Dakota, was the certain winner of the presidential nomination.

Hale and I had known Senator McGovern and his delightful wife, Eleanor, since he came to the House in 1956. He served two terms there, headed President Kennedy's Food for Peace program for one year, and was elected to the Senate in 1962. Following the 1968 convention, he was active in a successful drive to rewrite Democratic Party rules to open the party to more women, minorities, and young persons. The traditional bases of city political bosses, labor union chiefs, and elected and appointed officials were greatly reduced. As a sign of the change, Mayor Richard Daley of Chicago wasn't even a delegate in Miami.

Another initiative to open the party saw more states holding Democratic primary elections to choose convention delegates and to vote their presidential preferences. Senator McGovern used the state primaries to build enough strength to win the presidential nomination on the convention's first ballot. Neither former Vice President Humphrey nor the popular Senator Edmund Muskie of Maine had won enough primaries to remain in the race.

The platform supported amnesty for those who had refused to enter military service, busing of school students to foster racial integration, banning of handgun sales, and nondiscrimination because of an individual's lifestyle. Many moderate and conservative Democrats criticized it as being too liberal.

Disruption pervaded the convention, with serious divisions splitting almost every state delegation over whether to support Senator McGovern and which planks of the platform to approve. Some delegates were simply dissenters and protesters in general, unwilling to do anything for the party, while others made a serious effort to find compromise that would end the discord.

Senator McGovern's first choice as his vice presidential running mate was Senator Thomas Eagleton, the junior senator from Missouri, where he had also been lieutenant governor and attorney general. A scintillating personality and accomplished orator, he brought the cheering convention delegates to their feet with his acceptance speech, dissipating much of the acrimonious feeling that had characterized earlier convention sessions.

Unfortunately, when it was disclosed that Eagleton had undergone treatment for depression, McGovern was pressured to replace him. My disappointment at losing this attractive, highly qualified candidate from the ticket was assuaged when my good friend Sarge Shriver became McGovern's new selection for the vice presidential spot.

Hale made a wonderful address to the convention, telling the delegates about the dreary communal life we had seen in China and contrasting that with the kinds of opportunities, rights, and freedom we enjoy as a nation. The Democratic Party could regain national leadership if its members would unite and work together toward that goal, he said.

The convention's schedule was so delayed that McGovern didn't deliver his acceptance speech until three o'clock in the morning, which was fine with us because our body clocks were still reversed. Besides, Louisiana's delegation, which included several black delegates, had voted for Representative Shirley Chisholm of

New York for president—a great candidate and the only one on whom all of the state's delegates could agree.

We had all come a long way since the 1948 convention, when Southern delegations walked out because of a civil rights speech. Our Congress, our courts, and our presidents, who so often quarrel with one another, had opened to all races in the United States the right to vote, ride a bus, eat in a restaurant, see a movie, buy a house, go to school, be a delegate to a national political convention, and be nominated for president.

In the Republican National Convention proceedings, President Nixon and Vice President Agnew were nominated again, and the president's campaign slogan was "Peace with Honor." On October 10, the *Washington Post* carried an article alleging that President Nixon's special Committee to Re-Elect the President (CREEP) had tried repeatedly to disrupt the Democratic McGovern-Shriver campaign. With major dissension among the Democrats, a Nixon victory seemed assured even without the alleged Republican disruptions.

Firmly established as House majority leader, Hale drew no Republican opponent at all in his 1972 race. His easily won primary election was tantamount to election. Speaker Albert announced he would retire in 1978, and everyone assumed that Hale would be the next Speaker of the House, a well-deserved crowning achievement to his career.

Because he had no race of his own to fight, Hale was speaking on behalf of colleagues all over the country, as was I. From mid-October, when Congress was expected to adjourn, until Election Day three weeks later, we had accepted fifteen speaking engagements between us. Hale went down to Texas for a speech, and President Clinton later told me of the next day, when he, as a Young Democrat from Arkansas volunteering in the Texas campaign, drove Hale to the airport for his flight back to Washington.

As soon as the congressional session ended, Representative Nick Begich of Alaska, his wife Pegge, and Hale and I had planned a campaign trip to Alaska in Nick's behalf, and from there Hale and I were going to California. Hale had a high regard for Nick and wanted to help him. But as often happens, the Ways and Means bill wasn't finished on time, and everyone had to come back on Tuesday, October 17. Before Congress could adjourn, the Ways and Means bill had to be passed to fund the projects and programs that had been approved.

Over the weekend Hale and Nick went off on an abbreviated campaign swing through Alaska. Nobody told them good-bye because everybody knew they'd be back Tuesday morning. I stayed home in Washington, as did Pegge Begich. Hale spoke at a fund-raising dinner for Nick in Anchorage Sunday night.

He had tried to telephone me that afternoon, but my line was busy, and when he finally got through, I explained why: An important football game had coincided with a Southern station-wagon campaign on behalf of George McGovern's candidacy. Knowing that all the Southern governors were home watching the game, I turned on the television, and whenever a commercial came on, I phoned a governor to ask that he officially meet the campaigners.

Hale laughed at my ingenuity, then told me that he and Nick would attend a fundraiser in Juneau the next day, October 16, and then he would be home.

CHAPTER FIFTEEN

⌖

I WAS SITTING in the kitchen, working on correspondence while I waited to hear that Hale was on his way home to Bethesda. I often used the time when he was away to catch up on my various projects, and I enjoyed working at the big kitchen table where I could spread out my papers within easy reach of the phone and the television set. It was a comfortable, cheery room with a large open fireplace, and it smelled of spices and herbs. A bay window across the back wall looked onto Hale's garden, now covered with dry autumn leaves. Our little Cairn terrier Cody, a venerable gentleman, lay sleeping at my feet.

The warmth and stillness of the room made me drowsy, and I put my head down. When the phone rang it startled me. I realized I had been half asleep. Before I could pick up the phone, however, Cody began jumping up at me trying to keep me from answering it. He jumped up on the telephone table, something he'd never done in his life, and when I reached around him to answer the phone he tried to knock the receiver out of my hand.

"Hello," I said, half laughing at my little dog's antics.

It was the Speaker, Carl Albert, telling me that Hale's plane was missing. It had taken off from Anchorage and had never reached Juneau. No messages had been received from it, and it was long overdue. It had disappeared. The military had begun to search: One plane had been able to start before persistent fog had closed in again.

Carl would have preferred that Tommy tell me in person, but he couldn't locate Tommy and had run out of time. He wanted me to know before I heard it on the ten o'clock television news.

All I could say was, "Oh, Carl!" I didn't feel sorry for myself at first. I thought, *Poor Carl, what a terrible task for you to have to do.*

I immediately began trying to call our children. Cokie and Steven were in California, Barbara and Paul lived in Princeton, and Tommy lived a few minutes away. I tried him first but he and his wife, Barbara, were out and the baby-sitter didn't know where they were. Not even the White House operators had been able to find him for Carl, and they made a practice of always being able to find members of Congress, the cabinet, the Court, and others of the Washington power structure.

I called California, but Cokie's line was busy. (A friend at *Time* magazine had seen the report on the wire and phoned her before Steve could drive home to tell her in person.) I was trying to reach Barbara when the news came on:

> Congressman Hale Boggs of Louisiana, the majority leader of the United States House of Representatives, is missing on a flight from Anchorage to Juneau. With him in the light plane were Alaska Congressman Nick Begich; an aide to Begich, Russell Brown; and the pilot, Don Jonz. Boggs is fifty-eight years old. A search is under way.

I remembered that Hale hadn't taken his overcoat.

Liz Carpenter was the first to arrive, thank God. She heard the news on television and came right over, like the strong Texas woman she is, like family. We had been together through so many tense moments on the campaign trail and on election-night vigils. It was a great comfort to have her there.

Then a strange thing happened, when a young reporter with the *Washington Evening Star* came to the back door. The boxwood had grown so tall at the front door that all of our friends knew to use the back, and he saw me through the kitchen window. The reporter had been to our home previously so Cody knew him, but now that little dog got between me and the door and would not let him in. I had to put Cody in the dining room before I could open the door.

For the rest of the night, whenever I would go to a door to let someone in, Cody would try to get between me and the door. He didn't want anyone bringing me any more bad news. That night, he began sleeping in my room instead of downstairs in the kitchen, which had been his usual place.

More people began to come into the house. Liz put her press and White House skills to work and took charge. You can imagine the crowd—everybody from the press, our friends, Hale's colleagues, neighbors, friends of our children. People didn't know what to do, so they converged on the house. There were strangers, too—people I'd never seen before—curiosity seekers who heard the news on their car radios and just showed up. It was difficult to distinguish friends from strangers, but Liz sorted them out. She sent away the strangers, briefed the reporters, made certain I was all right, and in her spare moments, she brewed pots of black coffee. It would have been dreadful without her.

I was totally stunned, incapable of truly absorbing the news. The fact that I had to react physically and immediately to the people streaming into my house was good for me, I suppose. I became the one who was consoling them and saying, "Oh, look, now, they're going to find them. . . ."

The telephone was ringing constantly. Teddy Kennedy thoughtfully called to say he'd been flying with the same pilot, Don Jonz, and that they had been downed for several hours before they

Lindy and Hale in the Bradley
Boulevard garden, c. 1964.
(Boggs Family Archives)

Tuesday morning leadership breakfast
at the White House: Pierre Salinger,
Hale, Vice President Hubert
Humphrey, and President Lyndon
Johnson. *(Official White House photograph)*

Lindy as Chairman of
Democratic Dinner greets
Speaker John McCormack
and Mrs. McCormack, 1965.
(Lindy Boggs Archives)

The Boggses at the White House, 1962. (Boggs Family Archives)

Lindy, Tommy, Cokie, Hale, Barbara Denechaud Boggs, and Donn Anderson at the 1972 Democratic Convention.

(Photograph by Dev O'Neill/Office of Photography, U.S. House of Representatives)

Hale's Memorial Mass at St. Louis Cathedral in New Orleans, 1973. FRONT ROW, LEFT TO RIGHT: *former House Speaker John McCormack, Luci Baines Johnson, Speaker Carl Albert, Mary Albert, Lady Bird Johnson, former President Lyndon Johnson, Lindy, Archbishop Philip M. Hannan, Pat Nixon, Elizabeth Boggs, Judy Agnew, and Vice President Spiro Agnew.*

(Photograph by Frank Methe/Clarion Herald)

Tommy "The Cork" Corcoran, Lindy, and Ellen Marcus at Tommy's Washington fundraiser for Lindy, 1978. (Boggs Family Archives)

Spring Fiesta in New Orleans, 1974. Lindy receives visitors at her Bourbon Street home.
(Boggs Family Archives)

Lindy with granddaughter Elizabeth and daughter-in-law Barbara Boggs heading for the polls to vote for Lindy's first full term in the House, 1974.
(Courtesy of the Times-Picayune)

Lindy presiding at the two hundredth anniversary of the signing of the Constitution, Philadelphia, 1987. On the left and right, Senator Robert Byrd, Congressman Jim Wright. (Photograph by Keith Jewell/Office of Photography, U.S. House of Representatives)

Lindy, House Speaker Thomas Foley, Congresswoman Pat Schroeder of Colorado, and Congresswoman Nancy Johnson of Connecticut, at the dedication of the Lindy Claiborne Boggs Room in the Capitol, 1991.

(Photograph by Keith Jewell/Office of Photography, U.S. House of Representatives)

Cokie, Lindy, and Barbara. (Photograph by John Lowengard)

ABOVE: *Great-grandson Andrew Boggs with Lindy at her retirement party, 1990.*
(Boggs Family Archives)

Rebecca Roberts's graduation from Princeton, 1992. LEFT TO RIGHT: *Stephen Sigmund, Lindy, Rebecca Roberts, Cokie Roberts, Lee Roberts, Steven Roberts.*
(Boggs Family Archives)

Barbara Boggs Sigmund's sons and husband. LEFT TO RIGHT: *David Sigmund, Paul Sigmund IV, Stephen Sigmund, and Paul Sigmund.* (Boggs Family Archives)

LEFT TO RIGHT: *Tommy Boggs, Elizabeth Boggs Davidsen, Lindy, Douglas Boggs, Barbara Boggs, Hale Boggs, and Jacquie Boggs.* (Boggs Family Archives)

Last visit with President Kennedy in the White House, three weeks prior to his assassination. (Official White House phototgraph by Cecil W. Stoughton)

The Fords and the Boggses at one of the Bradley Boulevard garden parties, 1971.
(Photograph by Dev O'Neill/Office of Photography, U.S. House of Representatives)

Lindy Has Continuing Ties to the U.S. Presidents. (THIS AND FOLLOWING PAGE)

(Official White House phototgraphs)

(Official White House phototgraphs)

were found because they were in a mountainous place that radio beams couldn't reach. Hubert Humphrey called and said that Don Jonz was a wonderful pilot and that he'd flown with him many times. Alaska Senator Mike Gravel phoned with the encouraging word that his wife, Rita, had campaigned safely all over Alaska with Jonz as her pilot.

A psychic called from Ohio to say that he felt very strongly that he could make a connection with Hale if he had something that Hale had worn recently. I took his number and called Charlie Vanik, a loyal friend and an Ohio congressman. Charlie's principal aide, Mark Talisman, was a friend of mine and Cokie's, and I wanted to check out the psychic with him. I reached Mark in Ohio and he called me right back, saying that the psychic was reputable, refused to take money for anything he did, was not a publicity seeker, and had worked closely with the police in solving several cases.

I spoke with search coordinators with the Air Force in Anchorage and the Coast Guard in Juneau and asked if they objected to my using a psychic to help locate Hale and the others. One of them said that with the help of a psychic, he had recently found someone who had been missing for three weeks. I promised to pass on any information the psychic provided.

My parish priest, Father Gingrich, called and in a few minutes he was at my side. Before I embarked on cooperating with the psychic, I asked Father Gingrich if he thought it appropriate. He assured me that whether musical, artistic, or prophetic, people have talents that are totally unimaginable, and that the gift of prophecy is one of the seven gifts of the Holy Spirit that should not be ignored. I felt comfortable with that.

I didn't know exactly what to send that was small. I looked in Hale's closet and found his black tie and cummerbund in the pocket of a tuxedo, so I sent those to Cleveland in an envelope via an accommodating pilot on a regularly scheduled air route. The psychic reported he felt that Hale had last worn them at a party with me, and I had worn a "shimmering blue dress," which was correct. Regarding Hale, the psychic saw a peaceful water scene with a horizon, and he said he kept getting two names: Ruth Montgomery and Norma Iverson.

I said I didn't know and had never heard of Norma Iverson, although an explorer named Iverson had charted much of Alaska, but I did know Ruth Montgomery, an admired friend and a fine journalist who had written a book on Jeanne Dixon and Jeanne's psychic powers and discovered in the process that she too had some psychic powers. "Don't you know her?" I asked. He said he didn't, but that I should contact her. I immediately attempted to do so, only to discover that she was in Mexico.

When I did reach Ruth, she apologized for not concentrating on Hale's disappearance because she was recuperating from a fairly serious illness. She explained that she and her husband, Bob, pray over a situation or a person, and then she goes to bed. When she awakens she sits down at the typewriter and types automatically, without any plan or thought as to what she is going to write. "Would you be prepared for whatever news I give you?" she asked.

I said I'd be prepared for it, but I might not accept it.

When she called me back, she said she kept seeing "a beautiful horizon." Her feeling was that the plane had gone down.

I said, "Ruth, I would know if Hale were dead."

She said, "Sometimes, when someone dies suddenly, the shock of the death is such that they don't communicate."

I couldn't accept that.

I'm still confused about everything that happened that night. Barbara came from Princeton, and I talked with Cokie and she was coming the next day. Tommy got there, and he was upset that he hadn't broken the news to me. I was sitting on my bed with the phone and like the loving, unselfish son he is he said, "Oh, Mom, it's so unfair to you."

The search started the day that the plane disappeared, Monday, October 16, 1972, and by every standard, it was the most extensive formal search on record. More than 140 aircraft from helicopters to high-altitude spy planes were coordinated from Elmendorf Air Force Base in Anchorage and scores of Coast Guard boats, ships, and planes were ordered out from Juneau under the direction of the Coast Guard. The army sent special search teams on foot and Civil Air Patrol pilots searched from above. Commercial airline crews flying over the area and forest rangers in Alaska's vast national parklands were ordered to look for the plane. The operation was all the more remarkable because it was done with such devotion and with affection.

Our whole family went to Alaska the next night. We were already together, surrounded by loving friends in Washington, and the search was completely out of our hands, but I knew that if one of us were missing in Alaska, Hale would be there looking for us. We flew out of Andrews Air Force Base late at night, heading west- and northward across the continent, trying to comfort and reassure one another but frequently lapsing into private thoughts and prayers.

It was still nighttime when we landed at Elmendorf, on the edge of Anchorage, and were escorted to our rooms in the base guest house. The terrain was flat and the weather was unseasonably warm; it wasn't anything like the travel-poster Alaska. Unfortunately the warm temperatures were causing thick fog that still grounded the first fleet of search planes. We were torn between wanting the weather to stay warm so the men could survive better if they were in the water, and wishing for cold weather to lift the fog to allow the search to continue.

Pilot Jonz had filed a flight plan through Portage Pass, notorious for its sudden turbulent winds and extreme ice conditions, then over the icecapped Chugach Mountains to Prince William Sound and around the rugged, barren coast to Juneau.

Daily briefings were provided to us, most of the early ones taken up with guessing when it would be clear enough to allow search planes to take off. When it turned colder and the weather cleared, we saw firsthand the courage of those young pilots on some very trying flying days. It was such a heartful search. The pilots would stop a couple of hours before their eight hours were up so they could sign on for the next shift. They would come back and take my hands in theirs and say, "Don't you worry. We're going to find him." Some of the worst times were when we'd be resting in our rooms and we would hear planes taking off on another search mission. The girls and I drew support from one another.

Tommy was aware of some of the scientific marvels that the military was using in Vietnam, which were not yet public knowledge, and he helped persuade the administration to "bring in the big guns," so to speak, for the search. We couldn't talk about them then, but they included airborne infrared heat-sensing devices and the SR-71, a high-altitude spy plane with cameras that could read the letters on a small aircraft from eighty thousand feet up. The coastline maps of Alaska were later redrawn as the result of their imagery. Secretary of Defense Melvin Laird was a good and long-time friend of Hale's and mine, and he provided everything that this nation could offer.

The briefings began to take on their own rhythm as our young women—Cokie, Barbara, Tommy's wife, Barbara, and their daughter, Elizabeth, who was almost ten—would be very tough, while Tommy, Hale's brothers, Archie and Robbie, and the other men—friend Harry Lee, who was a reserve Air Force general besides his other accomplishments, Gary Hymel, Bill Monroe, the newsman of NBC-TV's *Today* show, and Jim Patton, Tommy's law

partner—smoothed things over. To them the military was authority, but not to our women. Their attitude toward the various majors and colonels was, "Get your act together."

One day we were told that special equipment had detected an
area of unusual warmth on heavily forested Mansfield Peninsula,
which sits high out of the ocean. "But," the briefing officer continued, "it would take ten thousand men walking in armlock to cover
it."

The three girls stood up as one. "So?" they said. Barbara provided a welcome light touch: "I can see the headline now," she told
us: "Boggs Found on Mansfield." (Mike Mansfield was the Senate
majority leader.)

Later I overheard one of the briefing officers say to another,
"You know, Mrs. Boggs is fairly sensible but those girls!—"

We were taken out to Portage Pass. The plane was not heard
from after it was to have entered that treacherous gap in the mountains, and as I looked at the stark glacial scenery, my first thought
was, *Oh Lord, please, they didn't go down here!* I didn't see how any
living thing could survive for long in that Arctic landscape. Fortunately for us, Elizabeth provided welcome comic relief. As we all
silently stood there, she gazed at the snowy mountains and declared: "Now, there's my Alaska!"

A Russian-American couple living nearby introduced themselves and invited us in for tea. Hale's grandmother had developed
the practice of stopping whatever she was doing in the late afternoon for her cup of tea. It represented relaxation, a little time out,
and Hale's mother had followed in her gracious footsteps. How
especially comforting this hospitable gesture was to me, my daughters, and my granddaughter.

The military thinks Hale's plane went into the water and that
it was questionable if it carried an electronic locater beacon that
worked. I was told that if a plane goes into very deep water, the

debris comes to the surface, but that in shallow water the soft bottom buries the sinking debris. Everyone in Alaska flies all the time, and they treat airplanes the way we do cars, taking off without checking that everything is aboard and operating properly, perhaps neglecting to fasten the seat belts if they're only going a short distance. They just get in and fly.

We stayed in Anchorage several days, and Robbie conducted Mass every morning. Even the people in our group who weren't Catholic seemed helped by it. Anchorage churches and synagogues offered special prayers for the safe return of the men. Everyone knew Nick as their state's only congressman, and many knew Russ Brown, his assistant. Don Jonz, from Fairbanks, was known throughout Alaska as one of its best pilots. I couldn't go up in a military plane, but the Civil Air Patrol pilots took me up in the same model twin-engine Cessna 310 that Hale had been in. I felt reassured when I was told it was a great "belly buster." (I maintained my interest in the CAP and years later I became the Vice Commander of the CAP Congressional Squadron at Andrews Air Force Base.)

In the beginning I was an encouraging cheerleader for the searchers, but as the days wore on and the news was still unfavorable, I didn't want them to think I was monitoring what they were doing. During the search they found a World War II plane that had gone down. That's how thorough they were.

I went home to the white-columned house in Bethesda where our children had grown up and where Hale had tended his garden. A hundred times a day I caught myself waiting for the telephone to ring, expecting it would be Hale or someone telling me he had been rescued. I listened for his step at the back door, for the sound of his voice as he came through the kitchen. There were no continuous news channels on television then, only the regular newscasts, which I watched for some word, some clue.

Every afternoon, Pegge Begich and I went to the Pentagon for a briefing arranged and often attended by Mel Laird. I was confident Hale would be found alive; it was simply a matter of time. Occasional reports of sightings of small planes or from people who thought they had heard a low-flying plane on the day of their disappearance continued to come in. One day we were told there had been a sighting that could be something definite. We waited at the Pentagon until it was checked out. My mind began racing and my emotions really collided: I was hoping that it was Hale's plane and afraid that all aboard would be dead. It turned out to be other debris. I took a deep breath and kept hoping.

A few days after Hale disappeared, Barbara won her first political race with election to the Princeton Borough Council. I know it was hard on her not having her father there to share that victory, but the rest of us made up for his absence as best we could. We were all so proud of her.

During the weeks and months that followed, I received letters from strangers who were remembering Hale in their prayers. The families of people missing in action and prisoners of war in Vietnam were so supportive that to this day, I have a close relationship with several of them. All of them kept saying, "Don't send him any negative thoughts. You keep believing. You keep hoping. We're all with you. Send only positive thoughts."

They imbued me with the feeling of fear about any negative thoughts that I might send to Hale. I realized with admiration that the MIA and POW families and friends had lived for so long, trying never to send their loved ones a negative thought, wondering what horrible situation they might be in, feeling frustrated at being helpless to rescue them or even to have the opportunity of looking for them. I felt that unless I had hope, I couldn't continue to give encouragement to the search teams that were flying under increasingly hazardous conditions.

When you're thinking about loved ones being close to death or in danger of death, what you hope for is that they won't lose hope because if they despair, then they're despairing of God's goodness. I began to have a feeling that all of these people were with me and my family, and that we were with Hale in a great communion of interest, prayer, and meditation that somehow or other could be helpful to him. In church parlance we call it the communion of saints.

Trying to keep myself geared up and console other people and send encouragement to those on the search missions and follow the advice given me by the POW and MIA families gave me some difficult times. One of my most poignant memories of this time is that of roaming the neighborhood with my precious grandson Douglas, as Hale had done with great frequency. Only five years old, Douglas missed his "Paw Paw" terribly and had difficulty in understanding his precipitous departure. I felt like a juggler keeping all the balls in the air. As long as I was physically and mentally active, I could keep my balance and send only positive thoughts.

On the day after Thanksgiving the search was officially suspended. Wretched weather—a combination of bitter cold temperatures, fog, and blowing icy rain, plus a recent snowfall and a lack of clues—forced the military coordinators to call a halt until spring. But by then every bush pilot and fishing-boat skipper had a description of the plane and would continue to look for it until it was found.

In Alaska they're so accustomed to people going off into the wild blue yonder that their state laws for declaring someone dead when their airplane disappears are very liberal. Soon after the search was officially suspended and after the election (in which Nick was reelected to Congress), an Alaska court convened by the governor declared Nick, Don Jonz, and Russell Brown to be legally presumed dead.

In New Orleans people began to ask me to run for Hale's seat, but I kept insisting we already had a congressman. I felt that we were going to find him and he was going to ask what took so long. His disappearance created an unusual legal situation in Louisiana because there, state law presumed a missing person was alive until he or she reached the age of one hundred years, and there was no method for declaring a congressional seat vacant if a person who was lost in an airplane had been duly elected to office.

Everybody was praying very hard for Hale. One day the pastor at Old Saint Mary's Church, a National Historic Landmark in New Orleans, called and said, "I hate to tell you this, Lindy, because I know you think Hale is still on this planet, but I have good reason to believe he is no longer on this planet. Remember the lady we were trying to persuade to give us that fifty thousand dollars for the restoration of the church? She came through with it today. Hale only could have worked that miracle in heaven!"

Hale's reelection to Congress in the general election marked the first time that a congressman who was "missing" had been elected in Louisiana. By coincidence Hale had helped resolve the death situation of a friend of ours who died in an airplane crash but whose body was never found. He was on a commercial flight from New Orleans to Florida that went down over water, and although many people saw the plane disappear, nobody could find it. Hale helped the family with a declaration of death.

The presumption-of-death difficulty was a legal never-never land for our family, affecting property taxes, the use of Hale's financial resources, insurance—everything. Louisiana authorities had to call on the House of Representatives to make the first move toward resolving our situation when Congress convened in January. In the meantime, selection of the House majority leader would take place.

Our longtime friend, Congressman Thomas P. ("Tip") O'Neill of Massachusetts asked if I would object if he ran for Hale's position. A member of Congress since 1952, Tip had been selected as whip by Hale and Speaker Albert two years earlier. The fact that the Democrats in Congress had to elect a new majority leader was disturbing to me, a tough realization. I assured Tip that I didn't object and jokingly added, "Because when Hale comes back and says, 'Thanks for holding it for me while I'm gone,' I know you'd be the only person to give it back to him."

I loved Tip more than ever for his sensitivity in wanting to be sure I wouldn't feel disappointed in him for assuming that Hale was dead and that he was going to take his place.

When Congress convened, Hale's seat was declared vacant. That allowed me to make a legal declaration of death in Louisiana and thereby proceed with the estate matters, including the freeing of assets that had been frozen since his disappearance. There was no method of appointing anyone to serve his term: Members of the House of Representatives must be elected. When Tip was elected majority leader, I called him with my congratulations.

Everyone needed a formal way to say good-bye to Hale. Members of Congress and Washington officials who were his close friends, his old friends in New Orleans, the children, his mother and brothers and sisters—all the friends and relatives needed a public, formal kind of memorial. I wanted to honor him, of course, but I still wasn't sure I wanted to send him those negative thoughts.

We decided upon a Memorial Mass of Resurrection at Saint Louis Cathedral in New Orleans the day after Congress convened. Once the decision was made, our family members and close friends planned the service, choosing favorite readings and arranging the seating and flowers, under the talented hands of Rose Monroe, selecting the music to be performed by the St. Louis Cathedral Choir, the renowned Xavier University Concert Choir, and the

Guitar Ensemble from Loyola University's College of Music, and giving roles to the grandchildren—now numbering eight with Cokie and Steve's beautiful two-year-old Rebecca—and to his family members and his sustaining friends, including his law class of 1937 (of People's League fame) and his fellow members of the Sons of Colonial Wars, the Sons of the American Revolution, and his confreres in the 4th Degree Knights of Columbus.

My old, dear friend Archbishop Philip Hannan prepared the Mass, which was new and emphasized resurrection and hope rather than death. The priests, who included Father Robbie Boggs and the Reverend Richard B. Stump, pastor of our New Orleans parish church, Saint Alphonsus, wore vestments of brilliant white and gold. The Reverend Edward Gardiner Latch, the chaplain of the House of Representatives, led the congregation in prayer, and the Speaker of the House, Carl Albert, offered beautiful and meaningful remarks.

It was one of the most meaningful ceremonies I've ever attended, filled with physical beauty and spiritual loveliness and people crowded in from all stages of Hale's life, from childhood and high school through Tulane, the Trade Center, the navy, and Congress—power brokers with whom he had worked and humble people to whom he had shown kindness and understanding.

Former President Johnson and Lady Bird and their daughters and sons-in-law Lynda and Chuck Robb and Luci and Pat Nugent came, as did Pat Nixon. Vice President and Mrs. Agnew and Hubert and Muriel Humphrey were there, along with the congressional leadership, the Louisiana delegation, and many other members of Congress. In all, four planeloads of colleagues and friends came from Washington. Louisiana governor Edwin Edwards and Elaine, New Orleans mayor Moon Landrieu and Verna, and all the state and city and parish officials were there as well.

I had been uncertain about inviting Lyndon, because I knew that his weakening heart put him in a perilous condition, but I deeply wanted him to be there and he insisted on attending. Before the service he and I stood in the back of the cathedral holding hands and looking into each other's eyes without speaking. I knew it was the last time I would see him.

The Marines provided an honor guard, and we used a catafalque with the American flag draped over it. My friend John Warner, the Secretary of the navy, performed his duty of presenting me with the flag.

After the Mass we all went out to stand in the sunshine of Jackson Square while a navy band played "The Navy Hymn," a Marine bugler played "Taps," and a rifle salute began. The first shots reverberated through my whole body until I didn't think I would be able to stand there without crying.

I was saved by the reaction of my grandson David Sigmund, who was looking at a flock of pigeons roosting, as usual, on Andrew Jackson's statue. When the first volley was fired, they all began to fly away. David, not yet six years old, pulled on the hem of my skirt. When I looked down, he turned his face up to mine and said, "Maw-Maw, how come they're shootin' all the pigeons?"

The following week Governor Edwards called a special election for March 20 in the Second District, which then as now embraced all the varieties of life in Louisiana.

I had come to know it like the back of my hand, beginning in New Orleans with its potpourri of spices, colors, and contrasts: jazz, opera, and Mardi Gras; shadowy intrigue and wrought-iron elegance; Andy Jackson and Jean Lafitte; shipbuilders and wharves in the curves of the river; prominent colleges and universities; streetcars and ferryboats; and a downtown surrounded by white and black suburbs bursting at their seams. The rest of the district was just as diverse, with oil drillers and fur trappers, sugarcane fields and sulfur mines, shrimpers and oystermen, rural Cajuns and African-Americans, good ol' boys and the remarkable women who sustain them all; and Zydeco, honky-tonk, and blues.

Everyone assumed that some long drawn out decision-making process led to my candidacy, but the truth is, I suddenly found myself running for Congress. It took me by such surprise that I called Archbishop Hannan and asked him if I should have had a period of agonizing self-appraisal, a sleepless night of self-examination, before deciding to enter the race for Hale's seat.

"No," he said, "what you're doing is all too natural. It's a natural progression of your life."

My children were in wholehearted agreement and pushed me. I couldn't have considered going to Congress without their support and their love. Mostly, their love.

CHAPTER SIXTEEN

*I*MPORTANT TO winning an election in uptown New Orleans was the backing of the Alliance for Good Government, a fairly new organization which had won Hale's approval. It was an enthusiastic political initiative made up mostly of well-to-do professional and society people, those persons sometimes referred to in the press and by the less affluent as "the silk stockings." When Hale was campaigning we used to call the opposite of the silk stockings, the blue-collar working men and women, "the mullets," for those wonderful little fish that follow their leader in droves.

Alliance support aided and abetted the success of any candidate because the membership would actually go out and work for those the alliance endorsed, registering people to vote, publicizing details of the candidates' positions on issues, organizing telephone banks to canvass for votes, and providing rides to the polls on election day. It also had a think tank type of committee that produced position papers on needs and issues in which the alliance was especially interested. While most of its members at that time were Democrats, there was a core group of Republicans as well.

The alliance hosted an annual cocktail party as its major fundraiser, and Hale and I usually attended. Before I decided to run for office, even though I didn't feel like going to any cocktail parties, I had accepted the alliance invitation.

By the night of the party, I had become a declared candidate. I had been stunned a few days earlier to discover that the cocktail party had been turned into a quizzing-of-the-candidates night, a forum with the alliance membership invited to decide right then which candidate to support. I didn't have time to prepare, but in Hale's last primary election campaign, he had been so busy in Washington he had sent me to campaign for him. He especially wanted the people in new areas that had been added to his district to have our interest and attention, and I met with them as well as with voters I knew in the old neighborhoods.

I had campaigned with Hale for so many years that I knew the aspirations and the problems of our constituency, and I was always open to their suggestions. Because of the Washington experience I had been privileged to enjoy, I was conversant with national and international affairs. Consequently, although I had no idea what the alliance would ask me, I had a substantial foundation of information.

Several other candidates attended the party. Among them was Woody Koppel, a real estate executive who had recently run a very fine though unsuccessful race for the City Council and who expected to be chosen. He was well known to the alliance executive committee, closer to their age than I was, and he had brought a group of enthusiastic young supporters with him.

During the program Rodney Fertel, another announced candidate, walked into the room accompanied by a huge man dressed as a gorilla. In a previous city race he had promised, if successful, to give the Audubon Zoo a pair of gorillas, and the gorilla had become a mascot.

The chairman of the meeting cleverly announced, "You may think you have seen a gorilla enter the room. I assure you he's really our sergeant-at-arms."

Toward the end of the evening, a man I didn't know rose and said, "Mrs. Boggs, you have an advantage over the other candidates."

I didn't know what he was going to say next. I asked, "Yes?"

"It's something called knowledge," he replied.

Hearing that, I felt much better about my chances.

When the session ended Larry and Kate Eustis and a group of us trooped over to Fisherman's Wharf at the Half Moon to be with our buddies "the mullets" while we awaited word on the endorsement selection from "the silks." Larry, our longtime affectionate friend, who had been Hale's first campaign chairman, kindly agreed to be mine.

The Half Moon was the gathering place for politicians from all over town, a corner bar that its owner, Mike Roccaforte, ran like a neighborhood club. It was the nearest thing to a pub in the Second District. Whenever there was any kind of political contest, everybody left the polling places and went to the Half Moon to wait for the vote totals and then to celebrate or drown their sorrows. It was between the Garden District, with its elegant old mansions of the city's first American residents, and the strongly ethnic Irish Channel neighborhood, original home to the Irishmen brought over to dig New Orleans's channels and basins and to build the railroad beds.

We lived on First Street in the adjacent Garden District, and my cousin Chep had lived on Coliseum Square, so we were all nearby neighbors. Pictures of Hale and Chep covered the walls of the Half Moon—the congressman and the mayor, the neighborhood's heroes. On one side of the pub Mr. Eddie opened fresh oysters at a little oyster bar, and across the street was Mike's restaurant, Fisherman's Wharf. That's where Larry and Kate and I were when the phone rang with the good news: I had won the Alliance endorsement.

The next day Mike Roccaforte put up a big sign declaring, WE LOVE LINDY! Even though my main headquarters offices were downtown, everybody assumed they were next to the Half Moon. The sign stretched across the building, and you could see it coming and going from all directions. In each of my nine campaigns, Mike put up the sign.

I was already in the race on my thirty-fifth wedding anniversary, January 22nd. To observe it I drove alone up to New Roads, to Saint Mary's, where Hale and I had been married. It was the only way I knew of marking this special anniversary, and after Mass, I stayed a while, praying and thinking about Hale and our life, our family, and the future. I realized how sorely I needed his advice and counsel. Every now and then someone would say to me, "You know, Hale's ready to help you if you'd like to have his help." I felt they were saying that just to make me feel better; I never consciously "talked" to him.

When I returned to New Orleans, everybody in my headquarters was acting peculiarly, as though something had happened and they didn't want to tell me. I thought they were being especially sweet because it was my wedding anniversary, but then someone told me that Lady Bird Johnson had called two or three times. When I reached her she told me Lyndon had died. I hung up the phone feeling sorrowful at the loss of one of my oldest, closest friends but thankful that we had said good-bye at Hale's service.

When Barbara heard the news, she called. "Mom, isn't it just like the two of them? They're the only two people having any fun on your thirty-fifth wedding anniversary!" For some reason my adrenaline rose that Hale and Lyndon had done such a terrible thing to me, and I got furious with them for not being there when I needed them. Then, abruptly, I realized I had only six weeks until the primary election. That was good medicine for me.

My strongest primary opponent was Woody Koppel. His supporters from the City Council election had stayed together and at thirty, he was much younger than I and telling voters he could build up seniority and bring people together. Three men who had run against Hale in the last primary also ran: Jules W. ("Ted") Hillery, who opposed the congressional seniority system; Joseph Ben Smith, an African-American teacher who wanted to improve education and to help the have-nots, and Rodney Fertel, the wealthy, flamboyant figure who this time was promising to give the zoo a pair of pandas if he was elected. All the men thought they were going to give me a good race and that one of them would surely win.

Mr. Alvin Alcorn, a great jazz player with his own well-known band, was devastated when he heard I was going to cross the Mississippi River one evening for a political rally in Gretna. "You're not gonna go there by yourself, are you?" he asked.

I said, "Oh, there'll be people over there with me."

That wasn't good enough for him. "I'm gonna bring my band, and we're just gonna come on over there with you," he said, so he and a few jazz musicians played for my campaign party across the river—where he couldn't imagine that I'd been campaigning with Hale for years and years.

Not long afterward I had an opportunity to repay the favor. Ella Brennan decided to offer a "jazz brunch" at her Commander's Palace Restaurant, and she asked Mr. Alcorn to bring his band. He called me the day before. "Miss Ella wants us to play 'soft jazz.' How could we play 'soft jazz'?" he wondered.

"Muffle the horns and tell the boys they can't sing loudly," I said.

I won 75 percent of the votes in the first primary. There wasn't even the need for a runoff primary. As Hale and I had done so often, I went to WDSU-TV for a live interview on election night.

Woody Koppel was already there, so hurt he had not done better in the race and so shocked he had lost that he could not force himself to congratulate me.

I waited for a minute, and then I walked over to him and said, "I know how dedicated you and your backers are, and I want you to know I admire the fact that you took the positions you did. You shouldn't feel unhappy." He never could make himself say "Congratulations," but in the years that followed we became friends. I wouldn't have run unless I had known I could win, and so many different groups had asked me to run I knew I was assured of victory.

The general election was an anticlimax. My Republican opponent's name was Robert E. Lee. I knew that as a Republican he couldn't possibly be a descendant of the original Robert E. Lee. The voters did, too, giving me 81 percent of their votes. I was on my way back to Washington—this time as Louisiana's first woman elected to Congress.

The most annoying charge during the campaign was the assumption that I wasn't truly interested in Congress, I was "just keeping the seat warm" until Tommy could run. The night that I won, I reminded the crowd at my headquarters that some people had said I was a stand-in for Tommy. "They are so wrong about that," I said. "I'm going to keep the seat warm, but I'm doing it for Elizabeth, my ten-year-old granddaughter!"

Looking back, I never expected to stay in Congress as long as I did. I didn't run for just that one term, but I thought I would finish Hale's agenda, concentrating on international trade, housing, taxes, civil, and equal rights. I never expected that I would develop my own agenda or that I would become a voice and a vote for many women during two tumultuous decades.

As a political wife and campaign coordinator for Hale, I had come to realize that women are the most efficient, honest, and loyal campaign workers a good candidate can have. There are dramatic differences between the politics of women and men. All of our lives from the time we are little girls, we are socialized to be compassionate, to think about the next generation, to be gentle and considerate of the smallest, weakest ones. We are the keepers of the culture, endowed with a nurturing quality that seeks to calm the waters, not roil them; to pursue compromise not challenge it; to think of the powerless not as problems or voting blocs but as people to be empowered.

Once we are committed to someone or something, we are loath to give up. Women are more alert to prejudicial practices and laws, more fiscally responsible, more open to international friendships, and have more understanding of ethnic distinctions. Women see in other women similarities, shared experiences. Men notice the differences between themselves and other men and sometimes end up feeling superior.

We hear so much about leadership and the quality of our leaders. To me it is very simple: People with ability should lead. The final consideration that led me to Congress was my conviction that experience is valuable and that I had a duty to use the experience I gleaned from three decades in Washington, as close to Congress as one could be without being elected.

Hale and I devoted our lives to this constitutional miracle that is the United States of America. I know the high cost of public service. It has always required personal and family sacrifice, but unless you are willing to participate in a democracy by serving, you cannot ensure the life, liberty, and pursuit of happiness that you have been promised.

More than a hundred family members and friends attended my formal swearing-in at the Capitol. In the 1789 ceremony, I was presented by the dean of our delegation, Congressman F. Edward ("Eddie") Hebert, and sworn in by the presiding member of the House, Speaker Albert. Surrounding us in the well of the House were the other members of the Louisiana delegation: Congressmen Gillis Long, Joe D. Waggonner, John Breaux, Dave Treen, Otto Passman, and John Rarick, and Senators Russell Long and J. Bennett Johnston.

Watching from the gallery were my mother, Barbara and Paul with their sons, Paul, David, and Stephen; Tommy and Barbara with their children, Hale, Elizabeth, and Douglas; my brother-in-law Archie Boggs and his wife, Sally, ever my sustaining friends; and Hale's niece Eleanor Ann Boggs Shoemaker and her family.

A huge group of Louisianians came, including many stalwarts who had been involved in my campaign: Larry and Kate Eustis, party leaders; Salina Burch and her volunteers, who ran the phone banks; and the volunteers who conducted polling, registered new voters, and staffed my headquarters. There was a mixture of friends from business and labor, mullets and silk stockings—every kind of voter.

Joining them were my Washington friends and the officers of the Congressional Club, the Women's National Democratic Club, and the Democratic Congressional Wives Forum. Their devoted presence buoyed my spirits, and I became excited as I really hadn't been before at the accomplishment and challenge of this bittersweet day.

That afternoon President Nixon graciously invited me and my family members to the Oval Office for a private meeting. I was especially happy to have Eleanor Ann along as my token Republican; her husband was the Republican district attorney of York County, Pennsylvania, and both of them were active in the county Republican club.

Over the mantelpiece was a portrait of George Washington. He must have been wearing his least comfortable set of false teeth, because it didn't look like the other portraits of him. Apparently President Nixon enjoyed quizzing visitors on the identity of the person in the portrait, and he asked my grandchildren, "Who do you suppose that is in the portrait?"

Little Paul Sigmund, age seven, piped up, "Mister President, that's George Washington. Didn't anybody tell you?"

Barbara told me that the hardest thing I was going to have to do in Congress was vote. "There's no 'maybe' button, Mama," she said, and she was right.

After all those years with Hale I more or less knew what to do, but you never know the ramifications until you're the elected one. The fact is, you have to make a yes or no decision, and you have to hurt some people in the process—behavior I found practically unacceptable. I was accustomed to appeasing the people Hale had to disappoint when he took a stand, saying this to one group and that to another—"on the one hand" and "on the other hand"—believing as I do that every side has some merit. There's no way of doing that when you're a member of Congress. You can listen, you can commiserate, you can agree, or you can disagree and then make adjustments so you can disagree less, but in the end you have to vote yea or nay. It's not easy.

As far back as I can remember, I smoothed ruffled feathers, beginning with my grandparents and then my parents. I find it is difficult to disagree with people I like and respect who have differing positions from mine. People would talk to me, and I could present Hale with the various positions or shades of thinking on the issue at hand. I was his listening post, his sounding board.

The first few months I was in Congress, my colleagues and the power structure naturally identified me with Hale. Congress was heavily male dominated; not much focus or attention was given to the role of women—within the Capitol or outside it. I set about trying to change that. As a freshman I had no seniority, so I had to use what leverage I had as the wife and helpmate of the former majority leader.

In many people's minds I was associated with political campaigning in different parts of the country—something I never would have done if it hadn't been for Hale. This gave me some prominence in my own right, and I was sometimes able to offer assistance or counsel, as I did with Marilyn Lloyd.

Marilyn Lloyd and her husband divested themselves of the radio and television stations they owned in Tennessee when her husband decided to run for Congress. He won the Democratic nomination, but he was killed in an accident before the general election, forcing the state's Democratic committee to select another candidate. Before the committee could meet, Marilyn started running. A Democratic delegation from Tennessee came to ask me if I would talk her out of being a candidate. For the first time in many years they had an opportunity to win that seat from the Republicans, they said, and they were afraid Marilyn couldn't win.

After I talked to Marilyn, I reported back to the delegation that they were incorrect in thinking she couldn't win: She would be their best bet. Fortunately they agreed because she is still in Congress, a leader on the Armed Services Committee and chair of its subcommittee on Energy Research and Development. She has been an outstanding credit to her state and district and to the Democratic Party.

Because of Hale I knew the ins and outs of the politics of leadership and the difficulties in keeping together a coalition of the polyglot group that is the Democratic Party in the House. I knew that sometimes the leadership simply had to be able to count on people for a vote, whether or not those members were taking a risk for themselves, so when push came to shove and the leadership needed me, I voted with the leadership, sometimes when I would have preferred not to do so.

Most of the time, the leadership respects the difficulties of individual members. However, they were correct in assuming I held a special place in the Congress and in the Second District. Despite unpopular stands I would take or votes I would cast, I would be understood by some and forgiven by many of my constituents and could win the next election. Many projects were obtained for my district because I was well-known to the committee chairman and to the leadership, and I received favorable decisions when issues were before committees that were important to my state or my district. It was only fair that I understood their needs as well and could support them.

Every successful politician will agree, as Hale did, with the adage that politics is the art of the possible; you put together what's possible or you can't go forward or reach any resolution. Having been initiated into the verity of this philosophy at an early stage in Hale's political career, I had little trouble in carrying it forward, but it wasn't easy to do without a wife who could pat people on the head and tell them I was sorry I had to vote that way because I really did think very highly of their proposals and there was a great deal of merit to them.

When I told Lady Bird Johnson, who had urged me to enter the congressional race, that I was running, she wondered aloud, "Do you suppose you can do the job without a wife?" The answer is "Not too well!"

As a member of Congress, I felt great responsibility: I had taken an oath to uphold the Constitution of the United States; I had to follow my own moral principles, and I would try to listen to and meet the needs and wishes of the people in my district.

A long-distance telephone call from a constituent tested me on each of these points. An elderly man called from deep in Jefferson Parish and, as did many persons of his generation, thought he had to scream to be heard "over long distance." He had to come see me, he said. I told him I'd be delighted. We made an appointment and he came, all scrubbed up and appropriately dressed "for the city," to my office in New Orleans.

It was the alligators, he said. He was a trapper, and he was having a terrible time with them. They had been declared an endangered species because so many had been killed for their valuable skins, but they were multiplying so fast they were eating up all the fur-bearing animals—mink, muskrat, otter, and nutria.

He trapped and farmed the same tract as had his father and grandfather, but he'd had to lease double the amount of land that sustained them and he was still getting fewer than half the number of animals he had trapped before. To supplement his income he had begun raising hogs on the levee.

A few days earlier an alligator had come up on the levee and eaten one of his pigs. "If the alligator comes again, I'm going to shoot it, and you're going to get me off with the Fish and Wildlife people," he said.

I told him that the ban against killing alligators as an endangered species was about to be lifted, and to please refrain from doing anything for the next ten days. "I know you've undergone a terrible struggle," I said, "but you'll be relieved of it very soon."

I was back in Washington when the next call came. "I told you!" he screamed. "The alligator came again, and I shot him. I hauled him down here to the Fish and Wildlife agent with my pig in him, and I told him that you would get me off!"

I asked to speak to the agent. I reminded the agent that the alligator ban was to be lifted in a matter of days and that this man had had such a terrible time, the government should be lenient with him. I had counseled him to be temperate until the ban ended, but he felt obliged to protect his pigs because he was raising them to supplement the income he'd lost to alligators. I pointed out that nobody had arrested the man—he had turned himself in and he had brought in the alligator. "Could you just give him a stern warning," I asked, "and tell him that if he does it again, he'll have to be punished?"

The agent agreed to take all these circumstances into consideration. But an uneasy thought came to mind; I asked to speak to my constituent again and when he got on the line, I asked, "Did you skin that 'gator before you brought him in?"

" 'Course I did, Chère. You think I'm stupid?"

Because I had been sworn in at the end of March and Congress had reconvened in January, I knew that only a few vacant places remained on committees. Before my swearing in, I eagerly accepted the Speaker's invitation to discuss my committee assignments. When I asked him what was left, he countered, "What committees do you want to be on?" I didn't hesitate: I knew where I needed to be.

Urban renewal had been an outstanding aspect of the Great Society program, but New Orleans was still waiting for its urban dream to come true. State legislatures had to approve of a city receiving federal urban renewal funds, and because minorities' rights were specifically included and protected in the program, Louisiana's rural-dominated legislature was reluctant to approve the project, and New Orleans was the last big city to receive urban renewal funds.

Under the enlightened encouragement of Mayor Moon Landrieu, the Tulane School of Architecture and Urban Planning and other private sector and university groups created a plan to revitalize the downtown and its adjacent riverfront properties, dovetailing the urban renewal project with the master plan. While awaiting the federal funds, they had already bought, expropriated, torn down, and bulldozed many existing structures. Only a few new buildings, including the gleaming white Lykes Shipping Line headquarters, were in place.

The Jefferson Parish council and the towns of Westwego and Harahan also were involved in a program which allowed towns and parishes to pass bond issues and with the participation of private enterprise and federal programs, to create new neighborhoods. With a minimal deposit, people could move into a new house and their rental payments became house payments, enabling them to own their own homes.

At the time the president could impound funds Congress had appropriated for specific projects. President Nixon impounded funds for urban renewal and for these low-income housing programs. New Orleans had begun this massive project and Jefferson Parish had created several new neighborhoods, when suddenly the money dried up.

They were my constituents now, left in the lurch with millions of dollars tied up and the dramatic centerpiece of our urban dream, Poydras Street and the riverfront, looking like an abandoned, bombed-out ruin. Westwego and Harahan were caught with bonds on their hands and neighborhoods only 15 or 20 percent occupied.

I realized that I should seek membership on the committee most directly involved in a solution, and I said, "I need to be on the Banking and Currency Committee. Under the president's impounding of funds, all of our urban renewal projects have come to a screeching halt, but if I'm on that committee, I can do something about it."

I felt a heavy obligation because Hale had participated in the New Orleans and Jefferson Parish plans. This was exactly what I had meant when I was running for Congress and said that I wished to continue his work.

Carl didn't once say to me, "Lindy, there is no vacancy on Banking and Currency." He talked to Tip, the majority leader, and to Jerry Ford, the minority leader, and they agreed to create an extra space for me on the Banking and Currency Committee. I was assigned to its Financial Institutions and Housing and Urban

Development subcommittees, the ones most pertinent to my district's needs.

The day after I became a member of Congress, I was sworn in as a member of the Banking and Currency Committee, Hale's initial committee assignment, by the committee chairman, my old friend Wright Patman of Texas. Reality set in. I was now a member of Congress, sworn to uphold the Constitution and charged with the duties and responsibilities and the accountability for my votes and my actions. It was a humbling realization.

In my personal life I was a single woman getting credit in my own name for the first time. Going through all that rigmarole with banks, businesses, and credit cards, I began to realize the magnitude of the problems for women as I encountered them. I had not been aware of the discrimination against women until I became an easy prey to it myself. Now it became perfectly understandable to me why women business owners and executives, as well as individual women, were complaining that they were being discriminated against in matters of credit.

Representative Pat Schroeder of Colorado, who entered Congress two months before I did, applied for an American Express card in her own name and was told they would be happy to issue her a second card on her husband's account. I think the limit was something like a thousand dollars on the second card, and Pat said, "That's one trip to Colorado and back." That experience involved her in the movement for equal credit opportunities for women.

Another friend was a talented professional who, newly divorced from a senator, found herself unable to obtain credit: Everything was in her husband's name. To lessen the shock and her anxiety as she dealt with insurance, bank accounts, the telephone listing, their child's school enrollment, changing everything into her own name, she consulted her doctor, who prescribed a mild tranquilizer. She didn't have the prescription filled, but an insurance company tried to deny her coverage because, it said, she was "on tranquilizers."

This friend was a valuable member of the Congressional Club but as the ex-spouse, she was no longer eligible for membership. I thought this was cruel: Just when she needed her friends most, she was excluded from their company. We changed the by-laws so she and any subsequent ex-spouses could remain members.

Women bank employees were already complaining about credit discrepancies in home mortgages: Men usually got them; women usually didn't. A group of professional women from the District of Columbia, Maryland, and Virginia pooled their efforts and talents to investigate the situation. They talked with business and professional women's organizations and scores of individuals, doing their homework and compiling statistical evidence to prove their case. When they came to me they said they could document a terrible discrepancy in home mortgages.

Public disclosure of financial institutions' practice of "redlining" neighborhoods outraged other minorities who were also seeking fair treatment. Poor neighborhoods in which money would not be loaned for home mortgages were literally outlined in red on the loan offers' maps. Each of us sixteen women in Congress used our individual experiences for the breakthroughs we knew were needed.

I do not believe the men I served with were aware of discrimination against women, but when our committee took up the mortgage-lending aspects of a new banking bill, it upset me that women who were married and supporting a husband and family couldn't get a mortgage in their own right. It struck me as especially unfair because reactivation of the draft had motivated men to stay in school on student deferments during the Vietnam War and women were supporting the families. Despite these social and economic realities, the wife's income was not considered stable by lending institutions—"Suppose she got pregnant!" was their attitude. The home mortgage situation was the straw that broke the camel's back for many women.

We were marking up a new lending bill that included an amendment protecting people from discrimination on the bases of race and age, and their status as veterans. I thought we should add, "or sex or marital status." I wrote that addition on my copy, and without saying anything I ran to the copying machine in the side room and made a copy for each member. When I returned I strongly depended on Southern charm to get my additions included in the bill.

I said, "Knowing the members composing this committee as well as I do, I'm sure it was just an oversight that we didn't have 'sex' or 'marital status' included. I've taken care of that, and I trust it meets with the committee's approval."

The amendment passed unanimously, forty-seven to zero, and that's how the Equal Credit Opportunity Act of 1974 reads. It wasn't that it was Lindy Boggs making the difference, it was the fact that there was a woman at the right place at the right time to make a difference.

The committee chairman, Wright Patman, was an old-time, straightforward, honorable politician who never minced his words. There were some people he disliked, and he held vehemently to his own economic and financial persuasions, but he was a straight shooter.

One of the people with whom Wright sometimes sparred was Arthur Burns, the chairman of the Federal Reserve Board. Arthur and his wife, Helen, were trusted friends of mine, which placed me, a freshman member of the committee, in the unusual position of sometimes being a go-between for the chairman and the head of the Fed.

The most delicate negotiation came after Wright made an off-hand comment about a proposal by the Fed and what dire effect it might have on the American economy.

Arthur said to me, "He impugned my patriotism."

I said, "Oh, Arthur, you know Wright didn't mean to do that!"

Arthur didn't mind Wright's usual remarks but the fact he "impugned his patriotism" was more than he could take. Through all of this Mrs. Patman calmly played bridge with the Burnses once a week, something she had been doing since before she married Wright. Politics was important, but their bridge game was not to be missed.

Though I experienced some sense of achievement in those first few months in Congress, I missed Hale sorely. And I didn't really say good-bye to him until a trip to Nairobi.

We had been together on many extraordinary trips abroad, and I had always been the working accompanier helping him. This time, I was the delegate and I was alone. As a member of the House Banking and Currency Committee, I was part of the U.S. delegation to a World Bank meeting in the Kenyan capital.

As I prepared for the sessions, I couldn't help but relive, in a way, some of Hale's experiences with Lend-Lease and the Marshall Plan, international trade and economics. He was an expert on so many things, a tremendous intellectual. I was more or less saying to him, "I need your briefings."

My Kenyan hostess was a lovely woman, the chief librarian of Nairobi. Her family was from the Great Rift Valley, where the United States had economic aid programs to improve the cattle herds. Before the conference opened she invited me to go with her to see the country from the point of view of the native families. We went out to the valley where herdsmen with their grazing cattle followed the growth of grasses up the hills all day. At night they descended into camp, where they cooked their meal over open fires. The children were allowed to stay up and listen to the grown-ups talk and tell tales. It was an enchanting experience, made beautiful with the sounds of their voices and magic of the firelight.

My hostess said, "I sometimes wonder what civilization is all about. I get up in the morning and send my husband off to his office. I get my kids off to school, and then I get ready and go to work all day. Sometimes I think, *What am I doing here? Why am I not out in the valley?*"

We returned to Nairobi and the conference opened. Henry ("Joe") Fowler, a former secretary of the treasury and an old and close friend, was there and that was a boost to me. He and Hale had worked together many years. Subjects came up that Hale had been involved in for years, but I kept reminding myself that now I was the one who was responsible; he was no longer there to be responsible. Though I worked hard and felt I was doing a competent job, I realized how much better Hale would have been at it. Unexpectedly I experienced a firm coming together of all my difficulties: I knew I had been trying to stand in for Hale, but now I knew it had to be me.

Secretary of the Treasury George Shultz, a close friend who had attended the meeting, offered me a ride back with him as far as Tehran, Iran. He would meet a plane there taking him to the USSR, his next destination, and I could return to the United States from Tehran in another government plane. I gladly accepted, both to have a visit with George and for a first-time-ever visit to Iran. When I returned home, I could tell Ardeshir Zahedi, the highly popular Iranian ambassador in Washington, that I had finally visited his country.

I was stunned to recognize the extraordinary precautions the Iranian government felt were necessary to assure my safety during a brief overnight stay: a chauffeur and an aide riding shotgun in the car; a security guard on the balcony of my hotel room and another in the hall outside my bedroom door, and an accompanying guide within the hotel itself—all of them presumably armed. Surely the political situation within Iran vis-à-vis strong ties with the United States was a precarious one.

Going back on the plane, I explored my new realization that I was the person who had to carry the responsibility. Hale had certainly prepared and helped me, and I would always have his archives and my memories of him, but whatever there was to do I had to do myself.

He had been scheduled to address the international conference of the Holy Name Society Catholic Men's Organization in New Orleans, and after he disappeared they had invited me to do so. It would be the first time that a woman delivered the principal address at their international meeting.

I was sitting on the plane, dead tired, trying to write my speech, and I thought, *Well, Hale, this is really your speech. I'm going to go to sleep and you're going to write it.*

I woke up a few hours later, and as I began to write, the words flowed out as though the speech were writing itself. I suppose that was the moment when I finally said, *Hale, you really are in heaven. You're not here.*

CHAPTER SEVENTEEN

ༀ᠁ༀ

AFTER THIRTY-TWO YEARS on the Hill, I thought I knew my way around the Capitol, but in that first year after I was elected, I quickly learned that being a member of Congress means life is never predictable.

I offered everyone on Hale's congressional staff a job, and I tried to find jobs for those who had worked for him in the majority leader's office. The only placement problem was with Roger Brooks. When Speaker McCormack was leaving and Hale was becoming majority leader, he asked only one favor of Hale: that he hire his chauffeur, Roger Brooks. I called Tip O'Neill and said, "You've inherited Roger Brooks from Mr. McCormack and Hale, and it's a splendid inheritance." And so it turned out to be. Roger drove for Tip when he was Majority Leader and then Speaker and went on with him into retirement. When Roger could no longer endure the physical requirements of the task, his brother took over the "inheritance."

One of my first congressional efforts was an attempt to restore the desperately needed funds in my district that the president had impounded or deferred. Besides our urban renewal projects, President Nixon had curtailed the expenditure of moneys for the Neighborhood Health Centers and Model Cities programs.

The nursing schools at the University of New Orleans, at Charity Hospital, and at Our Lady of Holy Cross College were also affected by funds: Sixteen million dollars that had been appropriated for a national nurses' education program had been impounded. Under the leadership of Nurse Nancy Halloran and the concerted efforts of other congresswomen, the funds were restored in the next year's appropriations bill.

I frequently saw the influence of intelligent, well-prepared, and talented women in writing the laws of this nation. There were only sixteen of us in the House, and only Nancy Landon Kassebaum in the Senate, and each of us became a surrogate congresswoman for the thousands of women who had no female representation and felt more comfortable making their suggestions for legislative or administrative proposals to other women.

The extent of women's problems weighed on our hearts and our consciences. We felt we had to band together to ferret out their valid suggestions and to engage the services of experts to advise us. We formed the Congresswomen's Caucus, not a caucus in the sense that we all decided on a legislative agenda and adhered to it, but simply a means of organizing ourselves into an efficient entity. We had to have an organized plan that we could implement in a coordinated fashion so that we had the support of all of our membership.

We met with members of the cabinet, heads of government agencies, and the White House congressional liaison staff, most of whom came with a retinue of experts to answer our questions. Arthur Burns was the exception, so knowledgeable that he invariably appeared before congressional committees accompanied only by his pipe. After we determined what cooperation we could get from the departments and agencies—what measures we could possibly pass—we proposed our legislation. Our initial successes led us to adopt the same procedures in subsequent years.

In order to find out if our suggestions were valid and what type of legislation and programs could ensue from them, the caucus set up a research arm at George Washington University's Women's Center in Washington, D.C., with Charlotte Conable, wife of Republican Congressman Barber Conable as our liaison.

To meet the caucus budget, we depended on foundations and other philanthropies interested in our work. While I was in New York to solicit a grant from the Ford Foundation, I was advised by its attorneys that a recently passed law prohibiting tax-exempt contributions to lobbying organizations applied to our caucus status. We tax reformers were "hoist with [our] own petard"!

This led us to completely separate our research activities from the caucus, and we formed what became the Women's Research and Education Institute (WREI), which is still going strong under the continued effective leadership of Betty Dooley. The caucus enjoyed the privilege of hiring the institute's "fellows," women pursuing graduate studies in subjects pertaining to women. Their theses became WREI working papers, which we sent to universities and to the students' sponsors. They were so well received that the institute began publishing them annually in book form as *The American Woman*, which gave them additional importance and popularity.

An early caucus interest was the equal credit for women from lending institutions—actively pushed by Banking and Currency Committee members Congresswomen Peggy Heckler and Lenore Sullivan, Congressman Parren Mitchell, and me—giving women equal conditions with men in the commercial credit category. This led to financial and credit legislation for women, the elderly, and minorities as embodied in the Equal Credit Opportunity Act.

The act was extremely complicated, with detailed regulations for banks and other financial institutions in granting individual and, we assumed, commercial credit. Our caucus listened to spokespersons for all the women's organizations as well as to outstanding women in banking and finance, and we incorporated their ideas and suggestions in our recommendations to the Fed. We spent many days in study and conferences until we had a proposed draft.

Actual writing of the regulations was given to the Federal Reserve Board, which was allowed thirteen months to finish because of the precise language required to cover all situations.

After the preliminary draft of the act was published, the women who had met with us were extremely pleased, but they failed to express their approval formally to the Fed. When the preliminary draft hit the people in banks, mortgage companies, and credit unions who would have to administer the new regulations, they jumped on it and flooded the Fed with objections that it was too complicated and detailed to be workable. As a consequence the final draft of the regulations reflected changes the Fed made to counter the protests and did not follow the first draft, which the women had approved.

These women assumed that they had been deceived, and they were absolutely furious. They descended on the caucus for an explanation and, they hoped, a rewriting of the regulations with their original input. We asked for a meeting with Arthur Burns in the Congresswomen's Reading Room, and this time, instead of coming only with his pipe, he brought five experts, three of whom were women. A great many details were worked out, although not to their complete satisfaction.

But we weren't finished. It had been our understanding on the committee that equal commercial credit to enable women and minorities to start and maintain businesses was inherently covered in the new act. That turned out not to be so, and we went back to work. Not until the year before I left Congress were we able to rectify that omission.

Because the majority of businesses in the United States are small businesses, many of them run by women who were treated differently than men when they needed to borrow money, the caucus took up their situation. Eventually a small business act more comprehensive than the one we proposed was developed under the leadership of Representative John La Falce of New York, giving special attention to even the smallest women- and minority-owned businesses and making certain that they had equal opportunity to receive government contracts.

Until the 1974 Equal Credit Act was passed, government agencies assumed from past experience that women-owned businesses were incapable of handling the contracts because there were few large businesses owned by women. Once the government acknowledged women's rights to the contracts, many businessmen realized that if they had female or minority participation in their business ownership, they would be more likely to receive government contracts, all other things being equal. What was started as an almost token consideration on the men's part fostered the development of many businesses, with more than 50 percent women's participation.

The fallout from these efforts encouraged all of us to keep the issue of women's equal rights before the Congress. Projects were initiated in all parts of the country. The National Businesswomen's Organization created a database to monitor whether equal credit rights legislation was working and if the government and private sectors were complying with it. Women business owners in New Orleans compiled their own *Women's Yellow Pages*, a directory of businesses owned by women, and professional women in the District of Columbia and adjacent areas of Maryland and Virginia compiled an inventory of women-owned businesses.

Equal opportunity for home mortgages for the elderly was another area of need, and its champion, as in all senior citizens' causes, was Representative Claude Pepper of Florida, through his Select Committee on Aging. He was ardent in his support and we worked to have his bill passed, giving seniors the same lending requirements as their juniors.

A deep feeling of relief settled on Washington when a peace plan for Vietnam was agreed on and signed in Paris on January 27,

1973, by the United States, South Vietnam, North Vietnam, and the Vietcong. At the same time the military draft was ended and U.S. prisoners of war held by the North Vietnamese began coming home. On March 29 the last of our troops left Vietnam, and by April 1, 590 U.S. prisoners of war had been released and returned to tearful reunions.

I was honored to share the joy of the families of Vietnam prisoners on the occasion of their homecomings. Those families and the loved ones of the missing had reached out to me when Hale had disappeared, and I felt forever close to them and one with them.

But as Vietnam was passing from the front pages, the Watergate affair took its place. I had too much to learn and to do in Congress to spend a great deal of time thinking about Watergate, but it was clear to everyone that serious problems were ahead for President Nixon and Congress would be affected.

But at this time I was enjoying the effects of the other great change in Washington—the changing role of women. Helen Thomas, the now famous dean of the correspondents' corps, and I were female trailblazers into the Washington Gridiron Club's annual banquet and show, the first women invited by that all-male bastion. Helen had covered the White House over many years for United Press International, and she was an excellent and respected reporter. We had been together on trips with Lady Bird and became good friends along the way.

Hale had always been invited to the Gridiron Club's big Saturday-night affair, when men of the Washington press corps presented their version of the year's memorable events to an audience of public figures and power brokers, including the president and vice president. Women were invited to a Sunday brunch and an abridged performance, but not to the Saturday-night show.

That first year when Hale wasn't there, I was invited by the *Times-Picayune* correspondent Edgar Poe, a respected friend, to take

Hale's place. Helen had been invited and she accepted, but many women in the press were protesting their exclusion from Gridiron membership and from the banquet, and they planned to demonstrate at the Capital Hilton the night of the event. I thought it was better to go than to decline because it would show that the club was accepting at least some women guests from Congress and journalism. I also thought that Edgar's invitation was especially gracious.

The night of the banquet I didn't want to insult my friends by walking past their protest as Gridiron members and their guests were arriving. I didn't know how I was going to get in until I remembered a back elevator that I had used for political and charitable events, when I needed to get to the ballrooms quickly. It had been installed when the hotel (then the Statler) had been built during Franklin Roosevelt's third presidential term to shield his wheelchair entrance from the public view and it conveniently went directly to the "holding room" for dignitaries awaiting entrance to the Ball Room.

Helen and I were the only women at the dinner, and the men were pleased to have us there. If anyone was offended by our presence, we didn't know about it. Neither Helen nor I thought anything in the show was raunchy enough to exclude women, and we had a delightful time helping the Gridiron open its door to change. A few years later during the Reagan administration, the principal banquet speaker who stole the show was Secretary of Transportation Liddy Dole, Senator Bob Dole's wife.

We had our good times, but most of my life involved all too "serious business." The Yom Kippur War resulted in the Arab oil embargo, which affected all Americans—but members of Congress saw it as a particular threat to their own constituents.

Following the imposition of the embargo, special-interest bills were passed in Congress for farmers because they couldn't work their lands or deliver their produce to market without fuel to run their tractors and trucks. If they signed up with the government, they could receive extra rations of fuel, and they could apply for emergency low-interest, fifteen-year disaster loans.

Fishermen, shrimpers, and crabbers in my district were also suffering from the diminution of the energy supply, and I was able to have them included in the legislation as "farmers of the sea." All the boat owners had big mortgages on their boats, and they would have lost them and their livelihood. My shrimpers were hit especially hard by falling shrimp prices and the fact that the big prawns—the money crop—were running far out to sea, about a ten-day-per-trip catch.

Because compliance with the regulations for the loans was a somewhat difficult process, I set up a meeting in Louisiana with several federal officials from Washington, sophisticated men well versed in the intricacies of the program, who came down to explain it to the local people.

They suggested I should not accompany them to the meeting, "because it might be a little rough," one of them said. I said, "I have to accompany you to protect *you*." They didn't realize that where we were going, strangers were often met with suspicion, and government people were never welcome. I was concerned about what kind of reception they might get from the locals.

We drove down to the town of Lafitte, where we'd reserved the American Legion Hall. The town sits astride lagoons and bayous above Barataria Bay in the salt-grass flats and cypress groves that were sanctuary to an illustrious hometown boy, Jean Lafitte, the pirate and smuggler, who helped Andy Jackson win the Battle of New Orleans.

The hall was already jammed with people when we arrived. Because so many of the fishing boats are family enterprises, with the wives actively involved onshore and on the boats, the audience included many women. The government men, who had brought only thirty loan applications, talked mainly to boat owners, explaining to them how to fill out the forms.

I said to the feds, "Don't ask anyone for a tax form. It will make them suspicious of the program." But of course they did ask, because their rules required them to do so.

Many of the oystermen are from parts of the former Yugoslavia, and they tend to be very large in stature. After a while one of them—massive even among his peers—leaned over the chairman's table and said, "Okay. You've done what you had to do for the boat owners. What are you going to do for us oystermen and the other fishermen?" The crowd cheered and yelled. Without the boat owners being able to keep their boats, there wouldn't be any work for the fishermen who leased and operated them. The officials finally got that through their heads and attended to everyone.

It was quite a meeting. I considered it a success because my constituents received as much relief as possible—and because the Washington people got away unharmed.

One of the compensations for working doggedly and carrying heavy public burdens is the wonderful feeling of camaraderie in the Congress; it's similar to lawyers fighting in court and then going to lunch together. Nothing would get done if members of Congress didn't get along individually, and I always seemed able to get along with everyone. Out of the blue Joe D. Waggonner, who had become the dean of our Louisiana delegation on Eddie Hebert's retirement, asked me to run for the Appropriations Committee.

I said, "Joe, I'm very happy where I am. I'm going to have a subcommittee chairmanship on Banking next year, and besides, what happens on Appropriations? Don't the members simply stamp or not stamp approval on what somebody else has already done?"

He said, "It's a very important committee. Louisiana has had someone on it for twenty-eight years, until Otto Passman's defeat, and we need someone on it now."

"If it's so important," I replied, "why don't you get someone else to run?" Joe said, "Because you can get elected."

I ran, I was elected, and I loved being on Appropriations. It's the last stand between the people and how the government spends their money, its job being to appropriate the funds that have been authorized to run government departments and agencies and for other specific uses.

For many years on an Appropriations subcommittee, I sat next to Louis Stokes of Ohio, who with his brother Carl, the longtime mayor of Cleveland, has been a leader in the African-American community. Between us we protected the women's and minority rights in various pieces of legislation. I also was on the Energy and Water Resources subcommittee, an exciting place to be when a great push for alternative sources of energy occurred after the oil embargo.

I was aware that solar energy was highly workable in certain climatic situations and in conjunction with other forms of energy, but ocean thermal energy was new to me until I learned about it and ate the first delicious hamburger ever cooked with that type of heat at a convention of ocean thermal energy specialists in New Orleans.

When the oil embargo began it seemed ridiculous to people who believed in nuclear energy that we weren't developing it as fast as possible. France seemed to have mastered the technique of building and using nuclear power plants, but France had only one plant design, whereas each nuclear plant coming on-line in the United States was different from the others and had to be approved at every stage of development and construction.

The effects of the oil embargo convinced our subcommittee that we must take the lead in seeking alternate sources of energy—and in all areas of science and technology. We have the resources. Three major government laboratories—Livermore, Argonne, and

Brookhaven—and National Science Foundation programs are all prominent in basic research, and most basic research in universities and regional laboratories is largely funded by the government and done in collaboration with universities and scientific institutions.

Considering the scope of the programs of NASA and of the National Institutes of Health, the enormity of the research and development by our government becomes evident.

My first year in Congress coincided with a terrible flood year for Louisiana. Even rivers and bayous that weren't out of their banks were running dangerously full and carrying all kinds of flood detritus. The Corps of Engineers called and told me they wanted to open the Bonne Carré Spillway, a major waterway, to divert Mississippi River water into Lake Pontchartrain, which has outlets to the Gulf of Mexico.

Fishermen and -women who depended for their livelihood on the oysters, crabs, and fish in the lake pleaded with me to prevent the diversion, saying that the influx of debris-laden river water would ruin their catches. I repeatedly relayed this message to the engineers, but finally the general in charge called me and said, "Well, Mrs. Boggs, is it your oystermen in Lake Pontchartrain or Avondale Shipyards that you're worried about?" The shipyards were in danger of being flooded unless the river water was released.

"Could you open the spillway gently?" I asked. Barbara was correct. There was no "maybe."

As floodwaters poured over wetland plants growing in the spillway, an amazing thing happened: The plants acted as a filter for chemicals and other impurities, and fresh water flowed into Lake Pontchartrain, renourishing it. The fishermen had their biggest catch in years.

The next year one of my fishermen said, "Mrs. Boggs, can't you get the engineers to open that spillway again?"

Just as I was beginning to feel comfortable in Congress, not even a year after Hale's plane had disappeared, one of my best friends left to go to the "other end of the Avenue." The Nixon administration was the first to use the Twenty-fifth Amendment to the Constitution, when Vice President Spiro Agnew resigned from office on October 10, 1973, the day he pleaded no contest to federal income tax evasion charges relating to kickbacks from Maryland contractors. The amendment, which had been passed after the assassination of President Kennedy, provides for the replacement of the president in the event of his disability, and of the vice president when there is a vacancy. President Nixon nominated Congressman Jerry Ford, our good friend and the House minority leader, to be his vice president.

I enjoyed the honor of making one of the speeches seconding his nomination, and I talked especially about our trip to China. I wanted to emphasize his familiarity with, and expert handling of, foreign affairs. All of us in Congress felt that Ford was the most representative of all of the Republicans in the House because his colleagues had elected him to the highest position among House Republican members, that of minority leader.

The House and Senate approved Jerry's nomination, and he was sworn in as vice president before Christmas 1973. In that respect things seemed to be settling down.

With Watergate hanging over the White House and our government, I was gratified to be planning patriotic activities that would make people feel proud to be Americans. Many of the intellectual delights I had in Congress were based around Bicentennial activities, and the two hundredth anniversary of the first Continental Congress—from which our nation was born—was coming up.

My personal relationship with the Smithsonian Institution started when Benjamin Read, the director of the Woodrow Wilson International Center for Scholars at the Smithsonian, and several of its scholars, approached me with their earnest desire to have the 1974 Bicentenary of the First Continental Congress commemorated by a joint session of Congress. I thought it was an excellent idea, and I helped in arranging a meeting for them with Majority Leader Tip O'Neill and key members of his staff, all of whom were pleased with the suggestion.

However, Tip was apprehensive that by the time the anniversary arrived, the Senate might be engaged in an impeachment trial of President Nixon, a cause for embarrassment instead of pride. I reminded him that the First Continental Congress had been a unicameral one, and I suggested that we hold the ceremony in the House and invite the Senate to attend.

"Since it will be a congressional celebration, we won't have to invite the president," I said, "and the Speaker would be the presiding officer." We would hold the celebration by a "Special Order" session of the House, by which the regular session is recessed for special events. After consultation with Speaker Albert and the renowned parliamentarian Lew Deschler, the format for the celebration was agreed on.

We planned a magnificent program over which Speaker Albert would preside. The army's Old Guard Fife and Drum Corps from Fort Myer would provide rousing patriotic music, Congresswoman Barbara Jordan, who later became the heroine of the Judiciary Committee's impeachment hearings, would give the opening reading, and historical remarks would be delivered by the distinguished professors of government and history Dr. Cecilia Kenyon of Smith College and Dr. Merrill Jensen of the University of Wisconsin, and by Alistair Cooke, the creator and narrator of the popular television series *America*. Already known as the host of PBS's *Masterpiece*

Theatre, and of the 1950s series *Omnibus*, Cooke—a naturalized U.S. citizen who was born in England—had now become instantly recognizable to and admired by millions of Americans.

When the time came, the program fulfilled its promise to the Wilson scholars and lifted the sagging spirits of our nation in the midst of the Watergate difficulties.

We also made a concerted effort to lift the sagging spirits of the Democratic Party. In the summer of 1974 we held a miniconvention in Kansas City, Kansas, with the broad purpose of rewriting the party charter in order to bring Democrats back together. I was a delegate to the miniconvention, which was held in Kansas City two years after Miami and two years before the next national convention.

Our national chairman, Robert Strauss, was magnificent in his success in pulling together all of the factions and in focusing the divergent points of view on where the Democratic Party should be. With the Vietnam War behind us, it was easier to find a common ground for agreement on other issues. A major decision reached was that it was time that a woman chair the 1976 national convention, and that the chairmanship should rotate between men and women in future conventions.

The politics surrounding the national party conventions in the selection of site and the choice of convention officers dominates the Democratic National Committee's agenda. The site selection means millions of dollars and jobs to the host city and it can foster the candidacy of one or another potential contender. Officers of the convention—the permanent chairman, co-chairman, keynote speakers, chairman of the platform committee, and the parliamentarian—represent the political direction that the national committee wishes to pursue in the general election and reflect the fighting for dominance among the officers of the national committee. Conventions hold additional interest for members of the House whose campaigns for election coincide every other term with the national campaign.

While the battle over President Nixon's tapes was working its way to the Supreme Court that winter and into the spring of 1974, the House Judiciary Committee began determining whether impeachment proceedings should be considered. On July 24, 1974, the Supreme Court ruled that President Nixon had no right to withhold the tapes and that they be given to the special prosecutor. The Judiciary Committee began public televised hearings that day on the impeachment of President Nixon.

Representative Barbara Jordan of Texas, a freshman member of Congress and of the committee, was a black lawyer and former Texas legislator whose political mentor and friend had been Lyndon Johnson. She was the right woman in the right place, and with her clear and electrifying presentation of facts and history, she "kept the Republic," as Benjamin Franklin had admonished the women to do so long ago, as she explained to a watching nation and world what our Constitution meant.

Members of the Judiciary Committee voted twenty-seven to eleven to recommend three articles of impeachment against President Nixon for his obstruction of the Watergate investigation, his cover-up of other illegal activities, and his repeated misuse of power to violate the constitutional rights of American citizens. The committee's action prompted the president to release additional tapes; one disclosed that he had approved the Watergate cover-up only six days after the break-in, when he was vehemently denying White House involvement. With that revelation most of his remaining congressional support collapsed.

During this time Vice President Ford made a trip through the South that had been scheduled for many weeks. Like the old-time party leader he was, he lambasted the Democratic Congress at every opportunity, trying to blame it for all the nation's problems. His final speech was in New Orleans, and he had invited me to ride back to Washington on the plane with him. I happily accepted.

When I was called to meet with him at a specific, to-the-minute time during his New Orleans visit, I knew it would be a formal appointment—leaders of the Second Congressional District meeting with the vice president. I determined that I was going to talk with him about some of my political concerns. There would be ample opportunity for happy talk about families on the plane.

"You know, Mister Vice President, I have been appalled by the tone of the news reports from your Southern visit," I said. "You can't be against the Congress. I know it's campaign talk and an old habit, but you are of the Congress and by the Congress, and you have to start being for the Congress, because in a very short while you're going to be president and you're going to need the Congress and all the support it can possibly give you."

He was stunned that I, his old friend, was talking to him like that instead of saying how much I loved him and Betty and the kids and asking how everybody was getting along.

As we were flying back, he received a call to go directly to the White House on arrival. A helicopter was waiting for him when we landed. (I don't remember the exact date on which the president decided to resign.)

President Nixon was in a frenzy, and Alexander Haig, his usually cool White House chief of staff and the last Nixon ally in constant contact with the president, was frantically distraught. For several weeks Haig, a career military officer acting in a civilian capacity, had been under enormous tension, first in trying to save the president and then in trying to persuade him to resign. He felt so responsible for the president that he was overreacting, taking charge of the Oval Office and practically running the presidency. It was a heartbreaking time.

On August 9 President Nixon resigned and returned to California, and Jerry Ford was sworn in as president. I was one of the few Democrats invited to his oath-taking at the White House. He had nominated former New York Governor Nelson Rockefeller as vice president, and after approval by Congress, the Twenty-fifth Amendment functioned again as Rockefeller was sworn in.

It was a unique time in our history: Although the voters had not elected Ford or Rockefeller, the people's elected representatives in the House and Senate had voted them into the highest offices in the land.

Everyone was ready to settle down and get on with their lives, and President Ford enjoyed a great deal of goodwill at the Capitol; he was a creature of the House, its longtime minority whip and minority leader. He was a good man who, it seemed, could do no wrong—until he pardoned Nixon a month after he was sworn in, and then it seemed he could do no right. That's an oversimplification, of course, but he did lose tremendous goodwill.

I felt that President Ford was well motivated in saving the country the trauma of any trial of Nixon, and I thought it was probably the right thing to do to heal wounds, but the decision seriously affected his popularity. The conjecture is that the promise of a pardon had been used to talk Nixon into resigning for the good of the country. There is no evidence of that, but it makes awfully good sense and it would have appealed to the ex-president.

I was sorry for any harm to my friend Jerry, and it was no affront to him that I strenuously endorsed landmark legislation before the Congress that year that wrested Constitutional power back to the Congress from the other end of Pennsylvania Avenue. By the end of the year Congress had passed legislation addressing the major problems of the times. In the War Powers Act, the president's power to commit U.S. forces abroad without congressional approval was curbed. In a measure that sought to avoid future campaign abuses such as those revealed by Watergate, limits were set on political contributions and spending by candidates, and Congress mandated the first use of public money to finance presidential campaigns. Added to the 1974 Budget Act restricting presidential impoundment and recision of congressional appropriations, the Congress created one of the Constitutional swings in division of powers that occur from time to time in our nation's history.

In an attempt to manage future short-term fuel shortages, a Federal Energy Administration was created, but disappointingly no long-term energy management policy was fully established. The dual problems of double-digit inflation and recession—unemployment had not been so severe since the 1930s—were partially addressed through an increase in the hourly minimum wage and extension of unemployment compensation by an additional thirteen weeks.

CHAPTER EIGHTEEN

꿍꿍

I WENT BACK to China in 1975 with a group of congresswomen, and the contrast between Hale's and my visit and this one
could not have been more striking. In the intervening three and a
half years, Deng Xiaoping, having been "rehabilitated," had returned from exile as deputy premier, and he was our official host.
Chou En-lai, the architect of rapprochement with the United
States, was desperately ill with cancer. We were free to walk about
unescorted, and we even took along our own television crew from
the States. The only similarity in the two visits was that both were
sponsored by the Chinese People's Institute of Foreign Affairs.

Dramatic changes had taken place at home since 1972 as well:
the military draft had ended and our troops were home from Vietnam; the last United States civilians had been evacuated from the
embassy in Saigon the previous April as Communist forces concluded their takeover of South Vietnam, and the United States and
China had opened permanent liaison offices in each other's country,
a step toward normalization of relations Hale had always supported.

Our trip was in the planning stages for several months, but finally we received the go-ahead from China. We all met in San

Francisco and flew out two days after Christmas. Among the members of our group were Peggy Heckler of Massachusetts and her daughter Belinda, Cardiss Collins of Illinois and her son Kevin, Bella Abzug of New York and her husband, Martin, and my grandson Hale Boggs and me.

From the moment we arrived, we caused a great deal of puzzlement among the Chinese wherever we went, mainly because of the appearance of our young people: Hale, a typical, white-skinned Anglo-Saxon fourteen-year-old with dark blond hair; Kevin, a handsome African-American kid with his football player physique, a modified Afro haircut, and skin almost the color of ebony; and Belinda who was twenty and had flowing, lustrous red hair and fair skin. Wherever they went these three created crowds. The Chinese didn't know what to make of us; we looked like a UN delegation.

We stayed in centrally located hotels, not isolated in official residences. I was especially honored when the distinguished wife of Chou-En-lai paid a courtesy call upon me in my hotel room. We were invited to see the Beijing air raid shelters, which no one would have seriously considered showing us on the earlier trip. They were spacious and extensive, well-stocked, and easily accessible to the general public through little shops all over town that had secret entrances to them. They probably couldn't have withstood a nuclear bomb, but they offered some protection against the conventional weapons of war.

One night was spent in a May 7th Cadre School where laggards and defectors from the Communist Party were educated and reindoctrinated, brought back to the "true" Chinese Communist way through an enforced regime of manual labor in the fields and intensive study of the writings of Mao Tse-tung. A "slow learner" we met said it was her third time to be sent to a school, although she was the entrepreneurial genius behind the Shanghai Symphony

Orchestra, its director of programming and publicity, and had traveled all over the world. She had been in Shanghai when Hale and I were there.

She was a great organizer of performances and put on a show at the camp for us. She engaged the assistance of Bella Abzug, an accomplished musician, wearing one of her famously elaborate hats, in singing a duet with her in that reindoctrination school.

Our group was the first official U.S. delegation since 1949 to be allowed into isolated, mountain-ringed Szechwan Province. We were permitted in because a woman was the chief engineer of a huge flood works project on the Yangtze River, harnessing waters, saving croplands, controlling flooding, and providing irrigation. The region still had some unhappy bands of people and it was a difficult decision for the government to allow outsiders in since the official point of view was that everything was simply splendid all over the country.

As a member of the Energy and Water Resources Development subcommittee of the House Appropriations Committee, I could understand and appreciate what China was trying to do in the massive river project. Basically it was not unlike our Corps of Engineers projects in Louisiana, except that there were hundreds of laborers building the dams and digging channels at the overflow spots so some water would flow into the fields, and in place of laying pipe with a crane and a crane operator, eighteen people carried each length of pipe and put it in place for another eighteen to cover with shovels of dirt.

The people worked hard and conscientiously. They usually didn't allow themselves to be distracted by anything, but when we suddenly appeared in a government automobile caravan, unlike any they had seen in years, they dropped everything to rush to the roadside. The Szechwan hotel that had been opened especially for us was surrounded by people, who stood in the roadway to stare at the cars.

Chou En-lai died during our visit to Shanghai. The television crew accompanying us called its New York headquarters every day and when they checked in, they were told about Chou's death. It was the middle of the night in China, but members of the TV crew called our rooms to advise us.

As soon as we saw our Chinese hosts that morning, we commiserated with them on the death, thereby inadvertently reporting it to them. They had heard nothing about it, and they couldn't understand why we were offering condolences. It was then that we realized that there was a blackout on the news in China; there was somber music on the radio but no announcement of any kind. The death was officially announced the next day, by the time we were prepared to leave.

I loved foreign trips but my heart belongs to the history and heroism of this country—which Hale and I and so many members of our families have served throughout the centuries. Thus, some of my most personally rewarding times in Congress were spent in historical endeavors, and my role on the American Revolution Bicentennial Commission was one of the most exciting and challenging ones. We began working well in advance to coordinate events at home and worldwide for the commemoration of the United States of America's two hundredth birthday on July 4, 1976.

Governments of many countries participated in the Bicentennial with a galaxy of star-studded programs. The Netherlands emphasized its unique role as the nation that had been the first to salute our new national flag. France presented outstanding programs, especially in cooperation with our commission's Jefferson and Franklin Exhibit in Paris, which honored the most respected American heroes of the French people. Spain made gifts of statues of Bernardo de Galvez, the Spanish governor of the Louisiana and Florida Territories, who squelched the traffic of British warriors and goods at Pensacola and through the Mississippi River system.

Egypt lent its King Tut treasures to several United States cities, among them New Orleans, where, under the chairmanship of Verna Landrieu, the wife of Mayor Moon Landrieu, a standard was established for the dramatic presentation of rare treasures through the uses of light, shadows, and space and effective crowd control. New Orleanians took the Tut exhibit so to their hearts that on its departure they provided an impromptu jazz funeral for the little king who had been denied funeral ceremonies at the time of his death.

The most ambitious involvement in our Bicentennial was by the people of Great Britain, who presented to the people of the United States a gold replica of Magna Carta, that original of English-speaking democratic documents embellished with precious and semiprecious stones, each of which had been personally donated by an individual. This stunning treasure was placed on public display in the Capitol Rotunda.

The British government determined, through its Bicentennial Committee, that its most appropriate gift would be the loan of the best of four surviving documentary copies of Magna Carta. Originally each of the barons at Runnymede, where it was signed in 1215, and every abbey and large city in the kingdom had received a copy, but only four remain extant. Exchange visits were arranged, a United States delegation to travel to England to receive Magna Carta and a British delegation to come to Washington to install it in Statuary Hall of the Capitol for the duration of the Bicentennial Year.

I was honored to be among our twenty-five delegates, headed by House Speaker Albert and Senate Majority Leader Mike Mansfield, to participate in the document transfer ceremonies in Westminster Hall in London. The Archbishop of Canterbury and the Lord Chamberlain were among the speakers, but it was Margaret Thatcher, then a leading Conservative member of Parliament, whose words were the most pertinent to the occasion, the most amusing and meaningful of them all. I had observed her on an earlier visit to the House of Commons, and from my seat in the gallery I had silently cheered her feistiness and her high intelligence. We were honored to be received by Queen Elizabeth at Saint James's Palace and to attend a reception in the House of Commons and at the 1776 Exhibition in the Maritime Museum.

The Fourth of July anniversary brought huge celebrations all across the nation, as communities large and small raised their flags and struck up the local bands. Most members of Congress participated in festivities in their home states. In Washington, a well-organized protest movement, "the People's Bicentennial," had announced its determination to interrupt any formal ceremonies at the Capitol. Our commission decided that the most satisfactory celebration was a Capitol open house with punch and cookies served to all comers as they strolled through the Capitol or roamed its grounds, listening to band music and pausing at booths to watch craftspeople making things as their colonial predecessors had two hundred years before. An atmosphere befitting the occasion was created, to everyone's satisfaction.

In addition to all the celebrations, 1976 was also a presidential election year, and as an outgrowth of Watergate, public financing was available for the first time for presidential campaigns. To qualify for matching federal funds, a candidate had to visit at least twenty states, raising $25,000 in individual donations of no more than $250.

The Democratic race attracted a multitude of candidates, among them Senators Mo Udall of Arizona, Birch Bayh of Indiana, Henry ("Scoop") Jackson of Washington, Frank Church of Idaho, and Fred Harris of Oklahoma; former Alabama governor George Wallace, Governor Jerry Brown of California, and former Georgia governor Jimmy Carter. President Ford was the favorite Republican candidate, but former California governor Ronald Reagan decided to enter the race. An actor, Reagan was a former New Deal Democrat who had become ultraconservative. He lacked close ties to the Nixon administration and, like the Democratic candidate Jimmy Carter, he had no experience in Washington. Both of them used their Washington-outsider status to advantage in the first post-Watergate national election.

Udall ran in twenty-two primary races in all parts of the country. I gave a party for him, which amazed Ashton Phelps Jr., who later became publisher of the *New Orleans Times-Picayune*. Ashton, who had been an intern in Hale's whip office, couldn't understand how I would have a party at my house for someone who had run against Hale for House majority leader. I explained that not only was he my friend, but I would do the same for any highly qualified Democrat who was testing the waters for the presidental race.

As I traveled around the country that spring, I discovered that Jimmy and Rosalynn Carter or their campaign workers were attending many state Democratic events, including Democratic women's meetings. Everywhere they went they set up booths or offices, where they served refreshments, handed out campaign literature, and answered questions about Carter's stands on the issues.

One trip took me to Pierre, South Dakota, to address the opening luncheon at a meeting of a national Democratic women's group. When I arrived the day before the meeting was to begin, I discovered that the only presidential candidate who already had a presence there was Carter. One by one, representatives of other candidates arrived after delegates to the meeting who supported them called their headquarters and complained about their absence. This was a clear example of the kind of thorough campaigning the Carters were doing.

On returning to Washington, I attended a party at the Iranian Embassy which Ardeshir Zahedi, one of the most popular ambassadors in the capital, gave to honor Princess Ashraf, the twin sister of the Shah of Iran. I was seated at a table with several important leaders, Democrats and Republicans, and they were all generally dismissing the Carter candidacy in amused terms.

I recounted my odyssey to Pierre, and I asked them to understand that the Carter candidacy was very serious. I said, "This is a dedicated group of people. What each of you needs to do is to reach out to Jimmy Carter and his advisers so that you will have influence and input into his campaign, and if he becomes president one day, which he very likely will, you will have influence in his administration."

I turned sixty that spring. I was none too happy about that until I received a telephone call from my octogenarian friend Gene Coulon, Charlie Coulon's uncle.

"I know what day this is," he said. He ignored my answering groan. "I called to tell you that you're going to have a wonderful time. The sixties are the teen years of old age."

How quickly I realized he was right! When I had vowed to continue Hale's work, I had no idea I would be chosen to chair the 1976 Democratic National Convention in New York City, a role which no woman had ever held. Being the permanent convention chairman was a great responsibility as well as an honor. I was selected by Bob Strauss, our national chairman, and backed by the national committee. One reason I was thrilled was because Hale had wanted to chair the 1960 convention and had been denied the privilege.

Because the previous convention had been so disorderly, I was determined that this first time a woman was in charge the convention was going to be run smoothly and fairly and we would bring the party together to nominate the president and vice president.

The day that my appointment was announced, a young House page came up to me and said in awe, "Mrs. Boggs, you have a telephone call in the cloakroom, from the president."

When I answered, President Ford said, "Hi, honey, are you going to pick a good one for me?" It was dear of him to congratulate me in that friendly way, and as it turned out, we did pick "a good one," and an equally good one for vice president.

As a member of the Bicentennial Commission, I was going to New York regularly because we had arranged to have the Tall Ships come in for the Fourth of July, and many other festivities were being planned as part of the city's celebration. The tall, multimasted ships with their billowing sails were used by many nations to train their naval cadets, and their parade would be the major international attraction of the festivities in New York Harbor.

On my New York visits, I was also able to work with the convention planners, the hotels, and the unions. The only frightening aspect was that all the New York City convention contracts came due July 2, the Tall Ships were coming in on the Fourth, and the convention's work started on July 10. If there were any disruption by any union, the result would be chaos, but I was certain that the euphoria accompanying the arrival of the ships would carry over to the next week for our convention.

Mayor Moon Landrieu of New Orleans was head of the National Conference of Mayors, and both of us had been strong supporters of an emergency federal loan for New York City to save it from bankruptcy, a loan President Ford had initially absolutely opposed, so I enjoyed the New Yorkers' respect and appreciation for my position on that crucial issue. The prominent New York Republican David Rockefeller had come to Congress to help explain the city's economic rescue plans; we were longtime friends, and I knew I could count on him for advice and assistance if necessary during the convention. Bob Tisch, a prominent New York investor, was chair of the host committee, which put my mind at ease about the potential problem of finding individuals, corporate sponsors, and groups to finance large parties and entertainments when the local economy was in such trouble. I was confident that Bob and his committee members would succeed.

I prepared as well as I could for my role as chairperson, working with the police, the media, the convention staff, and the staff at Madison Square Garden, our site. I learned how the electronic devices tallied delegates' votes and how I could communicate with each state delegation. I understood that while what was being said to the audience was important, it was a great deal more important to talk to the millions of people watching on television. That's a fine line to walk: to be as lively and enthusiastic as possible in the hall and yet to be presenting the right kind of calm, mature attitude to television viewers.

Speakers and dignitaries practiced standing on a little spot the television people marked on the floor and looking to one side and the other at the TelePrompTers. Practice rooms were available for rehearsing speeches, and makeup rooms were well staffed so that everyone would look good delivering them. I knew where all the exits were, where the TV cameras were set up, how the VIPs were going to get in and out, how long it took to walk from a car to the podium, and I had instantaneous communication with the convention's security headquarters.

During the Vietnam War bomb threats were frequently telephoned to federal buildings across the country and to other buildings housing federal offices, and New York City had its share. Despite the return of our troops and the passage of time, anonymous bomb-threat calls continued to be made. A week before the convention, I met with representatives of the Secret Service, the FBI, and other law enforcement and security agencies and with representatives of the New York City Police. They went over general precautions for the delegates and the party officials, security for cars, and the convention hotels. I finally said, "When are you going to tell me what I do when there's a bomb threat?"

They looked at one another and then an officer said, "We didn't want to make you apprehensive, so we were going to wait until the night before the convention to talk about this."

"The fact that you *haven't* told me about bombs has made me very apprehensive," I answered.

Special warning lights had been installed on the outside of the three major television network booths, ABC, CBS, and NBC, all of which could be clearly seen from my place on the podium. The police had a cadre of experts trained in handling threats and bombs. As soon as a threat was received, they went into action. All the important buildings in the city had evacuation routes.

Police could usually determine the seriousness of the call very quickly, and if they felt there was no imminent danger, "sweepers" would go through the building searching it but not ordering it to be vacated. If that happened, a yellow light would show on the booths.

For a more dangerous threat, a blue light would show. I was to say, "We're experiencing some smoke in the air-conditioning system, and we're going to have to leave the room. Please follow the people with white armbands. If we go out as promptly as possible, we'll be able to come back and reconvene quickly."

Everybody, I was told, understands smoke, whether they're from the farm or a sophisticated urban area. If there was an imminent threat of explosion, the red light would go on. I said, "Well, what do I do then?"

One of the agents said, "You're on your own, honey. The podium may be gone." We had three yellow lights during the convention, but no blue and thank God, no red ones.

A knowledge of parliamentary procedure helped me with my job as I worked closely with the convention parliamentarian. Early on, he said, "You know about Rule Thirteen?"

I said, "Rule Thirteen? What's that?"

"That's the one that says the chairman does whatever she wants to do."

Because I was brought up in the tradition of Southern women, I could easily be polite and gracious while being firm, and the long experience I had had in the Democratic Party and with its leaders provided me with the cooperation of many people who wanted the first woman chair to succeed. Bob Strauss had perfect confidence in me, and I had great respect and affection for him.

The hard work did have its bright spots. Because of the constraints of space and threats to security, the convention was cautious with passes, especially floor passes; they were difficult to come by and tightly controlled. I was at the podium presiding one day when I heard a little voice say, "Maw-Maw?"

I looked down to see my seven-year-old grandson, Stephen Sigmund, standing below the podium. He had a pass around his neck. I said, "Stevie? Where'd you get that pass?" He said, "I found it on the floor. It's a floor pass." He was by himself and since I couldn't leave and nobody else in the family was nearby to fetch him, he had a splendid time going from delegation to delegation until a kindly guard got him off the floor.

His mamma, Barbara, was off talking to somebody, and he just slipped away from her and came to see me. I asked him how he had gotten down to the podium. He said whenever he'd see somebody coming after him, he'd run. It took him a long time to get to me.

Jimmy Carter won the presidential nomination on the first ballot. He had presented himself as an outsider, a former peanut farmer and naval officer, a born-again Southern Baptist. His vice presidential choice, however, was a Washington insider and my longtime friend Senator Walter Mondale of Minnesota, who was quickly approved by the delegates.

Watergate had set the tone for Congressional elections two years before when many new members came to reform Washington, and it affected the presidential election as well. Despite Reagan's challenge, President Ford won the Republican nomination and chose Senator Robert Dole of Kansas as his vice presidential running mate. The ensuing race was very close: Carter and Mondale were elected by slightly more than 50 percent of the vote.

I had stayed in the house on Bradley Boulevard longer than I had intended, but my mother lived with me and she was comfortable and could entertain in familiar surroundings. I had enough space to permit a companion, Mrs. Pauline Zozicki, to live with her and still have room for children, grandchildren, and houseguests. My mother had accompanied me to the Democratic convention, and she had a delightful time, but when she died not long afterward, I no longer needed the services of her companion, and it was ridiculous for me to be in our big house with two and a half acres of garden to manage. Members of Congress went home to their districts almost every weekend, and the custom of big entertaining at home in Washington on the weekends had slackened considerably.

Cokie and Steve were living in Athens, where the *New York Times* had sent them from Los Angeles in 1974. Steve had the "quiet" little beat of Greece, Turkey, and Cyprus, and Cokie worked as a stringer for CBS-TV and Radio and wrote for magazines. Their children were young and accustomed to living abroad, and they all thought they would live overseas a few more years. They wanted to learn another culture, and they asked to be assigned to the newspaper's Thailand bureau in Bangkok, where there was an opening.

But then the *Times* decided it needed to beef up its Washington bureau. News from and about the capital, even after Watergate, had become the top stories in recent years, and the paper wished to have in-depth reporting on inside Washington happenings. Before Cokie and Steve could move to Thailand, Steve was asked to return to the United States, to Washington, in August 1977.

"It's a good thing we came home," Cokie said. "You were about to sell my house out from under me."

They stayed with me. Cokie went job hunting and was hired almost immediately by National Public Radio (NPR). She and Steve next began looking for a home of their own. They said they wanted my house, but I felt very strongly that they should look at other houses to make certain they really wanted to take on the Bradley Boulevard property.

Also I had to deal with the complication of Louisiana's community property law, which says that if one spouse dies, the remaining spouse owns half the property and has a usufruct over the other half—you can enjoy its use, but it belongs to the heirs. I felt responsible for the usufructuary because the monies eventually would go to our three children; houses around Washington were beginning to sell for a great deal, and I felt an obligation to get the best possible price. In the end Cokie and Steve prevailed. After all, it had been Cokie's house since the first day she saw it.

I bought a condominium on Connecticut Avenue that my daughter-in-law Barbara had found for me, and when I went to get a mortgage, I chose a financial institution that for many years had been owned by an old friend. I selected it because I thought of it as a solid and progressive institution, always promoting the city of Washington. I felt that I was honoring their reputation by giving them my business.

They chose a woman bank officer to handle my loan, which I appreciated. I knew my congressional salary was enough to cover the mortgage, although I had other assets. Until then I had not personally experienced the situation women often faced when they applied for a bank mortgage and did not have a working husband behind them. When the officer demanded that I produce detailed financial statements and insurance policies before I could be considered for a mortgage, I was stunned.

I said, "Why are you asking for all of this? I have a financial statement right here that's adequate for the coverage of this mortgage."

She said, "It's a federal requirement."

"My dear," I replied, "I am the author of the law that forbids this type of requirement for female persons and the elderly. You are not complying with the federal regulation, you are in defiance of it."

I felt badly because I knew it wasn't her fault—she was only saying what her supervisors had taught her—but in case she wasn't paying attention, I said distinctly, "There can be no discrimination because of race, veteran status, age, sex, or marital status."

She apologized and said, "May I discuss this with my superior officer?" I received the loan without complying with the request for the financial statements, of course, and I hoped fervently that the bank had learned a valuable lesson.

Years later Cokie refinanced the mortgage on the Bradley Boulevard house and was told by the banker, "Oh, this form is nothing, it's just a boilerplate saying we haven't discriminated against you because of sex, race, etc." She interrupted: "Nothing! It's not nothing! My mother wrote that law!"

After Cokie and Steve came home, I undertook a homecoming of sorts as well. Five years after Hale's plane disappeared, I returned to Anchorage in 1977 for a ceremony dedicating Mount Boggs and Mount Begich, twin peaks near Whittier and Portage Pass. None of my children wanted to go back, so my dear friend Liz Coulon went with me, and Moise and Phyllis Dennery, loyal friends since Hale's law school days, flew home from Europe via Alaska to be with me too. Pegge Begich attended with her Alaskan family members, buoyed by relatives from Minnesota.

I had a warm reunion with Colonel Pat Whittaker, director of the Alaska Air Command's Rescue Coordination Center and the first person in the air to search for Hale's plane, and with Colonel Russ Anderson, wing commander of the Civil Air Patrol who had spent long gray hours aloft in the search. Lieutenant Governor Lowell Thomas Jr. presided, and Senator Ted Stevens of Alaska, one of our long-term friends, made the formal dedication. Hale had been a strong advocate of Alaskan statehood, but when it came up for the vote in Congress, he was sick and in the hospital. Rebelling against doctors' orders, he got out of bed to go to the House floor to vote.

We were flown in two large helicopters out near the peaks, but by the time we reached them, clouds had lowered and we couldn't see either one. Someone wondered why we needed two helicopters when our group could have fitted into one. A young officer said the backup was used in case there was "an unscheduled landing" by either chopper.

I was glad I went back to Alaska. It was something I had to do for our family and for Hale, but I didn't blame the children for not wanting to go with me. Alaska had taken their daddy from them.

There were other "homecomings" of a happier nature. A serious Catholic sees any call to Rome as a homecoming, and following the death of Pope Paul VI in 1978, President Carter appointed Vice President Mondale to head a delegation on which I was honored to serve as his representative at the installation of Pope John Paul I. In addition to State Department briefings, I had a personal consultation in New Orleans with Archbishop Hannan so I would be well advised on the proper protocol and attire. For the installation I chose a long, high-necked black silk knit dress with long sleeves and a floor-length skirt which I wore with a black lace mantilla mounted on an antique tortoiseshell comb.

The glorious music, the pomp and ceremony, the excitement of enormous crowds of cheering people were exhilarating, but even more thrilling was the aura surrounding this physically tiny man who seemed imbued with the essence of goodness. At the diplomatic reception attended by heads of state and representatives of 110 countries, the Holy Father seemed to float among us as he went around the room, greeting each delegation, including several from Communist governments with many of the Communist representatives reverting to the practice of their youth to kiss the papal ring.

Later Vice President Mondale and several of us in the United States delegation had a private audience with the pope. I felt that he was a person of such intelligence, grace, and goodwill that he could serve as a true instrument of peace in our troubled world. Imagine my shock and dismay when, barely a month later, I awakened to the radio news that "my" little pope had died.

The election of Pope John Paul II, a Pole who was the first non-Italian pope in several centuries, brought to us a peripatetic leader who began to roam the world searching for ways to promote unity and peace. President Carter, who was always open to the religions and cultures of the nations of the world, invited the Holy Father to an official meeting and reception at the White House, where I was privileged to meet him.

Cokie was chosen to cover the pope's visit and because she knew the liturgy, the music, and the history of the Catholic church and the papacy, she produced thoughtful, in-depth reports that no one matched.

When she had been hired by NPR, Frank Mankiewicz was running it and some people thought she had gotten the job because Mankiewicz was a Kennedy family confidant and the Boggses and the Kennedys were friends. But at a staff meeting after the papal visit, Mankiewicz said to her, Cokie is a cute name, but don't you have a more formal name you could use?"

"Would you believe Mary Martha Corinne Morrison Claiborne Boggs Roberts?" she said.

"You're 'little Corinne'?" he asked.

In September 1978 a House Select Committee on Assassinations began hearings into the assassinations of President Kennedy and Martin Luther King Jr. Its chairman was Louis Stokes of Ohio, my colleague from the Appropriations Committee. The hearings were so extensive that more time was needed to complete the committee's work. Lou brought to the floor a bill to extend its life.

Before the floor debate my Louisiana colleague, Dave Treen, who had almost defeated Hale in 1968, and I had attended a luncheon with New Orleans high school students, at which a large majority of them expressed doubts about the conclusions of the Warren Commission. I felt that the Select Committee's work should be extended if even a small number of young people wished to be satisfied. When we went to the floor, I asked to be recognized by the chairman.

I began with a defense of the Warren Commission, which had several people nodding in approval, and I related Chief Justice Warren's comments about Hale's wording of the report. But then I recounted the expressions of doubt from the students, and I urged that the Select Committee's life be extended in an effort to satisfy this generation of young Americans. I was gratified that the life of the Committee was extended and that ample opportunity was given for its hearings to be completed.

The only consistent aspect of assassinations is that nobody is ever satisfied with the conclusions of the investigations.

Around this time, I was given another unusual congressional opportunity, this one to substantially help some of the most daring

U.S. participants in World War II. The Women's Air Service Pilots (WASP) had tested and ferried airplanes, carried troops, picked up the sick and the dying, and transported the dead, often flying dangerous missions in order to free the men pilots (many of whom they had trained) for combat.

Despite their uniformed duty under military orders, they had never received full military status. General H. H. ("Hap") Arnold, chief of the Army Air Forces during the war, was a great admirer and supporter of the WASPs, and he had promised them that he would promote legislation giving them that status.

When the European war ended, his proposal was presented in Congress, but the war in the Pacific continued and men combat pilots helped to sidetrack the bill, fearing that women would replace them. Hap repeatedly tried to push the legislation through Congress, but he died in 1950 before it could be passed.

His son, Air Force Colonel Bruce Arnold, enlisted the help of Senator Barry Goldwater of Arizona, a retired Air Force general and a great friend of Jacqueline Cochran, the renowned woman aviator who helped organize the WASPs. Colonel Arnold asked if I would see the bill through the House. I found his proposal exciting, a well-deserved accomplishment for the WASPs after all those years.

The House Veterans Committee, which had jurisdiction, included a woman, Peggy Heckler, among its members and its chairman, Olin ("Tiger") Teague of Texas, was not opposed to women having veteran status. He was bothered, however, because none of the former WASPs could find her military orders to prove the validity of their case. Tiger was reluctant to encourage his committee to approve a bill giving military status without written proof that the women had been under official military command.

President Carter had appointed a woman, Antonia ("Tony") Chayes, as the Air Force adjutant general, and Tiger invited her and the WASPs to a committee hearing. Still lacking proof of the WASPs' government orders, Tiger didn't want to be present as chairman in a negative stance so he kindly absented himself from the hearings that day.

The hearing became a love-in. Several WASPs brought along their husbands, among whom were several retired military generals and admirals, and the women who were still able to get into their WASP uniforms wore them. Tony Chayes was personable and informative, enjoying the opportunity to meet the famous women pilots. Members of the committee who had ever had contact with a plane or a war recounted stories about their flying experiences, swapping stories with the WASPs, introducing themselves to the adjutant general, going out of their way to show their support. The committee was won over, and before the bill reached the House floor for a vote, its success was assured when one of the former WASPs found her military orders.

During all this, one of my male colleagues approached me and said, "I don't know what your bill does, but there are so few of us WASPs left, could I sign on it, too?"

The bill passed by an overwhelming majority, and with every woman in Congress voting aye.

Congresswomen were beginning to see that there were so many areas of interest we shared—across ideological and party lines and across international boundaries. In 1979 I took one of the most fascinating and heartfelt journeys of my life. I joined a group of congresswoman under the urging and leadership of Representative Elizabeth Holtzman of New York, who felt a great urgency about feeding the children in Cambodia. It was a journey of conscience to Cambodian refugee camps on the border with Thailand, the first such humanitarian mission by the women of any national legislative body in the world.

In their attempt to convert Cambodia into a pure Communist state, Pol Pot and his Khmer Rouge were pressing their war against the population. The country was under the official authority of Vietnam, whose troops had invaded the previous year and from whom we had to secure permission to enter. Because of our country's recent involvement in Vietnam, we had to tiptoe around that diplomatic certainty, however; ostensibly our permission came from the Cambodian authorities. We were the only "officials" of the U.S. government allowed into Cambodia.

Our sole purpose was to find out what we could do to relieve the condition of the children and, particularly, to feed them. We traveled under the auspices of the Congresswomen's Caucus on an official "leadership mission," so designated by Speaker O'Neill to give us diplomatic standing and protection, if needed.

Peggy Heckler of Massachusetts was our coleader and the others were Millicent Fenwick of New Jersey, Barbara Mikulski of Maryland, Patricia Schroeder of Colorado, and Olympia Snowe of Maine. We had invited women parliamentarians from all over the world to join and two Australian senators participated.

We went first to Thailand. Under the leadership of Prime Minister Kriangsak, the Thais were courageously extending humanitarian help and political asylum to two hundred thousand Cambodians who overflowed the border refugee camps. Despite the fact that there was shelling every day and death was all around, hundreds of people were practically crawling across the border.

The camps' directors had organized a system in which aid groups were assigned to those areas of relief for which they were best suited and trained. For example, a group of Israeli doctors performed a tremendous service by setting up an admittance-clinic tent to diagnose all new arrivals. Until then sick people were placed with those who were well without any testing to determine if they might have a virulent malaria impervious to regular vaccines or a rampant new strain of spinal meningitis. The doctors then assigned as aides or nurses individuals who were most proficient in the type of care needed by the refugee-patients.

Associated Catholic Charities had major responsibilities for the children, especially for tiny infants. Along with everyone else who had been herded out of the cities by the Khmer Rouge, mothers had fled into the countryside with their children and babies. As long as they could breast-feed, the babies could survive, but as the mothers became dehydrated, their milk stopped flowing and the babies were left with nothing to eat. They were literally dying like flies. The children who were big enough to climb for berries or forage for roots did at least make it into the camps. Pat Schroeder had brought with her a home-district staff member, Sally Brown, who was a minister. She was valiant about going into the areas for people with dread diseases, to whom she brought great comfort in attending to the dying.

Remarkable organizational skills were displayed among the volunteer and medical organizations, many of which had been trying to get into Cambodia for years. Oxfam, the Oxford-based international relief organization, was an exception: A few of its people had been allowed in earlier. Some of the volunteer organizations were apprehensive that we, as members of Congress, might somehow upset their apple cart and perhaps undo some of the work they'd been engaged in for many months. To allay their fears we convened a conference and had everyone tell us what they could offer to Cambodia—in what quantities, with what personnel, and with what kind of delivery services from what locations. The presentations made everyone realize that there were areas of assistance in which one group was more qualified than another.

My most vivid camp memory is that of holding a six-month-old baby who was so tiny that she fitted into the palms of my hands. A nun said, "We don't let her cry because we don't want her to exhaust herself." Bouncing her gently in my hands, I thought, *This is a Cambodian baby, surely they sang French lullabies.*

I began singing "Frère Jacques," and then "Sur Le Pont d'Avignon"—any little French songs I could remember. I became tired, but the minute I slowed down the least bit, she'd cry "Waaah!" and I was compelled to start over again.

Once arriving refugees were processed and examined medically, they went to a holding camp, where they were prepared for transfer to other countries, including the United States, that were willing to take them. When they discovered that women representing the United States were present, they came to us with their problems. A common one seemed to occur when a family would be cleared to go to the United States and have a host family waiting there, but then a refugee family member would develop or be found to have tuberculosis or another contagious disease. None of them would be allowed to enter the United States until it was controlled; meanwhile, healthy family members were in danger of being put out of the holding camp because they had been processed and cleared; they had nowhere else to go.

The day arrived when we received the go-ahead into Cambodia, or the People's Republic of Kampuchea, as it had been renamed. Its capital, Phnom Penh, had been a gorgeous old fourteenth-century city, beautifully laid out, with highways and rivers connecting it to the farthest reaches of the country. It had been a prosperous commercial and manufacturing center with an international airport, and it was known throughout Southeast Asia for its fine educational and cultural facilities—universities, libraries, and museums. We had to fly during the day because, we were told, the Phnom Penh airport had neither a control tower nor lights. Fortunately we were in an old DC-3, the most reliable air truck in the world.

I said to the group, "I'll bet that the first person who will meet us when we step off is going to be an older lady who has worked with one of the international relief organizations. She will be our Communist chaperone to make us feel everything is simply wonderful in Cambodia." And that's exactly what happened: She was standing at the foot of the steps as we deplaned.

Most of the capital was a ruin, with just enough still standing to serve as ghostly signposts to its earlier glory. Blooming vines mercifully covered a great deal of rubble. We had tried to picture the people we were going to meet and what they were going to show us, but nobody could have been prepared for a country that had no communications, financial, or transportation systems and very little food. No cars were running; there were no cabs or buses of any kind. We were hauled around in government minibuses, the only vehicles on the street. No currency was circulated and there were very few goods to barter.

Farmers had no means of seeding and fertilizing unless they happened to have something left over in a barn. Fishermen had nothing with which to fish. There was no infrastructure whatsoever—neither highways, bridges, ferries, nor water treatment. There was absolutely nothing. The Cambodians are beautiful people, lithe of body and with lovely facial features. They used to be healthy and well fed because they enjoyed the protein from their fish diet and, for many years, a surplus rice crop, but now they were starving.

We were taken to an orphanage, which I'm sure was the only one in the country. Older children doted on a little child of about three because he was the only one of his age who had survived the wars. It was pathetic; he was the household pet. Still, in that dismal place, the children were being taught the traditional old legends and the dances and music of the Cambodian culture, thereby preserving and maintaining their heritage. They put on a show for us that was deeply touching.

At a so-called hospital, we were told that there were four doctors in the entire country; the French had recently successfully negotiated to allow in more, but they hadn't yet arrived. A member of our local group was a doctor in disguise, and I asked him how he had survived: Anyone who spoke French or had any kind of educational degree was done away with by the Khmer Rouge. He said, "I lied a lot."

We were guests of honor at a luncheon with the foreign minister of the People's Republic of Kampuchea, Mr. Hun Sen, and other officials seated stiffly at a long refectory table inside a barren hall. They tried very hard to put on a minifeast with many rice dishes. There were flies on everything, but we forced ourselves to eat every bite; it was an enormous sacrifice on their part to provide so much food, and we knew they probably wouldn't eat that well again for a couple of days.

Some months after we returned home, we learned that as a result of our visit, forty doctors had been allowed into Cambodia and that the population's rice intake had improved. Government officials began to accept more help from international organizations, and the help was coordinated for maximum success.

The only remaining heartbreaking aspect was our inability to get our own U.S. government to understand how desperate the situation was and to persuade it that there had to be some way we could at least support the people in the refugee camps.

There were other compelling interests at home and abroad to command the attention of the president and the administration. In President Carter's final year in office, inflation was high compared to previous years, and interest rates rose exponentially with each leap in the Index of Leading Economic Indicators. Congress had nearly completed its budget considerations on time when the president became so appalled at the condition of the economy that he demanded more budget cuts and greater restructuring of programs. This request meant that after many months of work, the whole budget had to be completely rearranged and rewritten and members had to fight for their programs all over again, this time with a slimmer chance of seeing them included.

After Eleanor Roosevelt, Rosalyn Carter was probably the first lady in closest partnership with the president. At his invitation she attended the cabinet meetings, and when her husband was preoccupied with compelling national and international problems, she went out (as Mrs. Roosevelt had) to be his eyes and ears.

A major shadow had been cast over the Carter presidency with the seizure of U.S. Embassy employees as hostages in Tehran in November of 1979, in retaliation for admission into the United States of the deposed Shah of Iran from his Mexican exile to receive medical treatment. The following April, eight U.S. servicemen were killed in an heroic secret attempt to rescue the hostages. Despite President Carter's further attempts to free the embassy people, they remained prisoners.

CHAPTER NINETEEN

❧❦❧

I WORKED HARD for President Carter's re-election. In some ways he seemed like "my" president—a Southerner, the first Democrat elected in eight years, and nominated at "my" convention. (I'll always remember the amusing story he told me when we were returning to the airport following his last big campaign rally in New Orleans, when I asked him about his mother, "Miss Lillian" 's, illness. He told me that he had stopped at her Atlanta hospital room on his way to New Orleans, where as an avid Dodgers fan she was watching three television channels for complete coverage of their games. Disappointed that he was not aware of the status of the team nor its star players, she inquired "What have you been doing with your time lately?") But the mood of the country had shifted to a more conservative bent—and people were worried about high interest rates at home and the humiliation of the hostages abroad.

And so—Ronald Reagan came to town and minutes after he was inaugurated the last fifty-two U.S. hostages held by Iran were flown to freedom. On that uplifting note, his presidency began.

The Reagans were the first presidential couple that I didn't know well, but I had known President George Bush and his wife, Barbara, since he was a young man. He had every imaginable kind of legislative and executive training in his career. His father, Prescott Bush, was a senator from Connecticut, and George, who lived in Texas, had served two terms in the House beginning in 1966. One of the special ways in which he had kept in touch with Congress was by maintaining his membership in the House gym. I knew Barbara as a valiant and effective worker in all the civic and social Washington enterprises.

President Reagan was not a Washington person. The executive officer of California, he was accustomed to dealing with a state legislature, and he enjoyed tremendous personal popularity. It was obvious from his record as a two-term governor that the more conservative wing of the Republican Party was going to be in control.

Recognizing this, several of the new Republican women were apprehensive about joining the Congresswomen's Caucus because they assumed that our members were going to be at loggerheads with the administration. Candidate Reagan had said that he wanted to drastically reduce spending for social services while increasing funds for defense and the arms race—a stance that was the opposite of many of our caucus priorities.

Obsession with the budget was the major thrust of the first year or so of his administration. When he presented his first budget request to Congress, the name of the game was budget paring. The House Republican conference adopted a legislative agenda that had been formulated with the approval of the White House, particularly in matters of the budget, an example of President Reagan's control over the Republican members of Congress.

He expected absolute, unwavering loyalty from all of them, and it was understandable that the freshmen women were apprehensive about joining the Congresswomen's Caucus when they feared that its legislative agenda would not fit in with his budget.

We always had a legislative agenda of the bills we thought were the most important for women, children, and families, but while the Reagan administration was in office, we realized that we stood little chance of getting those separate bills passed, so we decided to emphasize "economic equity" for women and wrap them all together. By taking bills already introduced with bipartisan and bicameral support and lumping them all together, we devised an Economic Equity Act without initiating anything new.

Among the measures that already had support from both parties in the House and Senate were Social Security improvements for widows, equal pay for women doing the same work as men, enforcement of child support reform, pensions payment orders, health care programs, and improved workplace conditions. Because they all came under the umbrella of "economic equity," the package was placed on the front legislative burner. Once the bills were passed, we had to make certain that they were implemented. This pattern has been followed every year since then.

Soon after President Reagan was inaugurated, he invited the congresswomen and the women he had nominated for high positions within the administration to a White House luncheon. He was new to the presidency and having such a wonderful time that his staff found it difficult to keep him on schedule.

When I arrived at the luncheon, one of his aides asked me to sit next to the president. I said, "I shouldn't do that, there are people here who outrank me."

He said, "We're aware of that, but we have to get the president to his next appointment on time, and we know you'll tell him when he has to leave." When we sat down I told President Reagan that I had been given a commission to get him out of the luncheon on time. He smiled broadly.

During the luncheon I said I was pleased that he and Nancy had attended the recent opening performance of his son, Ron's, ballet company. "I'm proud of Ron because he picked a tough ballet company to work with," I told him, "and he's obviously making a success of it."

The president replied, "You can't imagine what ballet did for him. Before ballet he was the messiest kid I've ever known. His room was such a disaster that we closed the door and wouldn't go in. Then he went to Yale and was on the freshman basketball team. His coach required the new members to take ballet, not only because it stretched their muscles and taught them measured movements, but because it gave them the kind of discipline they needed in order to be good basketball players. Ron fell in love with ballet and it changed his life. He became a disciplined, orderly person with a purposeful attitude. We couldn't miss his opening night."

Then he said, "When Nancy and I pulled up for the ballet performance, the theater's marquee extended all the way out to the sidewalk, and all I had to do was to get out of the limousine and walk under the marquee to go inside. I was getting out, and Nancy said, 'Ron, put on your coat.'

"I said, 'Nancy, I don't want to put on my coat. I'm only going to walk from here to there.'

"She said, 'It's a nasty night and you must put on your coat.'

"I said, 'I don't want to put on my coat. Nancy Reagan, don't you know I'm the most important man in the world?'

"She said, 'Yes, and that's why you're going to put on your coat.' "

Nancy was a strong woman, very much in love with her husband, and she protected him as best she could.

President Reagan addressed the luncheon and as soon as he concluded, I said, "Mister President, it's time to put on your coat." He looked at me, laughed, and said, "Okay, I know when I'm supposed to follow orders."

The president asked me to join him on another White House occasion, when I arrived with fellow members of Congress for a briefing in the Cabinet Room. I was surprised when he insisted I sit next to him, and I pointed out that more important people were in the room.

President Reagan said, "I know that, but they'll pass the jelly beans back to you." He is a gracious man.

Pope John Paul II made an historic journey to Asia soon after President Reagan took office, and he returned to Rome via a route over Alaska, which he was determined to visit for a day. My new friend, the president, appointed me as a member of the official party to represent him at the Alaskan ceremonies; heading our delegation was William A. Wilson of California, later named personal representative of the United States to the Holy See and, in 1984, our first ambassador after a 117-year gap in official relations between the United States and the Vatican.

The tension of flying over Alaska's snow-capped mountains stretching as far as the eye could see, and wondering where Hale and his companions might be, was relieved by the jolliness of two dear nuns and the unexpected entertaining humor of Cardinal Krol of Philadelphia.

The Alaskan committee, working under the constraints of a heavy schedule to be completed in a short time, necessarily tried to ensure strict crowd control, which included the movements of our delegation. We politicians in the delegation had watched television sequences in which the Holy Father reacted to crowds, and we felt certain that he would break away from his protectors to "work the fences"—reach out to the throngs held back from him by restraining fences. He did and, politicians that we were, we followed him.

At an outdoor public Mass I stood clutching hands with a fellow delegation appointee, Senator Jeremiah Denton of Alabama, who had been one of the Vietnam prisoners of war whose family members I had joined in sending "no negative thoughts" during the search for Hale and his companions. Because of the freezing temperature, the Holy Father said an extra Mass indoors at a home for the elderly, and then he visited an orphanage where he brought bright smiles to the faces of the children.

The very old, the very young, and the hearty Alaskans in between were enchanted by the personable pontiff. On his return to the airfield, he was even more expert and exuberant than we had suspected! He accepted the challenge of some eager young dogsled owners and gleefully drove their sled to the ramp of his plane as the farewell crowd cheered.

Whenever I am asked to name the major issue on which women vote when they choose a candidate for president, I answer that they vote their pocketbooks. Almost all women's issues are economic issues, a stunning idea to those persons who want to hear about "Great Women's Issues" and expect us to be preoccupied with the ERA or abortion or sexual harassment or whatever is being hotly debated at the moment when we vote for a president.

The major issues of importance that I've worked for are economic ones: equal rights for women in business, banking, and home ownership; the promotion of women in the workplace; better jobs in government and equal opportunities in government contracts; and equal opportunities for higher education, especially in science and medicine. Women vote their pocketbooks even more than do men, unless there is an urgent overriding question of war and peace. It boils down to that.

The most personal vote an American casts is the vote for president, and the only issue that has more influence on that vote than the economy is the feeling of trust. Pollsters know that trust transcends party and regional lines. They advise their political clients to use negative ads to break down the feeling of trust people have for an opposing candidate or party.

Trust and the solidarity of womanhood helped me through one of my tougher elections, in 1984. Pressures to have a black congressional district in Louisiana had been building and rightly so: population figures from the previous census showed that my district was becoming predominately black, and Louisiana was placed under court orders to create a majority black congressional district with the same proportionate share of the population as the other districts, based on the census figures.

The state legislature drew a majority black district for New Orleans, including a great deal of territory that had never before been in the Second Congressional District. Court cases kept the new district from being implemented in the first election after the census, but by 1984 it was clear that for the first time, I was going to have a really challenging race with a black opponent on my hands.

To my delight, a group of African-American women who felt strongly about any challenge to me formed themselves into "100 Ladies for Lindy." Their loyalty, enthusiasm, and energy in my behalf were infectious, and other women from across the social, political, and economic spectrum joined—university professors, Head Start teachers, patrons of the arts, parents in public housing projects, employees of big companies, the wife and daughter of Alvin Alcorn, the renowned musician who had helped me in my early campaigns—all ages, all backgrounds—until "100 Ladies for Lindy" had 268 extremely active members.

Those busy women banded together for my reelection because they wanted to do what they felt was right. It was another realization of that bond among Southern women, who through the years have endured a great deal together. Typical of these exceptional women was Leah Chase of Dookey Chase's Restaurant, a powerful civic and political leader who became one of the cochairs of my campaign. Celestine Cook, the co-owner of a large insurance company and an officer in LINKS, a prestigious national cultural organization, was another of these outstanding women.

Celestine's first husband, Bethel F. Strode, one of the heroic pilots of the famous Tuskegee 88th during World War II, was killed flying his own plane between Galveston and New Orleans. Upon Celestine's death, their daughter, Beth, bright of mind and endowed with a lovely singing voice, came with me to Washington, where she now works in the private sector as an accomplished public relations expert.

One day when I was campaigning in a public housing project, dozens of older women who were residents converged on me, some bringing letters of assistance they had received when Hale represented the district. They crowded around, inspiring me with their expressions of support and their recollections of how Hale and I had helped them and now they would help me. With all the strength supporting me, I knew I couldn't lose. I won 60 percent of the vote and was never again seriously challenged.

While I agree with Hale and Tip O'Neill that "all politics is local," all congressional campaigns seeking funds necessarily reach out for involvement with the Washington, DC community, the home of the leaders and best-known members of both political parties and home to the lobbyists. It is possible for a congressional candidate in a tough race back home to attend several Washington fund-raising parties many weeks prior to the election.

As long as I had minimal opposition, I resisted imposing yet another party on my friends and supporters, but as my opposition became more vocal and better organized, I reached out to my close friends, such as Ellen Marcus, Scotty Smith, Cece Carusi, Florence Hoff, and Marge Fitzpatrick, with whom I worked on a host of political, civic, and cultural endeavors, to organize the parties. My daughter-in-law Barbara and her partners in their party and convention service, "Washington Whirlaround," which later became

"Washington, Inc."—Ellen Proxmire, wife of William Proxmire; Gretchen Poston, who served as Rosalyn Carter's social secretary; Dorothy Michler, and Harriet Schwartz—also brought their professional expertise and high enthusiasm to party arrangements.

We knew that when the guests' pocketbooks had been massaged, they liked to rub shoulders with the leaders of Congress and the incumbent administration. With this in mind we attracted as many stars as possible to the magnificent homes of our hosts. House Speaker Albert, Majority Leader O'Neill, Democratic whip John Brademas and Democratic caucus chairman and fellow Louisianan Gillis Long regularly honored our requests to attend.

My first party was hosted by my good friend Carol Shapiro at her historic Georgetown mansion, Prospect House. All my life I had formed friendships with people of all political persuasions; as representatives of the people of the Second District, Hale, and then I, tried to represent all of those people as much as possible. Most affectionately pleasing to me among several Republican friends who came to Carol's party was the presence of Congresswoman Millicent Fenwick of New Jersey, one of the most admired members of the House, an elegant woman who was feisty enough to smoke a pipe as the result of losing a bet. (Prospect House, restored by my friend Thurmond Chatham, had been used as our nation's official guest house during extensive renovation of the White House during the Truman administration. The Trumans were moved for the duration into the usual site for official guests, Blair House, necessitating a substitute residence for foreign state visitors.)

Eunice and Sarge Shriver shared their home on Foxhall Road for a party at which Sarge honored me with a dear speech. I thought my affection for them had reached saturation point years ago; instead it continues to increase day by day.

My young friends Ann and Jim Free hosted a memorable party. They were part of a movement among young career couples to move into the heart of old urban neighborhoods and restore once-handsome town houses. The tasteful renovation of their lovely old house brought resounding accolades from their appreciative guests. I hope that I contributed to Jim's interest in preservation when he and Val Marmillion stayed with me in my old house on Bourbon Street while they were coordinating the 1980 Louisiana presidential campaign for Jimmy Carter.

The most personally meaningful party was hosted by my beloved friend Tom "Tommy the Cork" Corcoran, the famous lawyer of the New Deal era, at which all of the years of my Washington experience were represented among the guests. Tom expanded my knowledge of history and poetry and of the art of effective legislative procedures. With his brothers David and Howie and their charming wives, Joan and Esther, he enriched my life in every dimension. What fun we had!

In the same manner as my Wampa, Tom could play any tune all over the piano keyboard, adjusted to any key that accommodated the singers assembled around the piano. We traveled regularly to the Corcoran family's ski resort in Waterville Valley, New Hampshire, which is expertly managed by his nephew, Tommy, a former U.S. Olympics skier.

We also annually visited our friend, Gay Noe McClendon, the daughter of Governor Jimmy Noe of Louisiana, in Great Barrington during the Tanglewood Festival. There, Leonard Bernstein conducted not only the performing orchestra but also the music classes of talented scholarship students gathered from many countries, Communist and non-Communist alike. We were saturated with magnificent music and all of the political woes of Washington seemed far away.

Although Tom died before I left the Congress, his memory lives on especially in the person of my godson, Ned Kihn, the precocious son of Tom's daughter, Cecily.

The first election to demonstrate a "gender gap" was the election of 1982 as two million more women than men voted. The message was easily understood by my male colleagues. As soon as they returned to Washington after the elections, many male members of Congress suddenly "discovered" the Congresswomen's Caucus.

Because there was still only a handful of women—twenty-three—in the caucus, we had a constant and severe financial burden in trying to support our research, pay our dues, and get out a newsletter. Once the gender gap was identified and its significance understood by men as well as women running for public office, we decided it was time to dissolve the Congresswomen's Caucus, resolve ourselves into the Congressional Caucus on Women's Issues, and invite male members.

Women continued to comprise the caucus executive committee, but we began signing up men, including the Speaker, and since then we have maintained around 125 male members. With their inclusion, we had more help, more understanding, and more push for women's issues. Our expansion gave us new clout: We could go to the leadership and say, "Do we have a caucus for you!"

Men are rarely venal in their lack of interest or their opposition to legislative proposals that are considered women's issues. They are often simply unaware of the problems and the implications. With 125 men wishing to become aware, it was more important than ever to have a woman on each major House committee to push our projects and programs, and we met with the leadership of both parties to request that at least one woman be placed on every major committee.

I think many young women were lulled into believing that because we had gained so many rights for them in the sixties and seventies, they really didn't have to take much interest in politics. They weren't aware that equal opportunity and equal rights must constantly be exercised and protected or they are lost. That realization is always a shock to young women. Whether they're in

Congress or anyplace else, they cannot rest on the laurels of the past: To rest is to retreat.

Fortunately for the future, we are seeing more women all the time who want to make politics a profession. Quite often they co-alesce around a national problem or issue, such as environmental contamination or handgun control, and use all their expert organizational skills to fight for or against it. Politicians often are created when that occurs: They become candidates.

We also see political ambitions going along with an individual's contributions and achievements in other areas. Helen Gahagan Douglas was a successful actress when she was elected to Congress in California; she subsequently endured a great deal of unpleasantness in the McCarthy days, particularly at the hands of the newly elected Richard Nixon, who had defeated her for the Senate seat. Clare Boothe Luce, a playwright, author, and journalist, was appointed U.S. ambassador to Italy, where she served with brilliance. Margaret Heckler became the Secretary of Health and Human Services and went on to serve as U.S. Ambassador to Ireland.

Leadership in community and cultural activities is another valuable springboard for women to go into politics. Those active in voluntarism have gained expert knowledge about how to identify problems, how to organize to solve them, and how to impress upon elected officials the importance of doing something about them. They are successful in politics because they are widely recognized for their leadership skills, they have earned a reputation for caring, and often they are associated with organizations of good faith, community interest, or cultural development.

More young women are now willing to serve than we have seen in the last few years, and they're coming into politics earlier in their lives and careers, often running for the city council, school board, county commission, or state legislature so that they can raise their families and not have to be in session year-round. Later they can move into the full-time work of Congress or high state office.

When the professions, the halls of academe, and business management opportunities became available to women and women began to climb the ladder, it was hard for them to get off that professional, academic, or corporate ladder for a political position and believe that they could later pick up where they left off with their nonpolitical careers.

Women in Congress have been able in positive ways to apprise male members of situations, conditions, and inequities of which men are unaware. Men haven't been socialized to be aware. I always thought it was better to work from that belief rather than to be confrontational. We now know that legislation providing women with steps toward equality and perhaps a little bit of privilege, not harassment, in the workplace—laws that seemed almost unnecessary at the time—was particularly urgent.

My own young women were not to be left behind. Besides her work at NPR, Cokie anchored and reported for *The Lawmakers*, a PBS series on Congress. From there she went to a staff position on the popular PBS evening news program, *The MacNeil-Lehrer NewsHour*. Barbara, who was elected to the Mercer County Council, was the first woman to serve as its president, and two years later, in 1981, she was elected president of the New Jersey Association of Counties.

The following year she ran for Congress from New Jersey's Seventh District. She always felt that she was the person to carry on Hale's legacy, and she had a strong sense of competition, even within the family. At the same time she became a candidate, she discovered a melanoma developing behind her left eye and to prevent the cancer from spreading, the eye had to be removed immediately. It was a situation Barbara met with typical courage. What a remarkable trouper she was. The night she got home from the hospital—after her terrible shock of losing her eye—Barbara had a fund-raiser scheduled in Princeton. The Preservation Hall Jazz

Band from New Orleans was in town to perform on campus, and many of the old musicians had known Barbara since she was a little girl and they had agreed to play at her party. She valiantly got out of her sickbed to sally forth. For the occasion I brought her a new silk dress in her favorite vibrant colors of red and pink and purple, and a pair of matching, death-defying spike heel sandals. The party was on the second floor of the Princeton Arts Center, and I figured that anyone who saw Barbara walk up those steep stairs in those shoes would know that she could certainly still run for Congress. What became Barbara's trademark of wearing wild and funny eye patches—her characteristically brave way of turning what some would consider tragedy into showmanship—began that night as well. Rebecca, who was then eleven, made a blue velvet eye patch for her. That was it! From there on it was sequins, feathers—you name it.

A month after the operation, Senator Harrison Williams's seat suddenly became vacant and New Jersey party leaders prevailed on Barbara to switch to the Senate race. They thought she was the best possible candidate and she thought she could win. She entered the race too late to win, but she finished a respectable fourth in the primary. I would have loved having her in Congress with me.

A group within the Republican Party, including several ambitious young Congressmen, became determined to break down the Democratic leadership, and following the 1982 election its participants commenced a ten-year effort to take over the House of Representatives. Republicans had been the minority in the House since 1954, and for most of that time, they had been led by politically moderate leaders who worked with the Democratic leadership.

Representative Newt Gingrich, who was elected from Georgia in 1978, was part of the group seeking to change that bipartisan spirit of cooperation and to break into the leadership succession.

The "Newt Gingrich syndrome" is similar in some ways to the attitude of the liberals who wanted to break into the Democratic leadership succession when Hale was in line to be House majority leader.

In the process they expected to elect enough Republican members to be in the majority, and they worked solidly and steadily toward that goal. They ran television ads caricaturing Speaker Tip O'Neill and they took frequent special orders in the House—time at the end of the day after the session—to ridicule Congress and to denounce and decry the efforts of the Democrats and of the Democratic Party. Their speeches were primarily for C-SPAN television: The House chamber was usually vacant.

They worked to elect Republican state legislators so that when redistricting would be required after the 1990 census, they would have control of a majority of the state legislatures. For the same politically advantageous reason, they began grooming candidates for governorships: Governors can appoint U.S. senators when a vacancy occurs. Because a Republican was in the White House, the party controlled federal appointments, including those to the federal judiciary; if the Republican legislators' redistricting plans in the states were thrown into the federal courts, they were still in a positive position because of Republican judgeships.

When an opening occurred for Republican whip in the House, those running included Lynn Martin of Illinois and Newt Gingrich of Georgia. Newt, a leader of the anti-Democratic leadership movement, was elected. I was surprised that some Republican congresswomen voted for him instead of backing a woman, especially one as talented as Lynn, and when I asked them about it, they said, "We voted for Newt because he's willing to be tough, and the only way we're going to get the House back is by being mean."

Newt has some fine credentials for a leadership role. A historian with a master's and a doctorate from Tulane, he worked effectively on the House Bicentenary Commission with me. He is in line to be the Republican leader when Bob Michel retires. For the good of the nation and of the House, I know he will mellow by then, because although there are always countless personal and regional relationships in Congress, whatever tone the party takes is very much influenced by the leaders.

As a sign of the times, a 1983 article in the *Ladies' Home Journal* suggested that it might be time for a woman to be president of the United States. The article prompted serious discussions, its attitude being, "This is an idea whose time has come—what's taken us so long?" Other publications jumped on the bandwagon speculating on a woman president or vice president, all sorts of polls were taken, and that attitude of "Why not?" kept shining through.

I was among the Democratic women who were chosen as possible candidates by Myer ("Mike") Feldman, a former White House counsel to President Kennedy. He also cited the presidential capabilities of San Francisco Mayor Dianne Feinstein, now a senator from California, and my congressional colleagues Martha Griffiths and Pat Schroeder.

Republican women were chosen by William Fine, who named Associate Justice Sandra Day O'Connor, Secretary of Transportation Elizabeth Dole; Senator Nancy Kassebaum of Kansas; and Anne Armstrong, chairman of President Reagan's Foreign Intelligence Advisory Board and a former ambassador to Great Britain.

Representative Geraldine Ferraro, who had been in the House since 1978 representing Queens, New York, was a good member and a rising star, but Feldman didn't know her as well as he knew the others and it didn't occur to him to include her.

With a great many people such as Feldman and others of the older, experienced male politicians in the party, my background and experience, and their personal knowledge of my abilities, gave credibility to the idea. Their confidence was pleasing, but I knew that my age and my feelings regarding abortion, in keeping with my deep respect for all human rights, would preclude any serious consideration of me. To a young TV interviewer's suggested title for me of venerable Democratic hostess, I accepted if the criteria included putting together persons with important ideas, legisative clout, and funding capabilties.

I allowed the speculation to continue because in doing so I was carrying the idea to some who might not otherwise consider it— former Roosevelt, Truman, Kennedy, and Johnson people. I stayed within the mainstream of the consideration and talked to various groups, never about myself but always about the fact that a woman could be president or vice president. I wanted people to remain interested in that possibility.

Both of my daughters were well along in their professional careers, exemplary members of the women's movement: Barbara was elected as the first woman mayor of Princeton, New Jersey, later that year, Cokie signed a contract with ABC in 1988, while continuing her NPR work. She's an outstanding reporter and a fair person, which comes across. After many years with the *New York Times*, Steven was also ready to settle down in Washington, and he became a senior writer at *U.S. News & World Report* in 1986. They always had a completely professional and ethical relationship with me when I was in Congress: I didn't give them any scoops, and they didn't ask me any prying questions.

The political excitement of the possibility of a woman candidate carried over into 1984, and by the time we arrived at the Democratic convention in San Francisco, we were confident that Gerry Ferraro was going to be the vice presidential nominee. It had become apparent early in the campaign that somebody, either in the party hierarchy or in the House, was grooming Gerry, because when requests for speakers were received, she would be suggested for the role and then given a briefing, particularly on foreign policy and economic policy.

She was presented with great enthusiasm at a big women's meeting in San Francisco. She had been well-briefed, and she had splendid qualities. She was extraordinarily bright, a good lawyer fully capable of absorbing anything necessary to the leadership role. And, as a New Yorker, she brought all those electoral votes to the ticket to balance former vice president Walter Mondale, the presidential nominee from Minnesota. Gerry was sufficiently feminist, and she had also been a prosecutor and was tough on crime.

I went to New York to campaign with her and had the opportunity to spend the night and share her home life with her husband, John Zaccaro, their grown children, and her mother. When a big black limousine came to take me to the airport, the housekeeper who had worked with Gerry for years saw it drive up to the door and thought somebody in the family had died.

I didn't have any personal interest in being vice president, and I went along eagerly with Gerry's candidacy and worked hard not only to get a female vice president elected but also to bring Gerry's worthiness to the attention of the voters in Georgia, Florida, Delaware—everywhere I was asked to campaign—and of course in Louisiana. My heart went out to her a thousand times during the ordeal she had to endure during the campaign, with adverse criticism heaped on her family members and the difficulties that ensued.

Before we left the San Francisco convention, all the "super-delegates"—elected and appointed public officials—held a meeting and out of it was born an organization that became known as the Democratic Leadership Council (DLC). The idea was to have a politically centrist council of the super-delegates—those of us who had to live with the party platform—run with the party candidates and abide by and push for the rules. The DLC was seen as a way to give these experienced Democratic public figures a larger say-so in platform, rules, campaign direction, and candidate selection.

In the pattern set by Gillis Long when he was chairman of the House Democratic Caucus, the council corraled experts to define and discuss issues on which the party should focus; to ferret out problems and to propose legislation and executive measures for their solution. Seminars on the major issues were held in conjunction with DLC national meetings, and from them emerged such star participants as Bill Clinton, Al Gore, Chuck Robb, Sam Nunn, John Breaux, Bill Gray, and Dick Gephardt, and the formation of the Progressive Policy Institute, the party's think tank.

I had a newly drawn district and a difficult race for my own election in 1984. For the first time the Second District was predominantly black, by 58 percent, and a severe and sincere challenge against me came from a beloved figure, Judge Israel Augustine, an African-American of political prominence and substance. Hale and I had worked with Judge Augustine for many years, and he had been especially helpful in all my campaigns.

Because of that long association, and Hale's and my close ties to the black community, I felt some difficulties of heart and spirit as well as sense of political awkwardness in having Judge Augustine run against me. Most of the big African-American organizations supported him, although some smaller ones remained faithful to me.

I was personally and deeply involved in a pair of unusual historical events in New Orleans that year. One was the World's Fair. The other was the Precious Legacy Judaica Exhibit. For the New Orleans World's Fair, the Louisiana Exposition Authority received permission to borrow the original document of the Louisiana Purchase from the National Archives and to place it on public display.

Mr. Leblieux, the head of the archives section of the Louisiana secretary of state's office, and I were designated custodians of this precious document, and he came to Washington for our briefings prior to our flight with it back to Louisiana.

Experts at the National Archives were apprehensive about the safety of the manuscript in connection with possible theft or damage for publicity reasons. We were told that the manuscript would be placed in an ordinary package wrapped with brown paper, and that we were to do absolutely nothing to call attention to it. We were to act perfectly normal and casual while carrying it and to hold it on our laps in the tourist section of the plane. That was the most secure way to transport it, they said, and we carefully followed all the instructions.

A special display case with controlled humidity, illumination that would cause no damage, and shatterproof glass had been constructed to hold the priceless document and protect it as thousands of Louisianans and visitors passed by to see it. We were instructed to carry the document in our hands directly from the plane to that case at the fair site. Everything we were told made us aware of the mighty responsibility we had taken on in carrying the Louisiana Purchase from its safekeeping in Washington to New Orleans, and we followed our instructions exactly as they had been given.

But when we arrived safely in New Orleans and got off the plane, we had a big shock: Heavily armed guards outside the airport, an armored car, and a squad of motorcycle policemen awaited us. The guards abruptly took our package from us and put it in the armored car. We protested, but we were assured that orders were being properly followed as we were shown to a police car.

With sirens howling, we set off behind the armored car and its motorcycle escort, the whole procession followed by a police backup escort. Our cover was totally blown. It couldn't have been more obvious that there was something precious aboard as we went roaring off to the fair and drove right up to the building where the Louisiana Purchase was to be displayed.

New Orleans was also host that year to a collection of priceless articles that Hitler's armies had "requisitioned" in Czechoslovakia from that nation's Jewish community, among the oldest and culturally richest in Europe. Hitler had planned to build a museum of a "vanquished race" to display these treasures, and they were already cataloged for that purpose when the Allies rescued them. Eventually they were returned to Czechoslovakia.

Mark Talisman, an aide to Charlie Vanik, an Ohio congressman of Czech heritage, discovered the collection on a trip to Czechoslovakia. He met with government officials and suggested they put together an exhibition to travel to the United States. Eventually, the collection, appropriately titled "The Precious Legacy," became a reality, and New Orleans was on its itinerary because of our old and distinguished Jewish community and the New Orleans Museum of Art's reputation for excellence in presenting exhibitions.

John Bullard, the museum director, hosted a lovely reception, which was attended by the governor, the mayor, and members of the City Council. The Czech government sent its ambassador from Washington, and the minister of culture and the head of the country's Jewish community came from Czechoslovakia. John wanted them to be entertained also at a small, informal party by a public official. Ordinarily that wouldn't have been a problem, but these people represented a Communist government, and his usual coterie of party givers declined. He called me and asked if I would entertain them. I happily agreed.

We had the party in my home. The Czech minister of culture was the star, and at one point I thought the party was going to go on forever. It was a luncheon that began at eleven-thirty when I had some jazz musicians come in to play because the minister was a jazz buff. At four o'clock we were still sitting around the table.

I realized that the only way to get my guests to leave was to let them "second-line" out, which in New Orleans parlance means to follow the band, the band being the "first line." They happily followed the band through the house, out my door, and down Bourbon Street. Never before had I realized the full meaning of my colleague Congressman John Conyers declaration that "Jazz is a national treasure."

My New Orleans house is a private space of old brick arches and ironwork and a second-floor gallery, where I sit in the morning after Mass, drinking a demitasse of thick chicory coffee and resting my eyes on the garden. All you can see from the street are a pair of massive carriage entrance doors and French doors on the first and second floors, with those on the second floor opening onto a wrought-iron balcony, closed now as a protection from the noise of tourism.

The house was built in 1795 by Don Esteban de Quinones, an official of the king of Spain. As a young man, Don Esteban was secretary to the bishop until the king chose him as his royal secretary and notary public for the "Indies, Islands and Firm Lands of the Ocean," a position of importance and trust. He worked at the Cabildo, the Spanish seat of government a four-minute walk away, which was destroyed in a citywide fire in 1794 and rebuilt the following year. Next door to it is Saint Louis Cathedral, which was remodeled during that same decade.

I say it's a four-minute walk, but I always stop to talk with my neighbors. On a good day I can make it to Mass in seven minutes, passing Preservation Hall and Pat O'Brien's, the A&P grocery store, the neighborhood center open twenty-four hours a day, where I pick up the paper on my way home, and Faulkner House bookshop on Pirate's Alley, owned by good friends Rosemary James and her husband, Joe DiSalvo. When I was a member of

Congress, people always told me their problems and they still do that, but we talk more now about neighborhood happenings. The French Quarter is like a little town during early morning special hours before the tourists are out, much as it was when the French settled it.

My three-story house sits next to a Creole garden at the end of the covered carriageway that provides entry. A splashing fountain crowned with an angel casts a cooling spray, and antique iron settees from Paris bid a few minutes' rest. Even on the hottest days, it is cool in the shade of magnolia, banana, and laurel trees and an oversize ligustrum, which is supposed to be a bush but doesn't know it. Camellia, sweet olive, magnolia fuscata, angel trumpet, and Cape jasmine planted along the walkways permeate the air with their perfume.

The house was built with its front rooms on Bourbon Street. An arched loggia on the garden was glassed in to make a breakfast room off the entry. The formal dining room is in the middle of the first floor, and the parlor is next to it. In the old days the parlor's French doors could be kept open for light and air, but Bourbon Street has become so noisy and boisterous that I keep the doors firmly closed. The rooms are furnished with antiques, period pieces, and portraits of my family.

The second and third floors are larger, extending over the carriageway. The second floor had the typical four square bedrooms of Creole town houses until I turned two of them into sitting rooms because they're on the street and noisier: by closing the French doors on the street and double doors between the sitting rooms and the bedrooms, most sounds are eliminated from the bedrooms.

I inherited the house from Aunt Frosty, who died a month after we lost Hale. When Hale and I were married, Aunt Rowena had given us some caneback chairs to use as extra dining room chairs. We used them constantly, but in one of our moves, they disappeared. Rowena's attic was like a revolving door of furniture: Anyone in the family who needed something would go there and borrow it for as long as it was needed.

I always thought someone had seen our chairs and taken them away because I'd been guilty of doing the same sort of "exchange." After Frosty died and I flew down to New Orleans as the executor of her will, I conducted the required inventory. Our little chairs were in the *garçonnière* out back. I used them and other pieces that were in the house, plus the family pieces I had acquired through the years. Beautifully crafted antiques from the renowned New Orleans cabinetmaker, Prudhomme Mallard, are among the furniture mixed in with other pieces distinguished only for their sentimental value. My own antique bedroom set, however, was made for a young relative by an unknown craftsman; the bed, armoire, and dresser bear an angel motif designed for her. The beds are canopied with testers, whose hooks are placed high up for attaching mosquito netting.

Barbara once said that she was an adult before she knew there were furniture stores. She only knew that when some family member died, "furniture came in the mail."

The house is challenging to maintain, but thank heavens it has the charm, graciousness, and history to make it worthwhile. My renovation project took a long time, while I awaited approval of plans from the Vieux Carré Commission which is the authority over all buildings in the French Quarter. It was begun by Elizebeth Werlein as the first such preservation commission in the country.

I installed new wiring, central air-conditioning and heating, and a tiny kitchen on each floor. My major architectural change was to transform the back wall of the house, which had wooden siding and sash windows with awnings, into an old brick wall with floor-to-ceiling arched windows bringing in the sky, the sunlight, and a garden view. I worked with George Hopkins, a talented architect who was married to my cousin Corinne Morrison, and we submitted three separate plans to the commission, using the one they finally accepted.

I also wanted to remodel the sitting room next to my bedroom into a luxurious *salle de bain*, but George said he "couldn't do that to a dignified old room." I still needed an additional bathroom, so he ingeniously built a pair of closets into usable bathroom space. (Because the Spanish government assessed closets and extra rooms for tax purposes, the houses of 1795 vintage had no closets.)

My favorite place is on the third floor, a cozy two-room suite built with cypress-plank floors, pegged beams, and old exposed rafters. Dormer windows look out on rooftops and secret gardens, and a door leads to a sundeck where I love to go in the late afternoons and on nights when the moon is full.

A small, brick two-story house stands at the back of the garden, the upstairs used for servants or as a *garçonnière* for the boys of Don Esteban's family. The kitchen was on the ground floor in accordance with the building code enacted after the fire of 1794, which required that structures of two or more stories be built of brick with the kitchen wing separate from the main residence, an ample supply of water between them—the fountain—and fire walls connecting them.

Along the top of the brick garden walls are little "pigeonholes," spaces left for a natural cooling system: Hot air comes down and goes into the fountain, the fountain pushes it back out, and the holes let it out of the garden. When the government was avidly looking into ways to save energy, a group from Washington came to see several New Orleans courtyards, including mine, where this inversion-conversion system occurs.

I adore living on Bourbon Street, although it is not a suitable residential area in the opinion of some of my friends and relatives. New Orleans is such a neighborhood-oriented town that when

Aunt Rowena first heard that Frosty and Dr. Blackshear planned to move to Bourbon Street, she phoned me, sounding terribly agitated. "You must speak to Maybart!" she said—no one ever called Frosty Maybart—"She is thinking of moving to the French Quarter, and she was reared on Fourth and Coliseum in the Garden District!"

CHAPTER TWENTY

AFTER THE REELECTION of President Reagan in 1984, many of us in Congress felt a renewed sense of urgency to keep social service programs alive. The incumbent president had vowed once again to cut such programs—which benefited minorities, the poor, the young, the uneducated, and the sick—in order to avoid raising taxes.

Before I was Hale's community outreach representative or a member of Congress, I was one of thousands of wives who had come to Washington at the insistence of her husband's ambition. In a city that lacked any strong personal constituency, these women became its backbone, running the charitable organizations, working very hard to relieve some of the social problems, and helping to build many an edifice, such as Children's Hospital. So many congressional wives were involved in educational activities, civic projects, and neighborhood health care and rehabilitation issues that we became a major resource not only to the city but also to our husbands.

My early Washington experience prepared me well in helping to establish the Congressional Select Committee on Children, Youth, and Families, whose crisis intervention task force I headed. The committee was an invaluable resource, cutting across jurisdictional lines in a coordinated effort to obtain the most accurate, up-to-date information on what was being done for all facets of the family: the little child, the adolescent, the child in legal trouble, the family with diseases, children with educational difficulties, infant mortality, child and teenage suicide, drunken driving, child abuse, drug and alcohol use, addictions, and neglected and latchkey children.

Our committee members were among the first people in the government to talk about children with AIDS, because we could get the big picture and present the holistic view as no single committee or subcommittee could. We examined legislation that had been proposed for children and families as we tried to solve some of the problems they experience. We raised issues and questions that needed attention and we called on experts—including children—to testify. We had no money to pay witnesses or even their travel expenses, but people insisted on coming to testify.

We testified before other committees on the specific findings of our research and hearings. As a clearinghouse to pull together knowledge from various subcommittees and committees, we lacked legislative authority but we became compelling advocates before those who would write the laws. We were fortunate in having two successive dynamic and committed chairs, George Miller of California, followed by Pat Schroeder of Colorado.

At the same time, I asked every department and agency head in the government who came before the Appropriations Committee to defend a budget request how many women and minorities had been offered an opportunity for training and then promoted in that agency or department; how many had reached executive level; and how many contracts that agency had issued with female and minority participation.

Despite advances elsewhere, few women or minorities were hired to work on government construction contracts. To call attention to that situation, I focused on the enormous earthworks project that was planned for the supercollider, a multibillion-dollar investigation into the nature of energy that was ultimately (and, I feel, unfortunately) cancelled in 1993.

I supported the project because I don't think we can survive and compete in the world without pursuing every major scientific program that we possibly can, especially in the field of energy. As a member of the subcommittee on Energy and Water Development, I found it difficult to dismiss a proposal of such huge scientific magnitude and not go forward, at least with sufficient investigation on the feasibility of building it.

When the supercollider legislation came up, it was apparent to me that we should require that women and minorities compose at least 10 percent of those employed in its construction. I expected that the requirement would be annoying to the heads of the departments and agencies involved, but I discovered that those who were committed to female and minority hiring were ready with their employment statistics and answers when they came before us the next year.

Others, less interested in following the hiring guidelines, would say, "Oh, I don't have the statistics, but I will supply them," whereupon I would advise them that they were on the record, that the statistics had been officially requested, and that we expected to see them. Our alert and highly efficient committee staff members headed by Hunter Spillan on Energy and Water Development, Ed Lombard on Legislative, and Dick Mallow on Veterans, HUD, and Independent Agencies would follow up, and if the statistics on minority and women employees still were lacking, I'd tell the agency chief that before we could write the committee report, we had to have their figures. Some agencies were subsequently grateful to me for the discipline of having to be accountable to us.

For many years men's construction jobs were not open to women because they paid more than women could make as domestic help, and men were considered the family breadwinners. The thrust of legislation on my part was to make certain that women had the opportunity to be trained for any government job and the opportunity to hold it. My granddaughter Rebecca Roberts worked at a Chicago training center to help women get off welfare and into traditional as well as nontraditional jobs, such as construction work and carpentry. She was rewarded when, out of a dozen women trained in construction work in the first class after her arrival, eleven passed the union examinations. She phoned me and exultantly declared, "Thanks, Maw-Maw, for your help."

As women were entering the job market at all levels and gaining equality elsewhere, the Congressional Caucus on Women's Issues took up the need for medical research on women, for women. Almost all the medical testing and research in the United States has been on men, for men; neither lung cancer research nor heart research at the NIH had included women, nor did a widely publicized five-year study on the relationship between heart attacks and smoking. Gradually attitudes and actions at the NIH and the National Institute of Mental Health (NIMH) are being changed through the appointment of a woman surgeon general and the presence of more women in Congress.

Because the women's movement continues to push forward strongly on goals not yet fully achieved, it has led to ignorance of the successes we now take for granted and distracts attention from issues that demand our attention and urgent action. Child care, day care, and greater protection for medical leave, which secures the job of an employee who is absent because of health, violence in the home and in our neighborhoods, are matters clamoring to be addressed and refined by the women's movement.

I've always worked hard for science education, pushing it especially for women and minorities. The National Science Foundation (NSF) offered graduate fellowships dedicated specifically to them, but we discovered that they weren't being sought because under-graduate students had not taken the proper college courses to be able to obtain them. Similarly, when undergraduate college schol-arships were introduced, we realized that many high school stu-dents lacked the proper background to apply for them.

This led us to institute a master's program for middle school teachers, with the provision that they return to the classroom for at least two years so that they could whet the appetites of their students and send them properly prepared into high school, col-lege, and those fellowships for graduate schools.

By the year 2000, which isn't that far away, more than one-half of our work force is going to consist of women and minorities. Un-less they are trained and educated, the United States will be in a difficult position in the global society and the global economy—and vis-à-vis the global competition. Scientific and technological ed-ucation and training must enjoy a national priority status.

While I have promoted the advancement of women in all fields, it was a special thrill to me when Sally Ride became our first woman astronaut. I'd always been interested in the space program. With the rest of the world, Hale and I sat glued to our television set when astronaut Neil Armstrong became the first human to walk on the moon on July 20, 1969. I had been fascinated by the space program since its inception, believing that the unraveling of the mysteries of God's universe was the proper way to proceed into the latter part of the twentieth century. I believe we have to continue to build on the basics in aerospace science. Going all the way back to the Mercury program, every time there was a space shot, I would always sort of sink to my knees and "pray them up into the air."

As a member of the Appropriations subcommittee dealing with NASA, I had come to know Sally as a superior human being, a magnificent scientist and professor, and a brave and enterprising woman. When she was assigned to fly aboard the *Challenger* shuttle, all the congresswomen were invited to the launch.

A space shot is a fascinating experience that makes everything connected with it more dramatic and exciting. Flying into Cape Canaveral from Washington in the deep darkness of four o'clock in the morning, I looked out of the window and as far as I could see were the headlights of hundreds and hundreds of cars bringing people to watch the shot. When we landed and reached the cape, there on the launch pad, gleaming white in the light of early dawn, was the *Challenger*, mounted onto the big external fuel tank that was made at the Michoud plant in New Orleans.

As the countdown began over the loudspeakers, we could all feel our hearts beating faster. Astronaut Judith Resnik and I held each other's hand with fervent hope and prayers. Thousands of people were on the beach waiting for the liftoff. Like them, we held our breath.

As the count neared zero, everyone on the beach began to walk toward the water, as if they were going to help send the spaceship on its way. Fat brown pelicans were roosting on a cluster of pilings, and when the shuttle lifted off, the people surged forward and the pelicans opened their wings as if to push them back, to say, "Stay out of the way," all this happening as the great scientific "bird" was rocketing off toward outer space.

Three years later, on the morning of January 28, 1986, when the *Challenger* blew up, we lost Judith Resnik, a remarkable woman, a strong promoter of women in space, and one of the sparkplugs in seeing that women were included in the space crews. I had the television coverage turned on but at the crucial moment of launch, I was called to the phone. By the time I got back, I knew that something awful had happened.

Our subcommittee held hearings and questioned whether the

money to build the shuttle had been spent incorrectly, or if there had not been enough spent, or if NASA had not spent enough time on the launch. When departments and agencies involved in the space program came before us, they were questioned very carefully about their budget submissions. One of the big problems—not only in legislative decisions confined to the space program—is that the Office of Management and Budget sets budget schedules and rides herd on the same agencies and departments over which Congress has authority, and it sometimes arrives at different conclusions and cuts back in areas where Congress thinks it is important to go forward.

Among my closest ongoing relationships with the Challenger program is that with June Scoobee Rogers, the widow of Frank Scoobee who commanded the failed flight, and with other family members of that crew. As a memorial to their loved ones, they are setting up Challenger Centers around the country where interested young people are taught about flying and space engineering. An intensive course in math and science introduces them to basic physics and space engineering, and they use simulated control rooms, liftoff chambers, and other installations related to the space program. June and I worked together getting the project before the proper subcommittees of Congress for federal assistance.

While weighty matters are the daily fare of Congress, we are often called upon to help constituents in a most unusual way. In the summer of 1985, such a call came from one of our Louisiana "national treasures," Chef Paul Prudhomme.

Paul takes a break from his popular K-Paul's restaurant in New Orleans every summer to lease or borrow a restaurant for a few weeks in another city. He appears on local television, acquaints people with his Cajun cooking, and exchanges ideas with local chefs. Paul went off to New York City in July 1985, and the next thing I knew I was called off the floor of the House to take an urgent telephone call from him.

He was beside himself. City health inspectors had descended upon his borrowed Upper West Side restaurant, saying that twenty-nine violations were discovered on the premises and he could not be allowed to open.

"I have to open," he insisted. "People are lined up around the block. I don't know anything about these violations. I haven't been responsible for any of them. Is there anything you can do?"

I told Paul I would try to contact Mayor Ed Koch, who was once my seatmate on the Banking and Currency Committee, and that I would report the news to Charlie Rangel, the congressman from that district. When I called the mayor's office, thank heavens his secretary recognized my name.

I told her I had to get in touch with the mayor. "I'm sorry," she said. "He has left for the day." She didn't sense my urgency so I told her what had happened: "They won't let K-Paul open his restaurant." "Paul Prudhomme can't open his doors in New York City!" She was dismayed, as I'd hoped she would be, and she put me through to the mayor's car.

As soon as I explained the situation, Mayor Koch said, "Don't you worry, Lindy. I'll go by there. He'll open."

I hung up and went searching for my friend Charlie Rangel. When I told him what had happened, he declared, "That's in my district! They can't do that to him!" He hurried to phone his people in New York.

The New York media found out about Paul's plight and ran eagerly from one side of the dispute to the other. The head of the Department of Health threatened to arrest Paul if he opened; Paul vowed he would open. The Health Department would chain the restaurant doors closed; Paul would buy a chain cutter. With all the uproar, it was impossible to open the night he had planned to, and Paul promised the waiting crowd he would open the next day.

Mayor Koch called him the next morning and asked about the violations. After listening to Paul, Ed assured him that he trusted his veracity and that he would bring the heads of sanitation, electricity, construction, and health together to the restaurant.

It was a short meeting. The mayor directed the head of the Health Department to read each allegation and then he asked Paul to respond. Most of them were false. A couple of minor problems had been fixed. By the middle of the list, when the Health Department chief read the next violation, the mayor turned to him and inquired, "Is this life-threatening?"

"No, Mister Mayor," the man muttered. That ended it. Paul opened.

My daughter Barbara once said, "Hey, Mamma, you've got the best scam going. Everything is bound to be two hundred years old sometime." I like to think of my activities as preserving our national memory, but she was right.

As chairman of the House Bicentenary Commission in the latter 1980s, I worked with Senator Robert Byrd of West Virginia, the chair of the Senate Bicentennial Commission, to carry out a national program of publications and events to foster a better public understanding of the work of Congress. One accomplishment was the publication of a new edition of the *Biographical Directory of the United States Congress*, containing biographies of the ten thousand House members and seventeen hundred senators who have served, and we supervised publication of *Black Americans in Congress* and *Women in Congress*, projects in which I was especially interested.

Ken Burns, the prizewinning filmmaker who put together the remarkable PBS series on the Civil War, was persuaded to make a film on the history of Congress. He crafted a stunning ninety-

minute presentation that was shown on PBS and became a classroom teaching aid in American history, my favorite subject when I
taught school.

I guess I have always remained that teacher in my heart. I
worked with the National Archives on its National Historical
Publications and Records Commission, and as part of the Bicentennial of the Constitution, I helped to promote the creation of an
Encyclopedia of Congress.

These various projects made me realize our urgent need for an
official House historian and I was gratified when Raymond Smock,
with whom I had worked closely for years, was most deservedly
appointed as the first historian of the House.

I was a member of the commission on the Bicentennial of the
United States Constitution, and we celebrated the "Great Compromise," offered by a Connecticut delegate, which gave each state
equal representation in the Senate and representational numbers of
House members according to population. The preservation of
states' rights within a federal system and the protection of individual liberty were major concerns of the framers, as they are today.

More than two hundred members of the House and Senate
journeyed to Philadelphia on July 16, 1987, for special ceremonies
at Independence Hall, the site of the original Constitutional Convention. Fifty House members and senators plus the leadership of
both bodies participated in the commemoration, and I was overwhelmed at being unanimously elected by my colleagues to preside, sitting in the chair used by George Washington when he
presided over the Constitutional Convention in 1787.

When an awestruck woman asked me "how it felt to sit in
George Washington's chair," I acknowledged my sense of deepest
gratitude, but I couldn't resist telling her that it was uncomfortable
because Washington was a very tall man and my feet couldn't touch
the floor.

From the politics of the past to the politics of the present, I headed to Atlanta for the 1988 Democratic Convention. As a "super-delegate," an appointed convention official, I was not bound to any candidate ahead of time. When the Louisiana delegation tallied its votes for the presidential candidates, I voted with the delegates of the Second Congressional District, who were pledged to the Reverend Jesse Jackson. I got some reaction to my vote, mostly surprise, but I felt that I should vote with my constituents, especially because as I was the only white member of Congress representing a district that had a majority of black voters. In any case, I knew the ticket was going to be Massachusetts Governor Michael Dukakis and Senator Lloyd Bentsen of Texas and that I would enthusiastically campaign for it.

I have known Reverend Jackson for many years, and I admire his constant commitment to representative government. No other individual has registered as many people to vote as he has, and few have matched his sustained effort on behalf of minorities. While he was a student leader in North Carolina, he led fellow black students in demonstrations for their civil rights. Later he formed an organization to motivate inner city youth to get an education, and by the eighties, he was pleading with major-league baseball owners to hire more minority management personnel.

When the Republicans met that year in their national convention in New Orleans, I gave a party for the delegates. The convention results were predictable: George Bush was the presidential nominee, and he chose young, conservative Indiana senator Dan Quayle as his running mate. Despite the fact that I'm a Democrat, I wanted to be sure that the Republicans had a good time in my city, and I wanted them to see an authentic old house.

Early on the Sunday before the convention was to open, I had an urgent telephone call from a member of the host committee saying, "Lindy, can you help us? Our Indian chief who was going to give the invocation for the opening session can't come, and we're desperate. We didn't know who else to call."

I said, "Well, offhand I can't identify any among my acquaintances with the proper credentials, but I'll do what I can and I'll call you back."

Many members of several tribes lived in and around Jean Lafitte National Historical Park, so I called the park superintendent, Ann Belkof, and explained the dilemma, telling her that the Republicans required an Indian with political prominence among his own people and respected religious standing.

Sure enough, we got them all together—the Republican host committee, the arrangements committee, and the Indian chief— and the convention opened with a beautiful and unique invocation.

During the week, Kathleen Sullivan of *CBS Morning News* called to ask if she could interview me at my home. I quickly agreed, but I felt I should clear it with the Republicans; I didn't know if they would want a television show featuring a prominent Democrat during their convention. When I brought it up, they thought it was a grand idea.

Barbara was the mayor of Princeton, and she was such a political person that she had persuaded a New Jersey radio station to send her to the convention as a reporter. I was delighted to have her staying with me. I told her the TV crew was coming early in the morning and that they wanted to film in the house and then go out on the balcony to provide some Bourbon Street flavor. People were sleeping everywhere; in addition to Barbara and my granddaughter Rebecca, my house was full of relatives, friends, and my kids' friends, who wanted to be where the action was even though they were Democrats. The night before the television interview, I told everyone that they would have to get up very early and move into another room or go up to the third floor, because the television crew would have to pass through the second-floor bedrooms and sitting rooms to reach the balcony.

At three-thirty the next morning, the crew stumbled into my house lugging cameras, lights, and reflectors and trailing miles of heavy cable. I didn't mind them being there or the early hour, but I was apprehensive that when they plugged everything in they would knock out my power. I had rewired the house, but I didn't know how much it could take. I led the crew upstairs, and then I put the coffee on.

As Barbara described the scene later to her friends: "The New York TV crew came into this old house in the dark and, to be sure, they thought it was a Tennessee Williams operation right out of the faded South. Every place they looked were unmade beds and floors covered with bodies and people wandering about like sleep-walkers.

"The doors from the bedrooms out onto the balcony were locked, and we had to wake people and make them move out of the way in order to open the French doors onto the street. We had placed candles all around because we were afraid the electricity would be blown out and flickering candle flames were casting eerie shadows on the walls. I went around without my eye patch, looking like some weird apparition. We all laughed for days."

The next year Barbara made a gallant but unsuccessful race for governor of New Jersey. Then her cancer returned, this time behind her right eye, and no one thought it would go away again. Although she valiantly submitted to the innovative treatments by acclaimed doctors Jerry Shields of Will's Eye Hospital in Philadelphia and Steven Rosenberg at the National Institute of Health, I thought it was unfair—horribly, unspeakably unfair. She wrote poetry and continued to realize her greatest political success, serving with distinction as the mayor of Princeton, accomplishing an array of necessary and beautiful things, from a battered women's shelter and low-income housing to bicycle paths, children's play-grounds, and a book of poems.

I felt like I was on automatic pilot all week in Washington, and then on the weekends I would go to Princeton to be with her. Co-kie, who had become an ABC-TV correspondent the previous year, came from wherever she was on assignment to laugh or cry or simply sit with her sister, her best friend. Everyone wanted to comfort Barbara, even if for only ten minutes, and almost literally everyone did—longtime personal friends, many from faraway places, family members including members of our Sacred Heart and Jesuit families, political cohorts, and erstwhile political compet-itors, and we all came away feeling comforted by her. She was sustained especially by her friend Ed Baumeister, whose blood platelets were a perfect match to hers; by her enduring friends Ann Reeves, Susie Wilson, and Beth Healy, and by the beauteous three-some she called her surrogate daughters: Rebecca Roberts, Cokie's daughter, Lucinda Robb, Lynda's daughter, and Jamie Schroeder, Pat's daughter, who were fortunately students at Princeton Univer-sity at the time of her illness.

On July 20, 1990, I announced that I would retire from Con-gress at the end of the term. My children wanted me to stay, to run again, to keep working, but it was time to leave. I wanted to be relieved of the demanding burdens of a political campaign so that I could spend more time with Barbara. I thought we had more time together, but I was wrong. On October 10, 1990, Barbara left us for another dimension. As they had flocked to her bedside, hun-dreds of family members and personal, political, and academic friends poured into Princeton University Chapel to be uplifted by the magnificent funeral service she had prepared in every detail. Despite a spectacular thunderstorm that punctuated the recessional, large numbers of the congregation led by a jazz band playing "When the Saints Go Marching In" proceeded to her graveside in historic Princeton cemetery, located a stone's throw from that of Paul Tulane, the founder of my beloved university in New Orleans.

In one capacity or another, I had enjoyed the privilege of serving our nation in the House of Representatives, the greatest deliberative body in the family of nations, for fifty years, and I had been inspired to do so and trained for the task by Hale, who literally gave his life to the institution. In the doing he left a legacy that Katie Louchheim proclaimed in the sensitive poem she penned for his Memorial Mass: "Spendthrift—you've left us your grace, your balm, Trumpets to sound, hosannas to raise, Your heights to climb, your purpose proclaim."

And what has demanded my devotion and Hale's and that of over ten thousand people who have served in the House? The late D. B. Hardeman, accomplished historian and the longtime aide to Speaker Sam Rayburn and Hale's top assistant in the whip office, wrote: "More than walls, members, and parliamentary ritual, the House is a symbol of America's search for freedom and justice. During 184 years ten thousand men and women have wrought its history with heroes like Madison, John Quincy Adams, Lincoln, and Webster, along with the unnumbered whose unsung contributions are history too." During those years before and following D.B.'s statement, I found his assessment valid. It is the symbol that is ever before you during the long hours, the multiple demands upon your time and efforts, the voluminous stacks of mail and of required background reading, the ceaseless demands for necessary attention to the particular problems and promotions of your district's needs—all are endured, sometimes embraced, because of the quest to validate the symbol.

In the doing, the member of the House is aided and abetted by countless individuals and organizations inside and out of the institution and by the devoted staff members on committees, in their individual offices in Washington and in the home district and by the officers of the House and their knowledgeable crews. Hale and I have been blessed with association and cooperation from outstanding helpmates in all of these categories. Starting with Dave Mc-Guire (the ousted editor of *Reveille*) in Hale's first session, our offices have enjoyed a reputation for excellence because of the caliber of our staff members. When I was elected, Barbara Rathe was firmly established as the administrative assistant who had kept the congressional offices in Washington and in New Orleans running efficiently as Hale devoted more and more time to his leadership duties. She stayed on with me as did all of our office "family" members, the longtime associates such as the inimitable Pat Mahoney in our New Orleans office, who was a legendary wizard in accomplishing all challenges large and small, and those who had come more recently to the lure of the Hill, many of them experts in the legislative areas of my assignments. Jean Chippel came with me directly from my campaign organization and brought with her the knowledge of the new areas of the district that had been added following the 1970 census. Jimmy Nickens, our longtime staffer in the leadership offices, shepherded me through the intricacies of the physical plant that the Capitol truly is. Ann Marie Packo in the Washington office and Carol Fagot in the New Orleans office insured that my heavy professional and social schedules were well coordinated. Eva Stuart Voelker, one of the original Boggs Belles, assured the continuity of gracious reception of constituents and follow through on addressing their concerns. Donald Ensenat, once an intern for Hale during his junior year at Yale, arrived to be my legal counsel. (Years later, during the Bush administration, Donald became the U.S. Ambassador to Brunei.)

Throughout the years other knowledgeable and devoted staffers have performed outstanding services. Several of them came from the ranks of former pages and interns. Among them was my most distinguished legislative counselor and top legislative assistant, Jan Schoonmaker, who had assisted me when I worked on the Kennedy Inaugural Ball and who remains a constant source of information and advice. Other interns from our offices have gone on to future prominence, among them Walter Isaacson, editor of New Media at Time/Warner, Michael Lewis, the crusading best-selling author, Eric Wentworth, a prize-winning journalist, Donald Bacon, a noted journalist-historian who is one of the editors of the *Encyclopedia of Congress*, and Ashton Phelps Jr., who has followed brilliantly in the distinguished footsteps of his father, my lifelong friend, as publisher of the New Orleans *Times-Picayune*.

Without the support during campaigns and the continued assistance with constituent needs, government, corporate, and individual, throughout a member's service, no real contributions could ensue from an election. I was blessed with campaign chairmen and women who are not only devoted to me but also are honored citizens of our area—both of the Laurance Eustises, father and son (who is Hale's godchild), James Coleman (from our People's League and Tulane student days), Verna Landrieu, wife of Mayor Moon Landrieu and outstanding civic leader, Kathy Vick, who is now the Secretary of the National Democratic Party, Bryan Bell, longtime friend and outstanding business and civic leader, Leah Chase, cultural and civic leader and chef-owner of Dookey Chase's Restaurant, and Terry Alacorn, who now serves in the judiciary branch. Throughout my campaigns their efforts were aided by my trusted friend Ken Gormin, who for many years was president of Bauerlein Inc., a respected New Orleans public relations firm.

Devoted volunteer workers in Hale's and my campaigns have often become sustaining friends who have continued to help voluntarily in maintaining our constituent services and in accommodating the needs of our visiting congressional colleagues. Among them Michael Davis, Pat Denechaud, and Coleen Landry have continued to assist me through my sometimes frantic retirement schedule.

None of the campaigns nor the ongoing operation of congressional service can be successful without the necessary accompanying campaign funds. Many friends have assisted both Hale and me in securing the funds honorably and in sufficient amounts. Among them, Herman Kohlmeyer, the treasurer and chief fundraiser for Hale's campaigns and mine, has been our most constant source of support and the affectionate friend who has enriched our lives in many other dimensions. His multifaceted personality has embraced the high drama of the New York Cotton Exchange and the New York Stock Exchange, where his long-term activities earned him the designation of one of the "Four Sages of Wall Street" by *Money Magazine* (as cover person in the June 1987 edition), the frustrations of improving Louisiana's cattle herds and of expanding its agricultural yield, as well as a consistent, long-term interest, starting with the "Cold Water" committee, in uplifting the political quality of candidates and issues in our state and national campaigns. A bon vivant, he relishes the delicious cuisine and splendid service in New Orleans's famous restaurants and at the Fairgrounds Race Track, where he and his late brother, Charlie, have indulged for many years in racing their beautiful horses. A talented musician, who at one stage in his life played nine musical instruments, he has maintained the love of jazz and swing music. He is the only person I know who can sing along with me through all of the lyrics from the songs of the 1920s, 30s, 40s, and 50s. We just go "swinging along, singing a song, side by side." A great portion of whatever success I have enjoyed I owe to his wise counsel and his affectionate attention.

Favorable media coverage is vital to the success of Members of Congress, their staff members, and their supportive organizations. Throughout the years I have been blessed with positive associations and often deep personal friendships with many members of the media. I have marveled at their ability to accommodate to the radical technological advances that govern the gathering and dispensing of news and information from the days of limited international radio channels and no television capabilities to gavel to gavel TV coverage of Congress and instantaneous twenty four hour a day coverage across the media spectrum all over the world. It seems only yesterday that Hale inaugurated the Telstar program from the spot outside his Capital Whip office where Samuel Morse had sent his first wireless message. Among these friends have been chums from college and childhood days and their spouses, Bill and Libby Monroe, Howard K. and Bene Smith, Edmond and Barbara LeBreton, and Turner and Abby Catledge, and early acquaintances in Washington including Walter Lippmann, the Alsop brothers, Joe and Stewart, Walter Cronkite, Bill White, David Brinkley, Drew Pearson, Chalmers Roberts, Carol Rowan, Chris Sadler and Richard Coe, and Alfred Friendly. Added to them through the years have been Paul Wooten's admirable successor Edgar Poe and those who have followed him in the *Times-Picayune* Washington Bureau, Ken Weiss, George Hager, Susan Feeney and Bruce Alpert, my friend Joan McKinney, correspondent for the *Baton Rouge Morning Advocate* and several of my children's friends, Hodding Carter, Don Graham, Bob Kaiser, Nina Tottenberg, and Linda Wertheimer. Within the editorial and management departments I counted among my special friends Clayton Fritchey, once editor of the *New Orleans Item*, Charlie Manship of the *Morning Advocate*, C. C. Dejoie, editor of the *Louisiana Weekly*, Emile Comar, editor of the *Clarion Herald*, Walter Cowan of the *New Orleans States*, Jim Glassman, who edited his own paper in New Orleans, and then *Roll Call* in Washington, and Ashton Phelps, Senior and Junior, Donald Newhouse, Linda Dennery, and Jim Amoss of the New Orleans *Times-Picayune*.

Importantly, there were special members of Hale's staff and mine who were liked and respected by members of the media and who were knowledgeable about the journalistic profession. Argylle Campbell had worked on the *Item*, Gary Hymel had been literally lured from the *States-Item* by Hale, Mimi Griffiths had been on the public relations staff of Loyola University, and Beth Strode had promoted the numerous cultural and political enterprises of her mother, Celestine Cook.

In addition to their insightful coverage of National and International News, the Women's Press Corps in Washington has fostered the philanthropic, civic, and cultural activities of the spouses in the political, military, and diplomatic communities. So many of their interests match my own that some of my most enduring friendships have been among these remarkable women: Fran Lewin, Helen Thomas, Donnie Ratcliff, Elsie Carper, Marie Smith, Sarah McClendon, Sarah Booth Conroy, Betty Beale, Marie McNair, Helen Dewar, Mary McGrory, Esther VanWagonner Tufty, Nina Hyde, and the late Isabelle Shelton.

My greatest gratification in the wonderful work done by the Women's Press Corps comes from Kay Graham's brilliant stewardship of the *Washington Post*. When clubs in Washington were being integrated the Women's Press Club was sought out for membership because invitations to its annual January dinner, kicking off the political and social year, are the most sought after in Washington.

When I retired from Congress, the officers of the House honored me with a farewell party whose guest list was restricted exclusively to staff members—no members of Congress allowed!—that was given in the historic quarters assigned to my godson, the Clerk of the House, Donnald Anderson. It was there that the full realization of the enrichment of the House that they and their antecedents have contributed overwhelmed me. The Doorkeepers, the Legislative Counsels, the Parliamentarians, the Sergeants-at-Arms, the Architects of the Capital, the Attending Physicians, the Chaplains, the Postmasters, the Chiefs of Staff in the Majority and Minority Leadership offices, and those discerning clerks of the Majority and Minority rooms.

And I retired with the knowledge that the stewardship of the symbol and the substance of the House was in the trustworthy hands of the Speaker, Thomas Foley of Washington State, a thoughtful intellectual with a deep understanding of the complexities of the post–Cold War world and of the responsibilities and prerogatives in the solutions for them that the Constitution imposes upon the Congress. I rejoice as well that his wife, Heather, is his loyal partner who in the finest tradition of Congressional spouses manages his offices and assists him in the far-flung peripheral enterprises inherent in the Speaker's office.

I also retired with the confidence that the future of the State of Louisiana and its people were in the competent hands of the members of the Louisiana congressional delegation and that they also enjoyed the encouragement and cooperation of their wives (who happen to be the most beauteous women among all state delegations). Bennett Johnston, our senior senator, is Chairman of Interior Committee and a high-ranking member of Appropriations Committee; John Breaux, our junior senator, serves on Finance Committee and is a deputy majority whip; and House members Bob Livingston, Billy Tauzin, Jim McCrery, Jerry Huckaby, Richard Baker, Jimmy Hayes, and Clyde Holloway are all highly placed on committees with jurisdictions covering the most compelling economic and human needs of our state and nation. My confidence in a bright future for our state was further buoyed that fall with the election of State Senator Bill Jefferson, a brilliant Harvard Law graduate, as the new congressional member from the Second District, the first black Louisiana member since the post–Civil War Reconstruction period.

Although retired from the Congress, I keep in close touch with my beloved institution by service, as co-chair with Robert Tisch, on the Advisory Board to the Commission on the Preservation of the Capitol, and on the boards of the Folk Life Center, at the Library of Congress, where I work with my friend James Billington, the Librarian of Congress, the National Botanical Garden, the National Archives Foundation, the Former Members of Congress Association, and the Stennis Center, an organization established by the Congress to honor Senator John Stennis of Mississippi that encourages all people to participate in government service with a special emphasis on women candidates for public office.

I have also had the pleasure of serving on commissions devoted to fields of my enthusiastic personal interests. With the renowned New Orleans musician and professor Ellis Marsalis, I have co-chaired the Preservation of Jazz Advisory Commission and under the direction of Walter Massey I was a member of the national Science Board Commission on the future of the National Science Foundation.

At home in New Orleans, I have been reabsorbed into the cultural, civic, and philanthropic organizations that have consistently provided the gratifying underpinnings for a full and happy life. Among them I relish most my involvement of Tulane University under the skillful direction of its president, a nationally admired educator and administrator, Dr. Eamon Kelly. From a comfortable office whose window looks out over the Gibson Quad through the graceful branches of an ancient live oak tree I serve on the President's Council, the Board of the School of Business Administration, as honorary special counsel to the president, and as an Honorary Chairman with John Phelan, former chair of the New York Stock Exchange, of the university's capital campaign, Tulane for the New Century.

Easter Sunday 1994

When I retired from Congress at the end of 1990, I felt comfortable that Hale's and my years of service had come full circle.

The Cold War had ended, thereby easing the threat of a nuclear holocaust. The Soviet Empire had dissolved, and democracy was reborn in Eastern Europe. The Middle East was stabilized. The countries of Western Europe were implementing the economic union Hale and Bill Fulbright had envisioned years before. The space program had gone beyond the moon and was reaching for Mars, and in the doing the technologies developed from it had revolutionized the fields of communication, medicine, and weather forecasting, as well the aviation and automobile industries.

The diseases of polio, leprosy, and tuberculosis had been controlled. Free trade was being promoted through our rivers, harbors, and the Gulf of Mexico, and environmental safeguards were in place. The civil rights of more people than ever before in our history were assured, regardless of their creed, color, or condition.

I should have recognized the inevitability expressed in the adage that "the more things change, the more they remain the same," or as my grandmother Gom would say, *"Plus ça change, plus c'est la même chose."*

The government of Russia is in disarray. The nuclear threat remains within several countries formerly controlled by the Soviet government; in the suspected capabilities of North Korea, where resistance to inspection threatens a new war of aggression against South Korea and the United States; and in Iraq and Iran, with a destabilizing effect in the Persian Gulf.

A pervasive violence has disrupted the peace talks in the Middle East, the ending of the war in Somalia, and the first truly free elections in South Africa, and its effects can be seen in the neo-Nazi movement among skinheads of Germany and elsewhere in Europe, the horrible war of "ethnic cleansing" in Bosnia, and the very lives of American children in our own inner-city neighborhoods.

Trade talks with Japan have faltered, our economic and political ties to China are threatened by new evidence of the government's repression of human rights, and—circumstance by circumstance, country by country—many of the hard-earned rights of women are being eroded.

The consoling certainty that there exists a continuum of life is explicitly evident during this beautiful season celebrating the deliverance of Passover and the joyous hope of Easter. In true family tradition, Barbara and Tommy have gathered four generations of family members and friends for an Easter feast at their venerable old house on the Eastern Shore of Maryland, located only a few miles from Kent Island, which was settled by our ancestor William Claiborne in 1631.

The beauty of its surroundings is reminiscent of the Louisiana landscape of my youth: The flat, fertile land rolling into the river, the ancient cedars staunchly guarding the entrance to the long winding driveway, the rows of pine trees swishing in the humid breeze, the tall marsh grasses bowing slightly as a pair of wild white swans glides gracefully past—all these put everything into proper perspective.

My relationship with my great-grandchildren Andrew Hale Boggs and Caroline and Charlotte Corinne Davidsen is reminiscent of the relationship I cherished with my grandparents. It is exciting to know that my brilliant, beautiful brunette granddaughters, Elizabeth Boggs Davidsen, a United Nations official in Vienna, Austria, and Rebecca Roberts, a political consultant and television commentator in Philadelphia, are well on their way to seeing the dawning of the first century of the new millennium through a purple veil.

INDEX